S0-BZH-823

Suzy Gershman's

BORN TO SHOP

SAN FRANCISCO

*The Ultimate Guide for
Travelers Who Love to Shop*

1st Edition

Wiley Publishing, Inc.

For Bill Mindlin, with love and thanks for a million years of See's suckers, Fisherman's Wharf, and turtles named Carmi.

Published by:

Wiley Publishing, Inc.

111 River St.
Hoboken, NJ 07030-5774

ISBN-13: 978-0-7645-7886-1
ISBN-10: 0-7645-7886-3

Editor: Leslie Shen
Production Editor: Bethany André
Photo Editor: Richard Fox
Cartographer: Tim Lohnes
Production by Wiley Indianapolis Composition Services

For information on our other products and services or to obtain technical support, please contact our Customer Care Department within the U.S. at 800/762-2974, outside the U.S. at 317/572-3993 or fax 317/572-4002.

Wiley also publishes its books in a variety of electronic formats. Some content that appears in print may not be available in electronic formats.

Manufactured in the United States of America

5   4   3   2   1

CONTENTS

MAP LIST

ABOUT THE AUTHORS

Suzy Gershman is a journalist, author, and global-shopping goddess who has worked in the fashion and fiber industry for more than 25 years. Her essays on retailing have been used by the Harvard School of Business; her reportage on travel and retail has appeared in *Travel + Leisure, Travel Holiday, Travel Weekly,* and most of the major women's magazines. She is translated into French for Condé Nast's *Air France Madame* magazine. The *Born to Shop* series, now over 22 years old, is translated into eight languages.

Gershman is also the author of *C'est La Vie* (Viking and Penguin Paperback), the story of her first year as a widow living in Paris. She divides her time between an apartment on the rue du Faubourg Saint-Honoré (Paris's main shopping street), a small house in Provence, and the airport.

Suzy is currently working on a guide to the world's best shopping and also gives shopping tours; contact womantrip@aol.com for details.

Sarah Lahey retired from her career in home style to raise a family and recently rejoined the work force as news director for the *Born to Shop* series. Sarah also shows and sells English smalls at several Northern California antiques fairs. She lives with her husband and dog, Bentley, outside of San Francisco and wears the same size as Suzy (so they can share clothes).

TO START WITH

I did indeed leave my heart in San Francisco. I was 15 years old, I met a guy named Billy, and my world changed forever. I spent several summers in San Francisco (can you believe I had a job at a camp for teens called Camp Swig?!), and that's where I fell in love with big-city life. In those days, I thought dinner at Tad's (cheapie steak place) was a real discovery.

Tad's is still in San Francisco, where it always was—only now it's right near Anthropologie, Urban Outfitters, Sephora, and DSW. San Francisco has changed, but I am obviously on top of the changes. And I'm happy to compile them for this book, the latest first edition of a *Born to Shop* book in many, many years.

This book is very different from others in the series. For one, it's a domestic destination. And because I now live mostly in Europe, I see things differently. I also feel that today's reader brings a lot more sophistication to the page than when we began this series 22 years ago. So this book reflects only the things that I consider different or special or that you might not find on your own. If a place didn't impress me, I left it out. You'll also find less explanation and more geographic sprawl, because I figure you may be willing to drive or schlep a little for a good deal or an interesting shopping experience.

Of course, I couldn't do this without help from a lot of friends—big thanks go to Sarah Lahey, who earned her title of news director for the series and contributed enormously to this edition.

Thanks also to my son, Aaron Gershman, and his partner, Jenny McCormick, who have worked on other books in the series and who flew to San Francisco to check out Haight-Ashbury and tell me if I was nuts for hating it. In San Francisco, I relied on Paul Van Wijk of Warwick Hotels as well as all the women who participated in the first Born to Shop Tour in San Francisco at the InterContinental Hotel.

Finally, special thanks go to the Wiley editing team, who put a lot of extra care and attention into this new addition to the *Born to Shop* series.

See's suckers for all, with love and thanks.

Chapter One

·····················

THE BEST OF SAN FRANCISCO & BEYOND

The streets of San Francisco are filled with so many visual wonders . . . okay, so most of them are the people, but there are lots and lots of shops, too. You will have no trouble finding favorite places and creating your own "best of" lists. But first, we start with my list.

This chapter comes to you from both my heart and my own jaded eye—I see a lot of good stuff in my days on the road, so in order for a store to be included in this chapter, it has to be great. I mean world class. I hope to send you to a place that makes a statement about retail, or is simply something you won't find at home, or a destination you just gotta take time out to visit.

This mission is a little bit challenging in San Francisco because, while there are a ton of shops, I steer away from head shops, department stores, and branches of the big brands. I don't even much like the millions of vintage-clothing shops. My pickiness has affected the makeup of this list, but hopefully provides you with more that you can truly rely on. My personal passion for Southern Pecan flavored coffee from Cost Plus World Market has also affected this list. But you'll figure that out soon enough.

As you peruse the following chapters, you'll see that I hate Fisherman's Wharf and am not that keen on Union Square—so my opinions are out there in the honesty field and may not jibe with commonly accepted opinions on what's great in town or where the best places to shop are located. That's life in the big city. Now, who's pouring? You had the zin, right?

THE 10 BEST STORES IN SAN FRANCISCO

....

CITY LIGHTS
261 Columbus Ave., at Broadway.

There may be better bookstores in the world—certainly there are larger stores with wider range. What City Lights offers, however, is a selection with attitude and the politics of a generation. In short, City Lights has taught us how to be us. The store's creator and owner, poet Lawrence Ferlinghetti, is often on the premises. Note that the bookseller also publishes its own line of books, tomes that have been deemed too controversial or noncommercial by mainstream publishing. © 415/362-8193. www.citylights.com.

DIPTYQUE
171 Maiden Lane, near Stockton St.

Diptyque is a French maker of soaps and scents, with only two stores in the U.S. Thankfully, one of those stores is in downtown San Francisco. The packaging and labels have a distinctive style—the name of each scent is written in a circular pattern that is occasionally hard to read. Some of the scents are seasonal; some are old classics. Diptyque is a cult favorite, well known among fashionista circles. © 415/402-0600. www. diptyque.tm.fr.

FORGOTTEN SHANGHAI
245 Kansas St., between 15th and 16th sts.

You can't walk 100 yards anywhere in the Bay Area without being hit in the face with Asian influence, especially in home style. This store is in the Design District—nowhere near Chinatown, thank you very much (or *xie-xie,* as we say in Mandarin)—and gives area designers a workable touch of the Orient. Professionals get a discount, but this is not a to-the-trade source. Rather, it's a regular retail store with more than regular style, plus a great way of using fabrics and furniture to make chinoiserie user-friendly. Also available are some clothing items, fashion accessories, and many gifts, too. © 415/ 701-7707. www.forgottenshanghai.com.

GUMP'S
135 Post St., between Grant Ave. and Kearny St.

You will read so much about Gump's in the upcoming pages that you will wonder how it is I'm able to keep on going. Breathlessly, that's how. Gump's is one of those icons of retail for many different reasons, some of them coincidental and others based on genius in eye and in marketing. The beauty of the store lies in the way it takes the spirit of San Francisco and blends it with the mélange of cultures that make up the city, resulting in a look that is not only international, but also defines chic with an Asian twist.

Gump's is not really a department store, but a lifestyle store. It is a temple to local talents and well-selected objects that range from home scent and potpourri by Agraria (that's a brand, not a place) to beaded necklaces heavy with semi-precious stones woven with wood and wire. Items of beauty come from all over the world: Shop here as much for ideas as for actual merchandise. In fact, shop here as you would attend a museum or a shrine.

Do not go to Gump's if you are in a hurry. And do not write off Gump's because you do not buy expensive merchandise, because you are not rich, because you are not into luxe. This isn't just a place to shop; it's an experience. And it is one of the best stores in the world. Go with eyes and heart open, and worship quietly. © 415/982-1616. www.gumps.com.

HYDRA
1919 Fillmore St., near Pine St.

Soap stores are a dime a dozen—particularly in San Francisco, where sniff-and-swoon soaps were practically invented. What makes this store unique is its large selection of Devil

Ducks. These come in various colors and dress-up outfits and look like basic rubber duckies—but they've been anatomically altered (check out the shape of the tail) to serve m'lady as a private sex toy. Priced well under $10, they make the perfect gift for the woman who has everything—and perhaps supplant Rice-A-Roni as the definition of the most important San Francisco treat. © 415/474-9372. www.hydrasoap.com.

Outside of San Francisco, there are Hydra locations at 1710 Fourth St., in Berkeley (© 510/559-9796), and in Marin County at the Village at Corte Madera, 1618 Redwood Hwy., Corte Madera (© 415/927-2797).

JEREMY'S
2 South Park.

We shoppers know all about discounters and off-pricers and sample sales. What we may not be that familiar with is designer merchandise that has been discounted because it is slightly damaged. Meet Jeremy's, where men's and women's clothing, as well as shoes and accessories, are for sale—usually at a fraction of the original price. Often, prices are low enough that you find you can live with the damage. Or you can fix the damage yourself. Or who the hell cares, anyway?! I bought an Armani skirt for $13—some of the threads were unraveling, but you know what? I didn't care! I also saw Eskandar jackets for $112, Prada handbags for $230, and men's Italian jeans for $39. The oddball location is worth the taxi fare. © 415/882-4929. www.jeremys.com.

MARTHA EGAN
1 Columbus Ave., near Washington and Montgomery sts.

Martha Egan is the kind of store that thrives in an atmosphere where creativity and originality are rewarded. Her shop sells clothing and some accessories (even lampshades); most items are one of a kind. Many of the clothes—especially sweaters and jackets—are made from pieces of vintage fabrics. © 415/397-5451. www.marthaegan.com.

Mix
309 Sutter St., near Stockton St.

Mix is a small store, although it does have a mezzanine level. Its racks are filled with designer clothes from designers you have most likely never heard of—each item is simply chosen for its ability to provide a look. In this case, the look is uncluttered and untraditional. Drape and cut mean everything; oddball fabrics are important to the, uh, mix. Prices are not low. This is the kind of store where you can walk in, explain your needs, and turn yourself over to be "done." © **415/392-1742.**

Paper Source
1925 Fillmore St., near Pine St.

Visual and creative types will flip for the papers, note cards, greetings, shapes, sizes, and crafts lessons at this shop that doesn't care how much e-mail you get. The power of paper will never die—after a visit here, you'll have trouble resisting the urge to scribble real live letters again. Go to the rear of the shop, where you can mix and match colors for papers and envelopes of various sizes. © **415/409-7710.** www.paper-source.com.

There's a second location at 2061 Chestnut St. (© **415/ 614-1585**).

Silk Trading Co.
1616-A 16th St., at Rhode Island St.

The Silk Trading Co. is conveniently located right near Forgotten Shanghai (see above), perfect for those of you on a spree and out to see a lot of visual excitement in a short period of time. This is another source that appears to be a trade showroom, but is actually open to the public. You'll see a sales-and-bargains niche toward the rear along with a few items—such as tote bags—that are already made up and available for purchase. Mostly, however, this is a place to choose silk yardage from samples. There are silks from all over the world; the colors and possibilities are staggering. Note that Silk Trading also runs a catalog business and stores in other cities, so this may not be your only chance to ooh and aah. © 415/282-5574. www.silktrading.com.

THE BEST STORE OUT OF TOWN

TAIL OF THE YAK
2632 Ashby Ave., Berkeley.

Yak, yak, yak—how to describe a store that is anything but blah? This is a place that feels like a dream—it's not so much what it sells, but how it sells it, and what it looks and feels like. You'll find everything from soaps and scents to antiques and gifts and tabletop items. The atmosphere is almost ethereal—most of the merchandise is white (such as white-painted furniture, white soap, and white-rimmed picture frames), which only enhances the dreamlike quality of the premises. © 510/841-9891.

THE BEST GIFTS UNDER $10

- **Astrology soap** ($8), from Scheuer Linens, 340 Sutter St. (© 415/392-2813). I've seen all sorts of gimmick soaps in my lifetime of shopping, but this one was new to me: soaps based on your birth sign.
- **Chocolates from Ghirardelli,** one of the most famous of the San Francisco choco-makers. The company sells both cooking and eating chocolates in a variety of formats, from bars for under $1 to an assortment of multipacks. They make great destination-specific gifts. Available at the Ghirardelli Chocolate Manufactory at Ghirardelli Square, 900 N. Point St. (© 415/771-4903); Cost Plus World Market, 2552 Taylor St. (© 415/928-6200); or any branch of Walgreens (though only a limited selection).
- **San Francisco tote bag** ($10), available at the gift shop of the Mark Hopkins InterContinental, 1 Nob Hill

(© 415/392-3434), or the Westin St. Francis, 335 Powell St. (© 415/397-7000). Every destination has a tote bag, but this one features a nice line drawing of local icons, such as the cable car and Golden Gate Bridge. Mine has no artist's signature, nor brand; it's made out of recycled paper, lined with plastic, and has an inside pocket.

- **Chocolates from See's Candies,** the most California of brands. See's has stores all over the state, but is associated with San Francisco more than anywhere else. All of the products are good, but the best gift is a box of See's lollipops (ignore the newfangled flavors and stick with old-fashioned butterscotch). There are several branches in San Francisco, including one at Union Square, at 350 Powell St. (© 415/434-2771).

THE BEST GIFT FOR THE WOMAN WHO HAS EVERYTHING

I can't stop talking about the Devil Ducks from **Hydra,** 1919 Fillmore St. (© 415/474-9372; www.hydrasoap.com). Take a look at p. 3 for the inside, X-rated scoop on this bath toy.

THE BEST PET GIFT

Stop by **George,** 2411 California St. (© 415/441-0564; www.georgesf.com), to pick up a collar with your pet's name and your phone number woven right into it. You can choose any size and color combination. There's another store location in Berkeley, at 1844 Fourth St. (© 510/644-1033).

THE BEST NEIGHBORHOOD FOR A SPREE

If you can take time out to explore only one of San Francisco's retail districts, forget Fisherman's Wharf and Union Square—**Fillmore Street** is the one. It has an old-fashioned neighborhood feel, with stores created from small, low-slung stucco houses painted in pretty colors.

While there are some big brands and branches of multiples (such as L'Occitane), most of the shops feel cozy enough to be mom-and-pop establishments, and there is so much original retail that you won't get that seen-that-before feeling ("déjà-*view*"). Despite the fact that there is a Starbucks and even a big supermarket (Mollie Stone's), this is not a case of there-goes-the-neighborhood. The several thrift shops and many cosmetic and beauty boutiques balance out the offerings on Fillmore Street. It's a great blend of time and place and merchandise and people.

THE MOST HYPED RETAIL DISTRICT

First it was "The Haight," back when we were 20 years old (well, some of us were). Then we all became yuppies and shopped at J. Crew. Now we're our parents. But I digress: Your own social realities will very much affect how you feel about today's **Haight-Ashbury** district.

Haight-Ashbury recently came back into vogue as a retail area that caters to our kids. The more things change, the more they remain the same. But watch it, you don't call it a head shop anymore; and furthermore, that's a water pipe and not a bong—just everyday merchandise, friends.

For the most part, the businesses here today are branches of Los Angeles stores, so you don't get the feeling that anything is very fresh or new. There are a few fabric stores and great cafes, along with some interesting shoe stores. Of course, there are tons of vintage stores—but the prices are very high and the scene is, well, tired. Old. Used. You get my drift.

Academically speaking, it's fun to see the retro revision of the area—and to see the young folks respond to it as if this were something special. One of my friends has noted that kids from the suburbs think this is wild because they don't know any better. But any sophisticated shopper has seen this, done this, and traded in the T-shirt years ago.

THE BEST ONE-STOP SHOPPING

SAN FRANCISCO SHOPPING CENTRE
865 Market St., at Fifth St.

Yeah, yeah, it's a mall, and I am not usually pro-mall. So sue me. If your time is short, if the weather is bad, if you want to see a lot in a short period of time—then head over here. Bloomie's is nearby, but this vertical mall boasts Nordstrom as well as Abercrombie & Fitch, J. Jill, Club Monaco, and J. Crew. Bargain hunters should note that branches of Marshalls and Ross Dress for Less are about a block away. ✆ **415/512-6776.** www.westfield.com.

LOCAL HERO OF NOTE

WILKES BASHFORD
375 Sutter St., between Stockton St. and Grant Ave.

True grit prevents me from naming this one of the best stores in San Francisco, simply because it's not. What I'm really saying is that it once was, but it's not anymore.

However, shoppers the world over need to know how important this Union Square store was in making San Francisco shopping what it is today. I've heard that the store has been sold, which may or may not account for why it's not top-notch anymore. The other reason is simpler: There are now scads of designer shops in town.

Back in the day, Wilkes Bashford himself brought designers to San Francisco and proved there was a market for big names, expensive clothes, and chic and elegance. Today, the store has men's and women's clothing, a baby line, and a home-style department that carries the likes of Pratesi sheets. Everything is edited to a fare-thee-well and refined to meet the needs of the local population. © 415/986-4380. www.wilkes bashford.com.

THE BEST OFF-PRICE EXPERIENCE

JEREMY'S
2 South Park.

As I've already said earlier in this chapter (but it bears repeating), Jeremy's is different from every other off-price store in that it specializes in damages. That means the clothes might be dirty or have broken zippers or snags. But we're talking extremely big-time merchandise for men and women at very reasonable prices—such as an Italian hand-embroidered handbag for $35. © 415/882-4929. www.jeremys.com.

THE BEST THRIFT SHOP

JUNIOR LEAGUE NEXT-TO-NEW SHOP
2226 Fillmore St., between Sacramento and Clay sts.

In a town filled with thrift shops, this particular one stands out for its clothes, accessories, books, and small and large items of furniture. I saw a French country–style armoire for $400 that took my breath away. You have to get lucky, of course, but the basic donations come from very well-to-do families. © 415/567-1627.

THE BEST FLEA MARKET

ALAMEDA POINT ANTIQUES & COLLECTIBLES FAIRE
Alameda Point Naval Air Station, Main St. and West Atlantic Ave., Alameda.

This flea market takes place on the first Sunday of every month on the edge of Oakland. Plan for it. Believe me, it's the kind of event you should organize your trip around if you love flea markets. The market is what I would term "junky"—that's not to say it sells only junk, but the style is basically find-your-own-treasure as you prowl about. Because the market is partly outdoors, beware of the weather and the waterfront location, where it can be windy and especially nasty in the rain. © 510/522-7500. www.antiquesbybay.com.

THE BEST ETHNIC SURPRISE

KASHMIR HERITAGE
310 Geary St.; Westin St. Francis, 335 Powell St.; Renaissance Stanford Court Hotel, 905 California St.

Okay, so you didn't come to San Francisco to buy a carpet, and this isn't the place to do so—but with ethnic fashions raging, you'll want to explore this store's style of beaded, colorful, trendy, wispy, sometimes mirrored clothing and accessories. The shawls and fabrics are simply stunning. © 415/839-4077. www.kashmirheritage.com.

THE BEST CHINATOWN BUY

CANTON BAZAAR
616 Grant Ave., between California and Sacramento sts.

This store has so much merchandise that you could close your eyes, spin around, and point to something, and chances are good it might qualify as best Chinatown buy. For me, it was a silk-brocade book bag for $13. I was also quite keen on the travel shoe-bags for $10. © 415/362-5750. cantonbazaar@ aol.com.

THE BEST SOW'S EAR AS SILK PURSE

Despite my years as an old China hand, I'd never before—in either the U.S. or Asia—seen anything like the **silk fortune cookies** at Forgotten Shanghai, 245 Kansas St. (© 415/701-7707; www.forgottenshanghai.com), so I don't quite know how to describe or explain what they are. They look like silk-covered fortune cookies and snap shut like a coin purse. I put my son's birthday check inside a large baseball-size one. You can use them for gifts, party favors, place cards at a dinner party, anything your very creative brain can think of—and yes, you can even put condoms inside one and place it on your bedside table. Very, very chic.

THE BEST CHEAPIE SHOE SOURCE

SHOE BIZ
1420, 1422, and 1446 Haight St., between Masonic Ave. and Ashbury St.

You'll see a lot of discount shoes in this area and many chances to score. This small chain of stores gets my nod because it does great copies of the latest styles at very good prices. What you're looking at here are shoes that are made as knock-offs, not discounted big brands. You'll be able to find great shoes under $100. Promise. © 415/861-1674. www.shoebizsf.com.

THE BEST STORE FOR PLUS SIZES

HARPER GREER
580 Fourth St., at Brannan St.

Harper Greer features a nice blend of women's work, weekend, and dressy clothes, as well as outerwear, starting at size 14 and going up to where there are no sizes, only polite signatures. There's a mix of famous tags and not-so-well-known brands. This is where

I discovered Mycra Pac, which eventually changed my life. (As a brief sidebar, let me just tell you that Mycra Pac is a brand of microfiber raincoats with an outlet store in the East Bay. After drooling over all the coats at Harper Greer, I went to the Mycra Pac outlet, where I limited myself to buying only five. ✆ **415/543-4066.** www.harpergreer.com.

THE BEST PERFUME STORE

JACQUELINE
103 Geary St., at Grant Ave.

Jacqueline carries hard-to-find brands and real perfume, which is not easily found anymore. My friend Bonnie wears Sublime by Jean Patou and sends me here to fetch the perfume version for her. ✆ **415/981-0858.**

THE BEST MARKETING IDEA AS A STORE

OUT OF THE CLOSET THRIFT STORE
100 Church St., at Duboce Ave.; 2415 Mission St., at 20th St.; 1498 Polk St., at California St.

Called "Out," this thrift-shop chain also does HIV testing. Profits go toward AIDS research and community needs. There are multiple locations in the Bay Area, including one in Berkeley at 1600 University Ave. (✆ **510/841-2088**). For more information, go to www.aidshealth.org/otc.

THE BEST MUSEUM SHOP

SAN FRANCISCO MUSEUM OF MODERN ART
151 Third St., between Mission and Howard sts.

Much like the MoMA in New York, San Francisco's Museum of Modern Art takes a diploma in retail with a wide selection of paper goods, toys, games, art, books, textiles, and reproductions that make excellent gifts. You'll find merchandise from current exhibits, along with logo museum items, posters, and also statements in modern living, such as furniture and office supplies (i.e., stuff for the top of your desk). There is a house interest in fashion here, so look out for exhibits on fashion and accessories. Members get a discount. © 415/357-4000. www. sfmoma.org.

Runner-Up

LEGION OF HONOR
Lincoln Park, 34th Ave. and Clement St.

Do you remember the Hitchcock movie *Vertigo*? Well, some of it took place in the Legion of Honor—though none of it at the gift shop. Pity. The shop sells a wide selection of gift items that are sophisticated and elegant, not touristy or souvenir-oriented at all. There's an excellent stationery department, as well as very interesting collections of wearable art. Members get a discount. © 415/750-7649. www.famsf.org.

THE BEST HOTEL GIFT SHOP

FAIRMONT SONOMA MISSION INN & SPA
100 Boyes Blvd., Sonoma.

This is not at all a hotel gift shop—rather, it's clearly a spa gift shop. You'll find brands of local beauty and spa products, various sportswear outfits and gear, and even some color cosmetics from small local firms. You can easily spend an hour here. © 707/938-9000. www.fairmont.com/sonoma.

THE BEST HOTEL LOBBY FOR BROWSING

WESTIN ST. FRANCIS
335 Powell St.

Not only is this the most famous hotel in town, but it also features a partly redone lobby and several stores extending through the building and onto Union Square. Keep this place in mind for both a pit stop and a shopping spree. Options include Victoria's Secret, Harry & David, the hotel's own large gift shop, and a store that sells Vietnam lacquer ware and vases. © 415/397-7000. www.westinstfrancis.com.

THE BEST WINE SHOP IN A NAPA VINEYARD

Niebaum-Coppola
1991 St. Helena Hwy., Rutherford.

It's a mansion, it's a movie set, it's a store, it's—well, it's just plain amazing. Francis has built a shrine to Hollywood, his Oscars, his father, and his vines, and created a place where TV programs and movies can be shot, visitors can tour, and anyone can shop. The large store has a rustic Italian feel to it and is crammed with merchandise, from table settings and dishes to cookbooks by area chefs. Other members of the family get in on the action, although the Sofia brand was not created by daughter Sofia, but in her honor. You can do a tasting for about $15 for four glasses, or just shop and have fun. If you stop at only one vineyard store, this should be the one. © 707/968-1100. www.niebaum-coppola.com.

THE BEST FOOD MARKET

Ferry Building Marketplace and Farmers' Market
Market St. and Embarcadero.

Be still my heart! Oh me, oh my! And there goes the diet, too. Even if you aren't a foodie, you will love this combination of stores, stalls, style, and rehabbed architecture right down by the waterside. The best food purveyors and restaurateurs of the area have stores here, and the best growers show up for the Saturday farmers' market, when even the local chefs give tours, demonstrations, and food prowls to visitors. www.ferry buildingmarketplace.com.

THE BEST GROCERY STORE IN A TOURIST AREA

MOLLIE STONE'S
2435 California St., off Fillmore St.

This would be an excellent supermarket in any community— it's almost a parody of a California grocery store, with its health foods, fruit juices, homemade multigrain and sourdough breads, organic offerings, snacks, nosh items, coffees, picnic supplies, and real-people needs. If you like to save money while traveling, you can stop here for paper and plastic goods (recyclable, natch) as well as foodstuffs to enjoy in your hotel room or at your favorite picnic spot. ✆ 415/567-4902. www. molliestones.com.

THE BEST PLACE FOR ANYTHING

WALGREENS
Multiple locations, including 1301 Market St.; 300 Gough St.; 790 Van Ness Ave.; 1979 Mission St.; 499 Haight St.; and 135 Powell St.

There's a branch of Walgreens in every trading area in San Francisco. In fact, there are two within a block of the Four Seasons Hotel, right on Market Street. This drugstore chain sells everything you need in real life, including souvenirs, Ghirardelli chocolates, postcards, phone cards, and so on. I load up on a product called Emergen-C, a powder that makes a fizzy drink with extra vitamin C—great for that afternoon break when you've been shopping all day but must push onward. www. walgreens.com.

THE BEST DAY OUT OF TOWN

∙∙∙

BERKELEY
Fourth St. and environs.

While there are many sights to see in Berkeley and you can surely spend more than a day here—heck, I know people who have spent 4 years here—if you're going to make one single day trip for shopping, get thyself to the Fourth Street area. This particular neighborhood has tons of shops, many cafes, and so much energy that you just have to grin. You'll see branches of famous stores mixed with one-of-a-kind boutiques; there's enough that's fresh and new that it all feels great. This is what Haight-Ashbury should have become.

The shopping district is not particularly cute and certainly has no sense of neighborhood or anything charming like painted Victorian houses. Rather, it's a store-after-store district that grew up just past Emeryville and has a T-shaped flow to it. Most of the stores and cafes are right on Fourth Street, but don't miss **Anthropologie,** around the corner on Hearst Avenue. You'll also want to stop by **Lilith,** a branch of the Paris women's boutique, and then explore the only-in-America stores, such as **George** for pets, **Margaret O'Leary** for flirty clothes, and **The Gardener, Sur La Table,** and even the **Crate & Barrel** outlet for your kitchen and home. This neighborhood is so retail-friendly, **CP Shades** even left the city to open a location here.

Note: While you can get here by public transportation, you'll really need a car to transport all of your packages back to your hotel. See chapter 8 for details.

Chapter Two

....

SAN FRANCISCO DETAILS

WELCOME TO SAN FRANCISCO

The housing is expensive, the weather is strange (!!!), and the possibility of finding a job is small—yet everyone wants to move to San Francisco. If they can't live in the City by the Bay, then they're willing to settle for a visit. America's most popular convention city is also a top destination for international travelers and shoppers—San Francisco is the most yummy, mixed-up, funky, provincial, small big city in the United States.

With one giant bay, a couple of fabulous bridges, many airports, and far more than 49 square miles of space to play in, San Francisco today stands for not only the city center, but also the East Bay, Marin, Sonoma, Napa, and beyond. Silicon Valley's bubble may have burst, but there are still plenty of stores and plenty of places to eat, drink, and sleep in big-city style.

It's hippie, it's dippy, it's chic, it's counterchic, it's "You've got a tattoo, and I've got Gucci." Meanwhile food is more important than fashion, and fashion is what you make of it. But then, that's true only because the very definition of fashion is ever-sliding, as slippery as the San Andreas Fault. Step into my Painted Ladies and have a nice day.

On the surface, you may not consider San Francisco a great shopping town. That's part of what makes this city so unique: The good stuff is hidden. On the surface, you'll see places like Union Square, closer to a large outdoor mall than a great shopping destination. Please believe me, this is not the best part of San Francisco's shopping. While perched on the edges of Union Square are Saks and Macy's and Neiman Marcus—the whole American department-store experience right in one spot (with Nordstrom a block away and Bloomingdale's arriving next door to that)—the only real reason to shop these giants in San Francisco is that the selection may be different or larger than what's in your hometown. But the real secret to shopping in this city is to get away from Union Square and get out to the 'hoods.

Come with me; let me show you around. I've been a regular in San Francisco since I was 15 years old. I've changed, and the city has changed, but the beat goes on.

CHOOSING SAN FRANCISCO

While San Francisco is already a very, very popular destination, the city is eager to lure ever more visitors. The **San Francisco Convention & Visitors Bureau** even has a special program created to draw visitors away from Los Angeles. Check out www.notinla.com or call © **888/782-9673** for packages, discount hotel rates, and special deals—most often offered in winter—that are available when you book with a Visa card.

Another winter promotion you might be interested in is called **Dine About Town.** This deal is usually available only in January, when the best restaurants in town offer fixed prices: $22 for lunch, $32 for dinner. For more information, go to www.sfdineabouttown.com or www.sfvisitor.org; or call © **415/391-2000.**

GETTING THERE

By Plane

San Francisco International Airport, otherwise known as **SFO,** is the main airport in the Bay Area and serves both domestic

Maybe Miles

If you're planning to fly to San Francisco on miles that you have accumulated through your favorite frequent-flier program, remember that this is one of the world's most popular destinations. Book early! When it comes to freebie mileage tickets, it often takes 6 months' advance booking to get the dates you desire.

The major carrier for San Francisco is United, but because just about every airline flies here through a connecting city, the requests for frequent-flier tickets often jam up. You may want to use your miles to upgrade your seat rather than secure the ticket itself—this depends, of course, on availability and how long your flight will be.

and international carriers. While it is the airport most frequently used by visitors, you may find less expensive flights to alternative airports in the Bay Area.

Oakland International Airport (OAK) is the home of several low-cost carriers, such as **Southwest** (© 800/I-FLY-SWA; www.southwest.com) and **JetBlue** (© 800/538-2548; www.jet blue.com).

San Jose International Airport (SJC) was once an American Airlines hub, but since the Silicon Valley bubble burst, it has not been as popular or as active. Still, locals and suburbanites often research fares through this airport; insiders tell me that car rentals from San Jose are the least expensive among the area airports.

Without extra-bad traffic, drive time from San Francisco's Union Square to SFO is about 30 minutes; to Oakland, about 45 minutes; and to San Jose, at least an hour and probably more.

By Train

While it's possible, sort of, to get to San Francisco by train, the train doesn't actually stop at Union Square or anywhere in metro San Francisco. Not to fret: **Amtrak** (© 800/USA-RAIL; www.amtrak.com) does stop in Emeryville, in the East Bay (right across the street from some major shopping, as a matter of fact). Routes serving Emeryville include a cross-country train from Chicago as well as a coastal train from Los Angeles. Of course, in this age of $39 flights, who takes the train?

By Cruise Ship

Many of the cruise ships that sail the Alaska route begin in, end in, or pass through San Francisco. For many lines, San Francisco is a turnaround port with add-on packages available for those who want pre- or postcruise stays.

The cruise pier is in the center of town, obviously along the waterfront, and not terribly far from Fisherman's Wharf. There's even a mall, **Pier 39,** right next door, for those who can't wait to get to their shopping chores.

While all ships have onboard shops, it is illegal for those businesses to be open while in U.S. waters. The stores will open only once the ship has put into international seas. Besides, they rarely sell Alcatraz souvenirs on ships.

GETTING THERE FROM ABROAD

There is an entire chapter in this book specifically written for international travelers, beginning on p. 36. *Note:* While Oakland is considered an international airport, the bulk of the international carriers serve SFO.

Because San Francisco is more or less in between Asia and Europe, you can easily take nonstop flights here from any of the world's gateway cities.

ARRIVING & DEPARTING

If you're going to San Francisco, wear some flowers in your hair. Oakland? Well, never mind. Forget the flowers and check out the savings possibilities before you even book your arrival and departure details.

Since there are several different airports to choose from in the San Francisco metropolitan area, there are a few different arrival possibilities. Most transportation sources serve two major airports, SFO and OAK, but don't rule out other area airports. Check to see if your hotel offers airport-pickup service (most do); if not, ask your hotel concierge to call a shuttle service for you. Or you can contact **SuperShuttle** yourself by calling © 800/258-3826 or going to www.supershuttle.com.

SFO

I arrived at SFO on an international flight and was surprised to discover there were no free luggage trolleys. Many U.S. airports have free trolleys in their international terminals, but not SFO. Oh no!

The charge for a luggage cart was $3, and the machine that releases them was rather finicky: It wanted either single dollar bills in crisp condition (mine were rejected) or a credit card. Puhleeease!

But get this part: Rather than worrying about mechanical contraptions, my nails, and any lifting and schlepping, instead I flagged a skycap and gave him $5. This seemed a bargain, as I had two suitcases and a carry-on. For a $2 difference, this was a deal and started my trip out on the right foot.

There was no line for a taxi to the city, and traffic was not too bad in the mid-afternoon. My cab right to the heart of downtown San Francisco cost $40.

If you're the type to brave public transportation, you can also take **BART** (© 415/989-2278; www.bart.gov), which stands for Bay Area Rapid Transit. This commuter-train system connects SFO, San Francisco, the East Bay, and Oakland International Airport.

OAK

The Oakland airport is farther away from downtown San Francisco than SFO, but often has better flight deals—it's worth considering. There are a variety of methods to get from OAK into downtown San Francisco.

My 20-something kids came up from L.A. to meet me for a long weekend. Since they had little luggage, they were able to take a cheap flight to Oakland, and then connect to San Francisco via **BART** (© 510/464-6000; www.bart.gov). This involves taking the AirBART shuttle bus from the airport to the Coliseum BART station, and then the BART train to San Francisco, which, to me, requires being a very good sport. They said it was easy. *Note:* You must buy your BART train ticket before you board; get one from the vending machine at the airport before you even head for the AirBART shuttle bus.

If all that sounds like too much to bear, head for the official taxi line at the airport, and expect to pay between $50 and $60 for the ride into downtown San Francisco. Then add on a tip. *Note:* Taxi fares are comparable to fees charged by private car services (see below).

To save money but avoid the schlep via public transportation, you can compromise and go with the **Bayporter Express** (© 877/467-1800 or 415/467-1800; www.bayporter.com), a shuttle service with an unusual pricing system. The first person in your group pays $26, but each person thereafter pays $12. For a couple, this will cost $38. You must have a reservation to use this service, so call ahead or ask your hotel to do so for you. Giving 24 hours' notice is a good idea.

My flight departed from Oakland at 10am on a Monday, which made me a little nervous. Be at the airport 2 hours early? Battle morning traffic? On a Monday? I had way too much luggage to consider public transportation, so I decided to go with the suggestion of the front desk at the Warwick Regis Hotel and try town-car service. The concierge arranged it all with **Associated Limos** (© 415/703-9200). The flat fee was $60 (I used my credit card and tipped an additional $10), and I could sit back in style. This was not a budget ride, but it was so relaxing that I found comfort in the value. The drive takes about 30 to 40 minutes without heavy traffic. Other options include **Super Shuttle** (© 887/887-8819; www.supershuttle.com), which offers sedan and limo service, and **Virgin** (© 415/922-**LIMO**)—yes, the same firm owned by billionaire Richard Branson—which operates a limo service in San Francisco that does tours as well as airport pickups.

INFORMATION, PLEASE

I found one of the best ways to prepare for my trip was to simply read the San Francisco newspapers online—check out the excellent *San Francisco Chronicle* site at **www.sfgate.com**, or try other general-interest sites, such as **www.all-sanfrancisco. com** and **sanfrancisco.citysearch.com**. Once in my hotel, I studied *Where Magazine* (the freebie magazine) and, of course, the daily newspapers. For laughs, I changed the weather announcement on my e-mail account to San Francisco (enter ZIP code 94102), so I got to monitor the weather changing in the weeks before I arrived. *Tip:* If you're looking for the local-branch address of your favorite chain, try looking it up on the store's website before you leave home.

THE LAY OF THE LAND

San Francisco was built on the end of a peninsula and covers some 49 square miles of shopping ops, hence the name of the football team, the 49ers. But wait, there was a gold rush in 1849—maybe that's where the team name came from. San Francisco proper, most often referred to as, simply, the City, is made up of myriad neighborhoods (see chapter 5). There are numbered streets as well as numbered avenues, so pay close attention to addresses.

The best way to figure out where you want to be is to know the exact address as well as the two nearest cross streets. Taxi drivers will function best if you give them cross-street information, although you have to be a native (and a driver) to know which streets are one-way and in which direction.

If you remember that the City is traversed by Market Street, you'll easily be able to find the SoMa ("South of Market") district, on one side of the street, and Union Square and the main tourist shopping areas, on the other. Additionally, major public transportation routes use Market Street.

There are two major bridges to know about: The orange one is the Golden Gate (that will be on the final exam), while the "other" one is the Bay Bridge, which leads to Oakland and beyond, an area referred to as the East Bay. The Golden Gate takes you to Marin County, Muir Woods, and on to Napa and Sonoma, which are indeed two different places separated by a small mountain range (thus they are actually two valleys). Finally, when locals refer to the Peninsula, they mean those bedroom communities south of San Francisco in the direction of San Jose. The Peninsula is not the City, nor is anyone discussing one of the most famous hotels in Hong Kong.

GETTING AROUND

On Foot

The individual neighborhoods of San Francisco are walkable; it's getting to them that's the problem. This city is far larger than you think. The good stuff is not necessarily in places that are within walking distance or a cable-car ride from Union Square. In fact, while the touristy areas (Union Square, Fisherman's Wharf, Ghirardelli Square, Chinatown) are, without a doubt, touristy, it's the neighborhoods you've never heard of—and can't find—that are the good ones. The harder it is to get there, the better the shopping.

Much of the city plan is on a grid, so once you learn your cross streets, you can figure out where you are walking and

About Those Cable Cars

Yeah, sure, I know all about it: Visiting San Francisco is about riding the cable cars. So, if it's just you and you absolutely insist, be my guest—especially consider the basic tourist run from Market Street or Union Square to Fisherman's Wharf. But if there's more than two in your party, you may quickly find that a taxi is more economical! Cable cars cost $3 per person per ride. To make matters worse, there are no free transfers. The only cheery thought is that children under 5 ride free, and seniors can pay $1 if they ride before 7am or after 9pm (which is bedtime).

just how far it is. But this takes practice, especially since some of the main thoroughfares are many, many miles long. Also note that on some of the longer shopping streets, there are various niches of riches with wasteland in between. This is not the kind of town where you can walk from shop to shop and get to see everything.

Also remember that this city has more hills than Rome. In some cases, you can avoid a hill by cutting around it, but invariably, there's another hill lurking elsewhere. If you're walking, be sure to wear sensible shoes. Or buy a new pair at any of the city's various discount shoe stores, described on p. 163.

By Public Transportation

The good news: San Francisco thinks it has public transportation. The bad news: It's not too effective at getting you anywhere. Exception: **BART** (© 415/989-2278; www.bart.gov), which works great if you want to get to the East Bay.

I found my every other attempt at mass transit thwarted—often by time limitations. My recommendation: Budget for lots of cabs and just eat the costs.

While there is a bus network operated by **Muni** (© 415/673-6864; www.sfmuni.com), and its routes may serve the general direction you want to visit, be forewarned that the buses are slow (traffic is a killer) and don't run frequently, except during rush hours, when they move even more slowly.

But more about BART: I gotta tell you, the BART system—at least at Market Street—is not well signed and is, therefore, not easy to use. And I live in Europe and train travel constantly. Other than marking the way "TO TRAINS," there were no signs that helped me with directions and no indications of which trains I wanted. Your best bet may be to find a local to help you.

To get tickets: There are automated machines that will provide tickets for Muni and for BART. Note that Muni is separate from BART. Note also that in order to obtain a senior ticket, I had to stand in a long line, as none of the special-fare tickets (this includes tickets for travelers with disabilities) were available from machines. It's worth it, though—seniors pay $6 to get $24 worth of travel.

By Taxi

Taxis can easily be hailed mid-street in the center of town, although they become more difficult to snare in the rain or on holidays. The flag drops at $2.85; drivers expect a 20% tip. You will be staggered by how much of your budget can go to taxi fares. *Tip:* You might want to ask your hotel concierge for the phone number of a local taxi firm—that way, in case you're stranded in a faraway neighborhood and can't flag a cab on the street, you can at least call one.

By Car

A car helps enormously in terms of getting from 'hood to 'hood, but then you have the twin problems of traffic and parking . . . and paying a *lot* if you can't find a meter. If you are not a California resident, you might want to brush up on the various San Francisco–specific driving and parking rules, especially the one about curbing your wheels when you park on a hill.

San Francisco Mass Transit

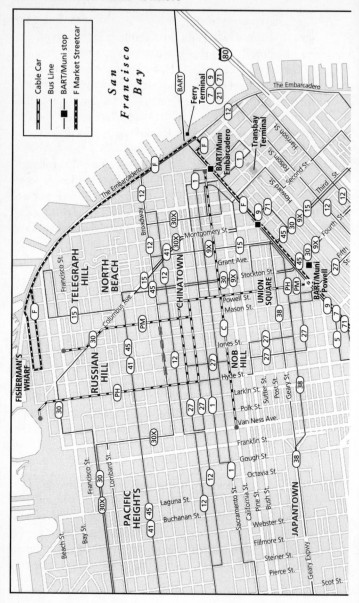

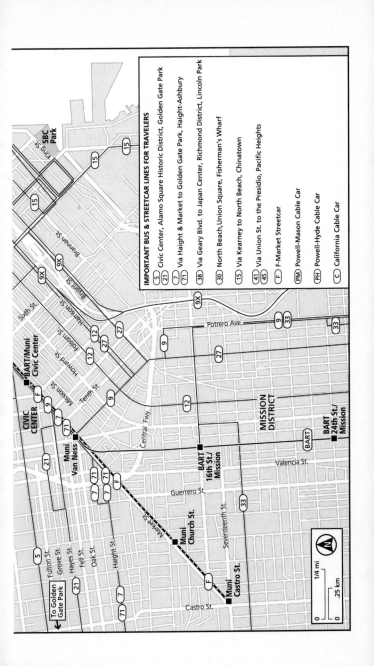

IMPORTANT BUS & STREETCAR LINES FOR TRAVELERS

5	Civic Center, Alamo Square Historic District, Golden Gate Park
21	
7	Via Haight & Market to Golden Gate Park, Haight-Ashbury
71	
38	Via Geary Blvd. to Japan Center, Richmond District, Lincoln Park
30	North Beach,Union Square, Richmond District, Fisherman's Wharf
15	Via Kearney to North Beach, Chinatown
41	Via Union St. to the Presidio, Pacific Heights
45	
F	F-Market Streetcar
PM	Powell-Mason Cable Car
PH	Powell-Hyde Cable Car
C	California Cable Car

SBC Park

BART/Muni Civic Center

CIVIC CENTER

Muni Van Ness

To Golden Gate Park

Fulton St.
Grove St.
Hayes St.
Fell St.
Oak St.
Haight St.

Market St.

Muni Church St.

Muni Castro St.

Castro St.

Guerrero St.

Seventeenth St.

BART 16th St./ Mission

Valencia St.

MISSION DISTRICT

BART 24th St./ Mission

BART

Potrero Ave.

Central Frwy.

Mission St.
Howard St.
Folsom St.
Tenth St.

Sixth St.
Harrison St.
Bryant St.
Brannan St.

King St.

1/4 mi

.25 km

Passing on the Savings

There is something called **CityPass** (© 888/330-5008; www.citypass.com) that offers many perks, including unlimited use of public transportation via cable car and Muni (though not BART) for 7 days, as well as discounts and free entry on some ferries and to attractions, such as the San Francisco Museum of Modern Art, Asian Art Museum, Exploratorium, California Academy of Sciences, and Steinhart Aquarium. This is a good deal only if you truly use it. The pass costs about $42 for adults and $34 for kids 5 to 17. To compare rates and value—which could be related to how many people are in your party—keep in mind that a taxi from Union Square to the Haight can carry up to four adults and will cost about $15 one-way, with tip.

There is also a series of transportation-only **Muni Passports,** good for travel on 1 day ($9), 3 days ($15), or a full 7 days ($20). The 7-day Passport is half the price of the CityPass mentioned above; one's good for transportation only, while the other includes museum admission and discounts—you decide which pass is ideal for your needs.

By Hotel Car

I was surprised to learn that all the hotels I tested kept a house car on hand to take guests to appointments, shopping destinations, or even dinner. The service is said to be complimentary, but you are expected to tip well.

By Ferry

You can get to Alcatraz Island, Sausalito and Tiburon (in Marin County), and Alameda (in the East Bay) by ferry. Alcatraz is an adventure unto itself; shopping in Sausalito is covered on p. 111. Shoppers should go to Alameda for the once-a-month flea market; ferry is not the best way to get there, but it can be done.

Ferries to Sausalito and Tiburon depart from Pier 41 (Fisherman's Wharf) and the Ferry Building. There are different ferry firms, so they use different piers.

PHONING AROUND

While the basic area code for San Francisco is now, and has always been, **415**, the addition of newer area codes for the greater sprawling region means there's a bouquet of choices: most frequently **510** or **925** for the East Bay, **650** for the Peninsula and suburbs south of San Francisco, **408** for San Jose, and **707** for Napa and Sonoma. Much of Marin uses the 415 area code as well. You must dial 1 plus the area code, even for local phone calls.

For information on prepaid phone cards and mobile phones, see p. 41.

MONEY MATTERS

Other than allowing yourself plenty of cash for the cable car and taxis, you won't have to worry about finding ATMs. They're readily available in all neighborhoods, although expect to pay a fee unless you find a direct affiliation with your home bank or have the kind of card that waives extra fees. You'll notice a plethora of freestanding ATMs, the kind not associated with banks; note that these usually have higher fees than bank machines.

International visitors can see p. 39 for more on money matters.

SHOPPING HOURS

The City has a reputation for being, uh, funky for a reason—nothing is ordinary here. This includes shopping hours, which

San Francisco, Segway Style

Want to have your picture snapped by weary tourists as you smoothly glide through San Francisco on a high-tech, self-balancing, gyroscopic gizmo called a Segway? Want to amuse your whining family bored with museums and fancy restaurants? Tired of shopping? (Of course not!) Take a Segway Tour with the **San Francisco Electric Tour Company**, based at Fisherman's Wharf at 757 Beach St., near Hyde Street (© **877/ 474-3130** or 415/474-3130; www.sfelectrictour.com). You'll have a ball, so will your kids (who must be 12 or older), and you can even turn this into a shopping experience the whole group will enjoy.

Our tour began with a 20-minute safety and operational practice session—that is, how to balance the thing, go forward and back, turn on a dime. The Segway moves by responding to simple body language: Lean forward and the machine glides that direction; lean back on your heels a bit and it slows to a halt. You steer by turning a knob with your left hand. Yes, it's that simple. You can master it, even if President Bush couldn't.

The standard tour takes 2½ hours and begins by maneuvering through some crowded Fisherman's Wharf traffic. We bypassed the T-shirt and junk shops and made our way to the public pier, where we could open up and let the Segways fly. Then we jumped up to a faster speed limit, whizzing past the tourists at just over 8 mph. (Segway envy is half the fun!) From there, it was up the hill to Fort Mason and then on to the Marina Green and Palace of Fine Arts.

The whole thing isn't cheap—about $65 per person. But then, remember that each of these deluxe Segways retails for over $4,500—which makes this tour a veritable bargain.

vary enormously according to neighborhood. Furthermore, some neighborhood merchants seem to band together, so as to form a unified front. For example, all the stores in one area may be closed on Mondays.

While major stores are open daily, expect hours—especially in small shops—to be oddball, such as 11am to 7pm.

Traditional big stores usually stay open Monday through Saturday from at least 10am to 6pm. On Sunday, they may open at 11am or noon and close at 5pm. But then again, they may not.

Some stores, especially alternative-lifestyle stores (Trader Joe's, Whole Foods Market), are open 12 hours a day, 7 days a week—or even longer. Whole Foods, for instance, is open from 8am to 10pm every day of the week.

SHOPPING & PEEING

You may think that your bathroom habits are none of my business. You may be right, under normal circumstances. But since I expect you to be on the streets a lot, and since I've had a fair amount of trouble finding friendly toilets, I thought I'd mention it.

For some reason, the entire city of St. Helena, in Napa Valley, is a no-pee-pee zone—and that's for people, not dogs. It is virtually impossible to find a public toilet or a store that will let you use theirs.

In the City, you'll have better luck in fast-food restaurants, department stores, hotel lobbies, malls, or public buildings. All California public toilets have facilities for those with disabilities.

SHOPPING & SALES TAX

California sales tax is a whopping 8.75%, one of the highest in the U.S. To avoid this tax, see "Charge & Send," below.

CHARGE & SEND

If you are looking to dodge sales tax, you must have the store ship your purchase outside the state of California. Furthermore, to be totally technical about the law, you can't bring that item back into the state of California for 90 days. But, if you live in a state other than California, remember this trick.

If you want to send packages to yourself, just to cut down on your luggage or schleppables, there are several branches of the **UPS Store** (www.ups.com), including one convenient location at 588 Sutter St., at Mason Street (© 415/834-1555), 2 blocks off Union Square. It's open Monday through Friday from 9am to 6pm, Saturday from 10am to 5pm.

ABOUT THAT WEATHER

I calculate that 30% of the clothes in my closet were bought on the road, when the weather was not what I was expecting. While San Francisco has plenty of stores to tempt you—and many bargain sources if you need to fill the gaps in your closet or suitcase—you might want to remember that the weather in the City by the Bay can be downright strange. Keep this in mind while packing, so you don't end up throwing away your travel budget on things you have back home.

To make sure you spend your shopping allowance on treats, check online weather sources (like www.weather.com) beforehand and prepare for the unexpected. Summer can be cold, and winter can be rainy. When it rains, it pours. Dress in layers and bring clothes that cover any possibility—that way, you can spend your shopping money on the things you really want to buy.

NATURAL SELECTION

You can make the argument that the shopping in San Francisco is a very closed system, that the good stuff is truly hidden, and that what's in plain sight and in easy-to-reach neighborhoods is merely a selection of American department stores and chains that have many branches dotted all over the

U.S. (and are most likely in your hometown, too). But wait. There is some good news hidden in here.

These stores differ from the ones in your mall in that they are often large, or even very large. They may have more range and larger selection in terms of styles and sizes in stock. They may test newer merchandise and rotate the stock more quickly than at home. For instance, while most Gap stores are created equally, the Banana Republic in downtown San Francisco is a flagship store—and is therefore better than just about any other Banana Republic in the U.S., except maybe the one on Fifth Avenue in New York. There are well-known brands that are still worth shopping while on your visit, as well as some majors that simply might not exist in your state. J. Jill stores, for one, are hard to find.

You may also have the chance to shop in the kind of chain store or multiple that has not yet come to your hometown. **Lush,** a British bath-and-beauty firm with a twist, is the best example I can think of. It has two locations in San Francisco, at 240 Powell St., off Geary Street (© **415/693-9633**), and 2116 Union St., between Webster and Fillmore streets (© **415/921-5874**); see p. 130 for a full review. **Sephora** (www.sephora.com), the French supermarket of beauty brands, is another, although by now it has pretty much spread across the United States. It has branches at 33 Powell St., at Market Street (© **415/362-9360**), and 2083 Union St., at Webster Street; see p. 132 for more information. As you must have already noticed, the San Francisco flagship branches of both these stores are located on Powell Street, right between Union Square and Market Street— an area you will be reading about a lot in these pages, and will doubtless be visiting as you do your own personal shopping. Just by testing a few stores on this busy street, you can get an idea of how similar or different the branch stores are from the ones you normally shop at home.

Chapter Three

....

SHOPPING TIPS FOR INTERNATIONAL VISITORS

Sitting midway between Europe and Asia, San Francisco has an international appeal that has long attracted visitors from across the Atlantic and Pacific oceans. Nowadays, with a weak dollar and a strong euro, more and more European visitors are headed to the City by the Bay. United Airlines recently began nonstop service from Paris to San Francisco, signaling that it's now easier than ever to see one of America's most interesting cities. Whether you have yen or baht, pounds sterling or euros burning a hole in your pocket, you'll find value to spending them in the U.S.—and joy in spreading them around San Francisco in particular. Just don't expect everyone to speak Chinese.

VISIT AMERICA

....

If you are planning to visit several American cities, ask your carrier about Visit U.S. fares, which are usually made in conjunction with a code share and offer discounted prices on domestic travel within the U.S.; they are available only to those traveling from overseas. Note that all travel must be made within the same airline network. For example, if you fly Air France from Paris to San Francisco, your intra-U.S. travel must be on Delta or another member of the Star Alliance network. If you want to use American Airlines for your connections within the U.S., then you should enter the country via American or one of its OneWorld partners. These fares are particularly handy because they allow for one-way travel and are not priced round-trip, as most domestic fares are.

But wait: Some of the discount domestic airlines also price their tickets based on one-way transit, or even by leg, so you might want to run a comparison. Connecting in and out of the Bay Area through the low-cost carrier **Southwest** (© 800/I-FLY-SWA; www.southwest.com), for instance, requires using the Oakland airport—but this can mean very low fares to a large number of U.S. destinations. Many foreign visitors have never heard of Southwest, but it has a reputation for excellent service and low everyday prices. **JetBlue** (© 800/538-2548; www.jetblue.com) is another such airline that a travel agent in Europe or Asia may know nothing about.

GETTING THERE: TRANSATLANTIC

Those who fly to the U.S. on a transatlantic route have a choice of stopping at an East Coast gateway city to change to a domestic carrier that serves San Francisco; flying through a Midwestern hub city (most likely Chicago, Minneapolis, Cincinnati, or Detroit) en route; or taking a nonstop from a European hub city, such as London, Paris, or Amsterdam.

If you have to make a connection through a hub, be smart and think about the time of year when you are flying—and if you have a choice, try to book through a southern hub city (like Dallas) rather than a northern one (like Chicago), which may be more adversely affected by bad weather.

You may also want to try picking a U.S. airport that is not as well traveled as your average big-city hub. Aside from the obvious reasons, remember that you must legally enter the country and clear Customs at your first point of arrival. It's a lot quicker to clear Customs in Philadelphia or Houston than

Atlanta or Miami. If you are not booked on a nonstop flight to San Francisco, explore your options for connections carefully. Also, make sure you have at least a 2-hour layover to clear Customs and to connect to your onward San Francisco–bound flight.

GETTING THERE: TRANSPACIFIC

Things have changed since back in the days when Pan Am owned the skies. United Airlines bought Pan Am's transpacific routes and has become the dominant international carrier at SFO; meanwhile, other airlines have also added to the air traffic that now links San Francisco to Honolulu, Beijing, Shanghai, Guangzhou, Hong Kong, Taipei, Tokyo, Osaka, Seoul, Singapore, Bangkok, and Sydney, among others. *Note:* United recently launched the first nonstop flights between the U.S. and Vietnam since the end of the war there.

ABOUT YOUR PASSPORT

Note that as a security precaution, the U.S. now insists on a special holographic passport. If you do not have such a passport, you will be denied entry into the country. Also, children may no longer travel on family passports, but must instead, have individual passports. I don't want you to freak out, but be sure to get this all cleared up long before you depart. Also note that specific countries were not able to meet the deadlines for these higher-security passports and were thus granted extensions. Ask for details before you're sorry. Further information may be found on the U.S. State Department's website at **www.travel.state.gov**.

ARRIVING SAN FRANCISCO

....

While your visit will center on San Francisco, you may want to consider using any of the other Bay Area airports, especially if you have domestic air connections from another U.S. city. See p. 19 for information on area options such as **Oakland International Airport (OAK)** and **San Jose International Airport (SJC)**. Most of the smaller U.S. airlines do not have advertising or representation outside the country, so unless you do some research, you may not even know what your travel options are or what kinds of opportunities you have to save money on your tickets.

If you are flying nonstop from a European or Asian city, you will arrive at **San Francisco International Airport (SFO)**. The other area airports mostly serve domestic flights within the U.S., although Oakland does handle some nonstop international flights to a limited number of destinations.

MONEY TALKS

....

Money Exchange

The single easiest way to get money in USD (U.S. dollars) is through an ATM. However, your bank's charges for using an unaffiliated ATM can be outrageously high; be sure to ask about these fees before you leave home. You may find that good old-fashioned traveler's checks, bought in U.S. dollars, offer ease and added security. Hotels and major stores will change traveler's checks. *Note:* If your traveler's checks are in a foreign currency, expect to pay a fee to exchange them and to use either a bureau de change, of which there are many in the Union Square area, or a hotel; your rate of exchange will also be less favorable.

One of the problems with exchanging money is that you'll be forced to make choices based on convenience, high fees, and security. Although you may want to exchange a large sum to avoid paying additional exchange fees, do *not* walk around with a lot of extra cash in San Francisco. While this city is no more dangerous than other large cities around the world, it does have its share of street crime.

Money Perceptions

Because Asian currencies are most often pegged to the U.S. dollar, the rate of exchange has remained more or less stable. However, the euro—introduced in 2001—has gained enormous strength over the U.S. dollar in the last year. As we go to press, the euro is worth $1.30. Sterling has also risen; at press time, the British pound was trading at just about $2 for £1. This means that those who are shopping from the euro zone will consider everything *cheap* in the U.S.

Price-Tag Realities

So if everything is *cheap* in America, are designer clothes—especially beloved European luxe brands—less expensive in the U.S.? Nope. Not at regular retail, anyway. Here's how it works.

The big luxury brands hold market at their headquarters to sell a season's worth of merchandise. They fix the prices to cover the spread of exchange rates over the next 6 months. With a rising euro and falling dollar, there is no way merchandise imported to the U.S. from Europe can cost less than it does in Europe. However, because sales in the U.S. tend to be more frequent and more dramatic, you may find something marked down to a better price. But this takes luck.

Tipping Tips

Service charges are rarely included in the U.S. While they are often hidden in room-service bills at your hotel, or added to a restaurant bill if your party has five or more people, in most cases you're on your own when it comes to tipping. And Americans not only expect tips—they think they deserve them, no matter how the service was. Americans rarely equate the amount of the tip with the quality of service. They just want 20% of the bill.

Note: When you figure 20%, do so from the price for goods or services before tax was added on. In San Francisco restaurants, you can use the easy trick of simply doubling the sales-tax amount. This actually gives you a tip of about 17%. Then round off the pennies or odd numbers.

Gratuities for luggage services are somewhat related to how fancy your hotel is. A tip of $1 per bag is considered normal in hotels rated below four stars. At fancy hotels, you're expected to tip around $2 a bag, or a rounded-up sum—say, $5 for two pieces of luggage and a tote bag.

For taxi rides, round the fare up to the next dollar and then add an extra dollar for short-haul rides, more for longer trips.

GETTING AROUND

See the sections called "The Lay of the Land," (p. 24), and "Getting Around," p. 25, for useful information on navigating the Bay Area.

If you don't speak English, don't fret. San Francisco is a very international city and there is every chance your taxi driver may even come from your hometown.

The international rule of foreign-ness also applies in reverse. Just because you see a person who looks Chinese, do not assume he or she is Chinese or speaks Chinese.

Mime will get you a long way, as will hand motions. Of course, if you are reading this book, you probably understand some English. When you find a listing you're interested in, just point to it and show the guidebook to someone who might be able to help.

PHONING AROUND

Using Phone Cards

Since you're probably well aware of the fact that most hotels charge an outrageous amount for phone calls (be they local, long distance, or international), remember to use a phone card to save money. Hotels will often charge a flat fee of $1 for each phone-card call you make (in that case, you may want to head to the lobby in search of a pay phone). On the other hand, many hotels now allow unlimited free local calls. Ask.

A phone card will require that you dial a series of numbers and access codes (and that you have the kind of eyesight that can read small print), but it will save you a tremendous amount of money. Phone cards are most easily bought near the cash register at drugstores such as Walgreens, Rite Aid, or Longs (all with numerous locations in the Bay Area). Most cards allow for international long-distance calls. Some cards can be used in both the U.S., as well as any other country in the world, so you can still use the remaining time on the card when you travel onward or return home.

Making International Calls

To make an international call from the U.S., the system is different from that found in every other foreign country. Dial 011 and then the country code, followed by the city code and phone number. Dialing 00, which may be your usual method of getting an international line, will instead get you an operator in the U.S.

Receiving Mobile Calls

If you have a three-way phone system, you can receive calls on your regular mobile phone and through your regular phone number. You will pay a large relay or roaming fee for each international call. To charge your phone—assuming it's 220 volts, as is common in Europe and many parts of Asia, and the battery charger is 110-220 volts—you'll need to use a simple plug adaptor. Note that if it is not, you will not be able to walk into a U.S. phone store and simply buy a new charger for your 220-volt phone.

Using Prepaid SIM Cards

Prepaid SIM cards for your own mobile phone are available through Virgin Mobile and T-Mobile; the latter has more stores and vendors in San Francisco. A SIM card, providing service and 2 hours of talk time with a local phone number (area code 415 in San Francisco), will cost about $50. You can add more minutes online, on the phone, in a T-Mobile store, or at any store that sells T-Mobile recharge cards. These are available in $10, $25, and $50 increments. Extra minutes are priced in bulk, so the per-minute rate is better when you buy $50 worth of time rather than $10.

The recharges to the phone are good for up to 2 months, which means that unless you return to the U.S. to use that SIM card again, you should be prepared to use all your minutes or lose 'em. The phone will tell you how many minutes you have left, so you can use the minutes appropriately.

Unlike many phone systems in Europe, U.S. phone companies charge you (in minutes used) to receive calls. Furthermore, with prepaid cards, it's unlikely that you can take advantage of common U.S. promotional deals such as free calls after 7pm or free weekend calls. Ask first. Assume nothing.

Although the area between Market Street and Union Square is dense with computer and phone stores, I tried several places before I was able to find a prepaid SIM card. I have visited most of them and suggest it's easiest to just pop into **T-Mobile,** at 50 Powell St., which is right at the cable-car turnaround and exactly in the heart of tourist tromping grounds between Market Street and Union Square.

Using Pay Phones

Pay phones in the U.S. will accept phone cards, but codes must be input manually—there are no electronic swipe cards at this time. You can swipe a bank card, but not all pay phones accept all bank cards. I have only Visa cards—one from a U.S. bank and one from a European bank—and I could not find a pay phone at SFO that would accept either. They all wanted

MasterCard. Go figure. And this was for a local call, not an international one.

SHOPPING AROUND

If you shop with euros, you may be so blown away by how low American retail prices are that you'll lose sight of additional ways to save money. Keep in mind that all stores have sales and markdowns throughout the year. In Europe and in some parts of Asia, sales are held only twice a year; there may be promotions outside those official sale periods, but they are nothing like in the U.S., where everything seems to always be on sale.

Aside from regular retail sources, there are many layers of retail stores that specialize in lower prices. Ask around, use this book, and find out about:

- **Off-Pricers:** Stores that sell branded merchandise (often from a previous season) at a reduced price—often 40% to 60% off the regular retail price. (Marshalls, Ross Dress for Less.)
- **Price Clubs:** You join the club by paying an annual fee, usually $30 to $50, and then get access to brand-name merchandise at low prices. Many items are sold in bulk, especially the foodstuffs. (Costco.)
- **Discounters:** Stores that sell branded merchandise at up to 20% off. (Target, Wal-Mart.)
- **Outlet Stores & Malls:** Factory outlets are usually owned by the manufacturers to clear out unsold merchandise; they're often grouped not within the factory itself but in a mall or village that provides one-stop, destination shopping. In San Francisco, there are a few freestanding outlets right in town (Nordstrom Rack) and more located outside of town, clustered into shopping centers.

GET THEE TO THE 'BURBS

For more than a sociologist's look at shopping in the Bay Area—and the United States—you should get out of San Francisco proper and into one of the upper-middle-class suburbs, where big-box, discount, and off-price stores are all grouped together.

You'll save time and money and have an understanding of a segment of American retail that simply doesn't exist in Asia or Europe. One example is those big-box stores—enormous stores that are somewhat like *hypermarches,* but are often devoted to only one segment of the market, such as Petco (which, believe it or not, sells only merchandise for pets).

Two of my best shopping experiences were in the San Francisco suburbs, in Marin County at a mall called **Vintage Oaks** (p. 157), and in the East Bay in Moraga, at the **Mycra Pac Designer Outerwear Outlet** (p. 230), a source for micropore raincoats. Moral of the story: If you care about saving the maximum amount of money, expect the deals to be located outside of the city center, and be willing to drive and search.

For me, having a car made everything suburban possible; driving around made me feel like I was really in America.

PAYING UP

If you do not pay cash for your purchase, you may be introduced to some of the newfangled technology used for electronic payments in the U.S. Debit cards are not as popular in the U.S. as they are in Europe, but credit cards are used frequently. The new technology includes swiping your card across a tablet and using a specialized stylus to sign an electronic screen.

SALES TAX

Visitors who are not used to shopping in the U.S. will be surprised when they discover that the price marked on a tag is not the final price paid for an item. At the cash register, state sales tax will be added. To avoid the nearly 9% additional charge, you must send your purchase out of state (p. 33). Although this tax is more or less equal to what Europeans refer to as VAT, there is no VAT refund in the U.S. for foreign visitors.

PENNIES FROM HEAVEN

Because of the addition of sales tax to the prices, plus the American marketing tradition of pricing items a few cents shy of a rounded dollar figure, you will most likely owe a sum that involves the use of pennies. While change will be given, if you are shy a penny or two, look around the cash register to see if there is a cup or container filled with pennies. You are invited to use a few of these pennies to provide exact change. In return, if you end up with a few pennies left over in your hand after a transaction, it is polite to contribute your two cents' worth.

BRINGING IT HOME

Be careful about sending yourself merchandise in your home country, as you will most likely be charged import taxes.

The best bargain is in excess baggage. For travel within Asia and Europe, one pays by the kilo. However, for travel from the U.S. to a foreign destination, one travels by the per-piece system—you are allowed two pieces of luggage with a total weight of 50 pounds (22kg) each. Airlines charge a flat fee for each additional piece of luggage; this fee is usually between $100 and $130.

It is usually less expensive to pay for an extra piece of checked luggage than to pay overweight charges on the two pieces you are allowed. Ask your airline before you begin to shop.

The items you bring home will, of course, be subject to local duties.

Chapter Four

....

EATING & SLEEPING IN SAN FRANCISCO

Along with Manhattan, San Francisco is one of those cities that defies the average laws of hotel stays and regular eats. The hotels are fancier or funkier (choose one), and the food is more important than the address. In fact, many of the local hotels are international landmarks, and the entire concept of gourmet food in America, with an emphasis on native-grown ingredients, was invented in the Bay Area.

The hotel scene is particularly confusing for a variety of reasons: Many of the city's most famous venues have been bought up by chains; several chains run numerous hotels in the area; and the big luxury players are putting pressure on the smaller fish.

WEATHER OR NOT

Hotel rates in San Francisco and the so-called season are related to times of year, not weather. Winter, the "off-season," usually has milder weather than summer. But because Americans prefer to travel in the summer, this is an expensive time for accommodations. Peak season is September and October, when the weather is glorious: not too hot, not too cold, not too rainy, and get this—many a blue sky. Note that those convention planners love September and October, too, so hotels will be jammed, sidewalks swarming, and prices at their least negotiable.

THE BIG HOTEL CHAINS

Because it's such a popular destination for business travelers and vacationers alike, San Francisco hosts most of the major hotel chains and sometimes has competitive rates at accommodations in good locations for seeing (and shopping) the sights.

If you're one of those people who consider Union Square the center of the world for visitors to San Francisco, then you'll find most of the big American chains represented in the near vicinity; even more have hotels located closer to the Moscone Center, only a few blocks away. While these hotels are often enormous and can be impersonal, they may also offer excellent rates and/or promotions. Yes, they get groups and tour buses, but yes again, they are in business to move rooms. There's also no guessing when you book with a chain; you know exactly what you're getting.

If you're staying at a chain hotel, please heed this warning that came from a taxi driver with whom I was discussing life, religion, and politics. He told me that very often a fare would jump in his taxi and demand to be taken to "the Westin" or "the Ramada" or wherever, naming the hotel's management company. Keep in mind that these hotels change management and ownership often—in fact, most of the major hotels in the Union Square area are now affiliated with new brands. Remember, the taxi driver knows the hotel as the St. Francis or the Mark Twain, not as the Westin or the Renaissance.

To add to the confusion, further note that a large percentage of the hotels in the downtown and Union Square areas have changed names entirely!

HILTON SAN FRANCISCO
333 O'Farrell St.

This hotel may be the size of a high-rise football stadium, but it's got an awfully good location—about 2 blocks from Union Square and another 2 blocks, in a different direction, from Market Street. It's possibly of the school of design best left to tour groups and convention goers, but you know what? It often has great rates, promotional deals, or rooms that can be booked with airline miles. Don't knock it. What the hotel lacks in charm, it more than makes up for in location and made-to-suit amenities.

When I checked online, I found a room with a king-size bed for $189 a night. There are also "weekend breaks," as well as special prices for groups, members of AAA and AARP, and military servicemen. ☎ **800/445-8067** or 415/771-1400. www.hilton.com.

INTERCONTINENTAL MARK HOPKINS
1 Nob Hill.

What becomes a legend most? Could be InterContinental, which has taken over the iconic Mark Hopkins as part of its rebranding. The hotel is famous for its Nob Hill location and the Top of the Mark, a restaurant and club with spectacular views.

Rooms are old-fashioned in a 1930s style, but have all the modern amenities—including view, view, view. While yes, this hotel *is* on the top of a hill, there's a cable-car line right outside the front door, and you can easily walk down to Union Square or to other transportation, such as the Powell cable-car line that heads to Fisherman's Wharf or the San Francisco Shopping Centre, a large vertical mall.

Club InterContinental guests pay a little more for special privileges, including a breakfast buffet and cocktails. The concierge desk offers many personalized services, such as a jet-lag recovery kit and a currency pack for international travelers who need U.S. dollars in small denominations. In fact, the hotel gears many of its amenities to international visitors.

Rates usually start at $300 and go to the top of the hill. But wait! There are often special InterContinental promotions (though it can be hard to get a deal because this hotel gets its share of groups, especially on weekends). ☎ **800/327-0200** or 415/392-3434. www.markhopkins.net.

OMNI SAN FRANCISCO HOTEL
500 California St., at Montgomery St.

This central location is a little more in the business district than the tourist world, but it's still within walking distance of Union Square, Chinatown, and the cable car. The Omni San Francisco is also just around the corner from Jackson Square, an area studded with expensive and fancy antiques stores. Teamed with this good location is a renovated grande-dame hotel with an extravagant lobby and moderate rates. Guest rooms come with marble bathrooms, fancy sheets, and the usual technology you'd expect from a luxury property. In fact, this is the poor man's Four Seasons.

The Omni is only 3 years old (well, the renovations are 3 years old), so this hotel may not be on your radar screen yet. But you'll especially like some of the promotional rates—Fridays can be as low as $159, while a weekend deal gives you 2 nights for $269. © 800/THE-OMNI or 415/677-9494. www. omnisanfrancisco.com.

WESTIN ST. FRANCIS
335 Powell St.

Located directly on Union Square, the St. Francis is the doyenne of old landmark hotels. It became a member of the Westin family relatively recently, so few people refer to it by its corporate affiliation. The hotel is and will always be, simply, the St. Francis.

Note that with more than 1,000 rooms, this hotel is downright huge—it will never pass for small or *intime*. Also note that the hotel has two sections—a newer tower was added in 1972, and while there is nothing wrong with its decor, it looks and feels very 1972. It is considered the déclassé part of the hotel, so you should specifically ask for one of the sublime rooms in the old section (and get that guaranteed in writing).

Because of the tower, the lobby also has two parts—the newer part (where you check in) is very, uh, 1972. But the part of the hotel that fronts Union Square, where you'll find Michael

Mina's restaurant, is sensually gorgeous. Shoppers will enjoy the gift shop, one of the largest and best of any hotel's, along with the small arcade of stores and the pure luxury of the velvet Biedermeier chairs in the classic part of the lobby. Don't miss the chance to pop in.

Rates vary with the season; there are so many promotional deals that it's hard to even know what a room regularly costs (about $250). Special offers may include romantic weekends, spa days and nights, or even a Girls'-Night Slumber Party. The less expensive the room, the more likely it is to be in "the tower." © **800/228-3000** or 415/397-7000. www.westinstfrancis.com.

LUXURY SHOPPING HOTELS

The very definition of "luxury" is in question here, since for years the St. Francis was considered the height of local luxury and location. Now a member of the Westin chain, it's still considered nice, but not the top of the mark (excuse the pun).

It's only within the last several years that European luxury standards have come to town; the very serious international and domestic luxury chains have now invaded and begun competing with one another. Often these hotels are filled with guests who are regulars within a chain—Four Seasons prides itself on wooing repeat customers, and the new Ritz-Carlton is so fabulous that even a drive-by will make you wistful for a room there. Sometimes a landmark hotel becomes a member of a chain, as with the aforementioned St. Francis, as well as the Mark Hopkins and the Stanford Court.

FOUR SEASONS HOTEL
757 Market St., at Fourth St.

Those who book hotels by brand won't be disappointed with the brand-new Four Seasons, which is the first local property to gain five-diamond status in a single year. Hidden in plain sight, the Four Seasons has an entrance right on Market, across the street from Emporio Armani and Walgreens, but its main entrance is off a tiny street no bigger than an alley. The hotel is situated in a tower block that also includes the city's fanciest gym and condominium residences, which are served by a different elevator. Guests must ascend to the lobby and then switch to a different elevator to get to the rooms—but this is hardly a chore since the lobby is grand, the gift shop is well stocked, and the people-watching includes a combination of fashion and corporate types.

The location is indeed prime—this is city dwelling at its best. The hotel is 1 block from the big department stores on Market Street, almost across the street from Ross Dress for Less, at the foot of Grant Avenue, and a short walk from Union Square. There's also public transportation outside the front door; SoMa is just beyond.

My room had an excellent view of the stores on Grant Avenue; other units feature views across the city. But I didn't come for the view. The location is great, the service is wonderful, and yes, the lemon-soufflé pancakes are on the menu. The hotel is known for its Bulgari bath amenities (which are also sold in the gift shop if you don't want to steal them from your room); my room had goodies from L'Occitane, the Provençal firm.

This hotel ranks number one on the Condé Nast Gold List for San Francisco. Rates are around $350 to $400 per night. © 800/332-3442 or 415/633-3000. www.fourseasons.com.

MANDARIN ORIENTAL
222 Sansome St.

Also situated in a high-rise, this hotel is located in the business district of the Embarcadero. It appeals more to travelers here for work or those who know the Mandarin Oriental luxury brand, which is growing in the U.S. The brand stakes its fame on its service philosophy, but the restaurants aren't bad, either. The decor is Asian, and guest rooms are high enough to offer incredible views in all directions.

The shtick with this hotel is that it's as fancy as the Four Seasons and offers excellent service, but it costs less; however, the Four Seasons has a better location for shopping. Rates here begin at $260. ✆ **800/526-6566** or 415/276-9888. www. mandarinoriental.com.

SECRET HOTEL FINDS

BECK'S MOTOR LODGE
2222 Market St., between 15th and 16th sts.

The "in" spot for the gay crowd, this renovated 1960s motel features camp style and a great location at the edge of the Castro. Rates are low (sometimes under $100 per night), and the scene is fabulous. Parking is free. ✆ **415/621-8212.**

BEST WESTERN CIVIC CENTER MOTOR INN
364 Ninth St., at Harrison St.

Yes, it's a real live motel! And it's very Ozzie and Harriet on the outside. I have done a thorough inspection, and while I haven't yet stayed in this motel, I like it enormously for several reasons: It's clean with a bit of style; it's a block from some terrific discount shopping; parking is free; and its rooms go for around $100 a night.

While the neighborhood is, uh, in transition, this up-and-coming SoMa area already has lots of home-style stores, a huge Costco, Trader Joe's, Pier 1 Imports, Bed Bath & Beyond, and Nordstrom Rack (the enormous outlet for clearance merchandise from Nordstrom).

Guest rooms are decorated in basic hotel chic; they've just been renovated this year, so everything is new and fresh and in perfect condition. Expect to pay between $89 and $139 per night. A number of promotional deals are available online and for members of AARP and other organizations. ✆ **800/528-1234** or 415/621-2826. www.bestwestern.com.

WARWICK REGIS HOTEL
490 Geary St., at Taylor St.

I wish I knew a hotel like this in every city. It would be the perfect hotel anywhere, but it's a true gem in San Francisco— where it's hard to imagine such a winning combination of charm, location, and price.

A member of the Warwick chain (based mainly in Europe), this hotel is most often called, simply, the Warwick, rather than by its full name. Located 2 blocks from Union Square, the hotel is small (with 80 units) and personal, elegant and cozy.

Guest rooms are plush without being too stiff to enjoy. They're decorated with French antiques; many have fireplaces as well. Most of the beds are canopied; the rest are four-posters surrounded by silk fringe and curtains. The upholstery and wallpaper have a William Morris Art Deco feel. There is a secret seventh floor with just two rooms, accessed by getting off the elevator on the sixth floor and walking up a few stairs. These rooms are junior suites, both far more lavish than my apartment in Paris.

Rates vary with the season, but are always under $200 per night; $180 is the norm. © **800/827-3447** or 415/928-7900. www.warwickhotels.com.

SNACK & SHOP

Finding a nosh while you shop San Francisco is not going to be hard. The city has all sorts of eating experiences and world-class world cuisine. Even the diners are great.

There are cafes in most of the big bookstores, such as **Borders** (right on Union Square), as well as in the music/bookseller **Virgin Megastore.** Many of the chic Euro designer shops have cafes—try the cafe at **Emporio Armani,** where the food and decor are super and the prices are moderate. Of course, all the department stores have places to eat, and **Macy's** has a gourmet-foodstuffs department to boot. Shopping malls have food courts—the one at the **San Francisco Shopping Centre** even sells Krispy Kreme donuts.

Note: The Grocery Store is not a grocery store and it does not have a cafe.

DEPARTMENT-STORE DINING

CHEESECAKE FACTORY
Macy's, 251 Geary St., 8th floor.

This is a tad confusing. To look at it, you will think the Cheese-cake Factory is in Macy's. Technically, it is not. The famous comfort-food chain does have its own entrance, which is handy considering that it keeps restaurant hours, not store hours. If you're at the main front doors to Macy's, look hard right for the entrance to the restaurant.

I am not saying that you've come to San Francisco to eat at the Cheesecake Factory. What I *am* saying is the location is convenient; there are great views overlooking Union Square; and the menu is extensive enough to include something for any palate at a modest-enough price. In terms of turnover, this is the single busiest restaurant in town. Location, location, location. ✆ **415/391-4444.** www.thecheesecakefactory.com.

NEIMAN MARCUS
150 Stockton St.

There are two restaurants at Neiman's: The Café is the quickie meal option, was recently renovated, and offers a curry-chicken salad and lemon soufflé to swoon for. You'll be surrounded by chic shoppers here. ✆ **415/362-4777.** www.neimanmarcus.com.

HOTEL DINING

Many of the city's most famous chefs work their magic in the city's best hotels. If you like to book by the cook, check out the list below, remembering that chefs frequently move on. In fact, as we go to press, there's a chef change at the Fifth Floor, the much-acclaimed restaurant in the Hotel Palomar.

Michael Mina: **Michael Mina** at the Westin St. Francis, 335 Powell St. (© **415/397-9222;** www. westinstfrancis.com)

Wolfgang Puck: **Postrio** at the Prescott Hotel, 545 Post St. (© **415/776-7825;** www.postrio.com)

Richard Reddington: **Masa's** at the Vintage Court, 648 Bush St. (© **415/989-7154;** masas.citysearch.com)

Ron Siegel: **Dining Room** at the Ritz-Carlton, 600 Stockton St. (© **415/773-6168;** www.ritzcarlton.com)

Hotels are often a good place to stop by for a meal, as it gets you in the door without feeling awkward and allows the opportunity to poke around a bit. **Silks,** at the Mandarin Oriental, is worth investigating, especially at lunchtime if you want to see the big wheelers and dealers. The **Four Seasons** is a good choice for Sunday brunch—and provides a chance to bite into those lemon-soufflé pancakes I keep raving about.

PICNICS

Whether you're headed for a day trip out of the city or simply to a bench in Union Square, a picnic is a great way to enjoy local foodstuffs—and to save your cash for another meal (or more shopping).

Naturally, there are plenty of gourmet stores in San Francisco, especially good for picnics in your hotel room or at nearby parks. For in-depth listings, see p. 144, or try some of the places mentioned below.

FERRY BUILDING MARKETPLACE
Market St. and Embarcadero.

The granddaddy of all gourmet shopping and picnic foods is the Saturday farmers' market at the Ferry Building. All kinds of food stores and stalls are open during the rest of the week as well.

MOLLIE STONE'S
Multiple locations, including 2435 California St., off Fillmore St.

For gourmet treats, try any branch of Mollie Stone's, which is a normal-enough grocery store for the local population, but has a multitude of only-in-California-style foodstuffs . . . and enough whole-wheat granola to make your day. More than just a supermarket, Mollie Stone's is that combination of grocery store and town hall where everyone shops, meets, promenades, and drinks Starbucks. The San Francisco store is located a—dare I say it—stone's throw from Fillmore Street and is, therefore, perfect for picnic needs or gift shopping. There's a selection of area wines, kosher foods, deli items, and even fresh sushi—the ultimate picnic food.

Now, here's one of my best tricks: Do your general shopping in the area, and then pick up your groceries. If you have a receipt that totals more than $20, head to the parking lot and wait for the free Molliebus, which will drop you off right at your hotel. Why shop and schlep, I always say. © 415/567-4902. www.molliestones.com.

TRADER JOE'S
555 Ninth St., at Brannan St.

While perhaps not one's first choice for a picnic, this is a must-do for any shopper or foodie. Because Trader Joe's does not specialize in prepared foods, you may not find as much selection as you'd like for a picnic. You will, however, find wine, frozen foods, low-carb diet needs, Soy Vay sauce, cheese, nibbles, and enough to put a smile on your face and a kilo on your tush. As you read further into this book, you'll learn why

I specifically suggest the branch on Ninth Street. © 415/863-1292. www.traderjoes.com.

There are additional locations at 3 Masonic Ave., near Geary Boulevard (© 415/346-9964), and 401 Bay St., at Mason Street (© 415/351-1013).

WHOLE FOODS MARKET
1765 California St., at Franklin St.

The main San Francisco branch of Whole Foods is on California Street and offers a variety of programs such as a lecture series and community meetings. But we come for picnic foods! And ye shall find prepared everything here, from salads to sushi, and plenty in between; much of it organic, healthy, and oh-so-California. Soy me, baby. © 415/674-0500. www.wholefoods.com.

There are additional locations in SoMa, at 399 Fourth St., at Harrison Street (© 415/618-0066), and in Berkeley, at 3000 Telegraph Ave., at Ashby Avenue (© 510/649-1333).

Chapter Five

....

SHOPPING NEIGHBORHOODS

People are quick to tell you how much they looooooove San Francisco. In reality, it's the various villages of the city that are unique and memorable, the lovable parts. If you don't get out into these areas, you haven't really tasted San Francisco. And sourdough never tasted this good.

As far as I'm concerned, you can skip some of the most basic touristy areas—and shop Union Square with the understanding that it's there, it's easy, and it's without charm. Permission granted to think of Fillmore Street as the heart of the best part of San Francisco. See below for why. And the Haight? Even our 20-something reporters haighted it. On the other hand, in an attempt to be evenhanded, I then sent some local 20-somethings over—*Return to Haight,* we'll call the sequel—and they loved it. Go figure. But with or without Haight-Ashbury, there's still plenty to prowl. And, I think, several surprises.

Getting to many of these neighborhoods will require either a wad of dollars for taxi fares; a car and the will to find a parking space or pay for a parking lot; or the saintly patience to navigate public transportation, which may or may not be convenient to your hotel or lifestyle while on the road. With all these challenges in getting around, it's easy to see why the touristy areas just get more and more traffic and offer less and less true style.

San Francisco Neighborhoods

San Francisco Bay

Exploratorium/
Palace of Fine Arts

GOLDEN GATE
NAT'L REC. AREA-
FORT MASON

Beach St.

MARINA
DISTRICT

Moscone
Playground

Bay St.
Francisco St.
Chestnut St.

GOLDEN GATE
NATIONAL RECREATION AREA-
THE PRESIDIO

Lombard St.

Greenwich St.

COW
HOLLOW

Lyon St.
Baker St.
Broderick St.
Divisadero St.
Scott St.
Pierce St.
Steiner St.
Fillmore St.
Webster St.
Buchanan St.
Laguna St.
Octavia St.
Gough St.
Franklin St.

PACIFIC
HEIGHTS

Pacific Ave.

Pacific Ave.
Jackson St.

PRESIDIO
HEIGHTS

Arguello Blvd.
Cherry St.
Maple St.
Spruce St.
Laurel St.
Walnut St.
Presidio Ave.

Washington St.
Clay St.

Alta Plaza
Park

Pacific
Medical
Center

Lafayette
Park

Sacramento St.

CALIFORNIA ST.
SHOPPING

SACRAMENTO ST.
SHOPPING

California St.

Pine St.
Bush St.

FILLMORE ST.
SHOPPING

CLEMENT ST.
SHOPPING

LAUREL
HEIGHTS

Sutter St.
Post St.

Geary Blvd.

Japan Center

Geary Blvd.
O'Farrell St.

Anza St.

Parker Ave.

Masonic Ave.

ANZA
VISTA

Ellis St.
Eddy St.

Steiner St.
Pierce St.

Fillmore St.
Webster St.
Buchanan St.

JAPANTOWN

Jefferson
Square

Laguna

Turk Blvd.

Golden Gate Ave.
McAllister St.

WESTERN
ADDITION

Fulton St.

Fulton St.

Conservatory

Fulton St.

Cole St.
Clayton St.

Central Ave.

Lyon St.
Baker St.
Broderick St.

Grove St.

Grove St.

HAYES
VALLEY

McLaren
Lodge

Hayes St.

Hayes St.

Alamo
Square

Octavia Blvd.
Gough St.
Franklin St.

John F. Kennedy Dr.

THE PANHANDLE

Divisadero St.
Scott St.
Pierce St.

Fell St.
Oak St.

HAYES ST.
SHOPPING

GOLDEN
GATE
PARK

Stanyan St.
Shrader St.
Ashbury St.

Masonic Ave.

HAIGHT-ASHBURY

Page St.

Page St.

Haight St.

Haight St.

Waller St.

Kezar
Stadium

Pavilion

Frederick St.

Waller St.

Buena Vista
Park

Duboce
Park

Hermann St.
Duboce Ave.

Market St.

Carl St.

14th St.

Noe St.

Guerrero St.

MISSION
DISTRICT

Parnassus Ave.

CORONA
HEIGHTS PLGD.

THE
CASTRO

Church St.

TOURISTY NEIGHBORHOODS

....

Union Square

Union Square is the most famous piece of real estate in San Francisco—hmmm, well, maybe Haight-Ashbury is, but then, that depends on how old you are. To me, Union Square is the center of the world, although this is more for directional purposes. Union Square is what we must consider "downtown": the heart of the action.

Emotionally, Union Square is not my favorite part of town, even though this is where most of the big name and major brand stores have their doors. In fact, I clearly recall standing on the corner of Sutter Street and Grant Avenue (everybody now, sing a chorus from *Flower Drum Song*) and thinking, as Bette Davis once put it in one of her movies: "What a dump." Talk about ugly sprawl. Ouch. I was far from dazzled.

The neighborhood is not swank—even though many of the stores are. The architecture is downright weird, in that there are some fabulous-looking buildings (from the outside), but the area, as a whole, has a low-built, urban-sprawl atmosphere without ever coming together visually. It has no feeling of fun or beauty, or even sense of place.

Nonetheless, Union Square is the major tourist and commercial hub of the city. Most major hotels and department stores are crammed into the area surrounding the actual square, which was named for a series of pro-Union war demonstrations at the outbreak of the Civil War (the "War between the States," as I was taught to say, growing up in the South). Few remember any of the wars commemorated by the park and the statue therein (for yet a different war). Today, Union Square means "shopping" to most visitors. And, after all, why are we here except to shop?

A plethora of upscale boutiques, restaurants, and galleries occupy the spaces tucked between the larger buildings. Every major department store in America is either on Union Square (**Saks, Macy's, Neiman Marcus**) or a block away on Market

Union Square

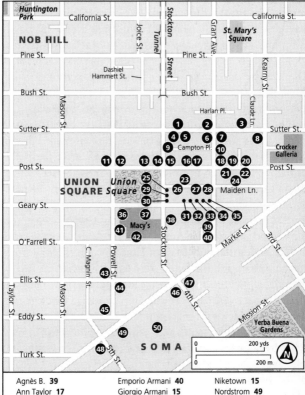

Agnès B. **39**
Ann Taylor **17**
Arthur Beren Shoes **25**
Babette **5**
Banana Republic **7**
Big Pagoda **2**
Bloomingdale's **50**
Borders **11**
Bottega Veneta **33**
Britex Fabrics **32**
Brooks Brothers **19**
Burberry **16**
Caswell-Massey **1**
Chanel **27**
Christian Dior **29**
Coach **18**
Cole Haan **9**
Diptyque **26**
DSW Warehouse **43**

Emporio Armani **40**
Giorgio Armani **15**
Gucci **30**
Gump's **22**
Henry Cotton's **35**
Hermès **28**
H2O Plus **31**
Levi's Store **14**
Loehmann's **3**
Loehmann's Shoes **8**
Louis Vuitton **37**
Lucky Brand Jeans **10**
Lush **41**
Macy's **36**
Macy's Men's Store **42**
Marshalls **48**
Max Mara **21**
Mix **6**
Neiman Marcus **38**

Niketown **15**
Nordstrom **49**
Old Navy **46**
Prada **34**
Ross Dress for Less **47**
Saks Fifth Avenue **12**
Saks Men's Store **25**
Salvatore Ferragamo **37**
San Francisco Shopping
  Centre **49**
Sephora **45**
Talbots **20**
TSE Cashmere **24**
Urban Outfitters **44**
Wilkes Bashford **4**
Williams-Sonoma **13**
Yves Saint Laurent **23**

Street (**Nordstrom, Bloomingdale's**). Most European brands have stores within a credit card's throw, as do all the major off-pricers (two **Loehmann's** stores, plus **Marshalls** and **Ross Dress for Less** almost next door to each other on Market St.). Don't forget all the mass merchants (an excellent **Banana Republic**), some of which are originally from San Francisco (like home-style and cookware guru **Williams-Sonoma**).

Note that the area—as a shopping district—refers to more than the four streets that frame the actual square called Union Square. Perhaps the fanciest doors are on **Geary Street,** the southern landmark street, but my favorite is **Sutter Street,** which doesn't even pass the park directly. **Post Street** is another goodie—this runs parallel along the north side of Union Square Park, with more big names and the famous **Gump's,** one of the most important stores in American retail. And one of the best.

The pedestrian-only **Maiden Lane** moves east away from Union Square for the length of a mere 2 blocks. It has a national reputation as one of the most adorable (and upscale) streets in America, partly because it is, indeed, a lane and not a through street for vehicular traffic. It was cuter 20 years ago, but is still home to many a high-end name (despite a somewhat constant turnover among the flavors of the month with the must-have Maiden Lane address). Several local heroes have been in the Union Square/Maiden Lane area for years, like **Britex,** the fabric store, newly reopened after renovations.

Here's an important tip: The lower part of **Grant Avenue,** south of the entrance to Chinatown, is considered part of this Union Square shopping district and offers rows of designer shops. Do not assume that just because a store has a Grant Avenue address, it must be in Chinatown. In fact, the Union Square part of Grant Avenue is the hottest new address for upmarket and international brands. The street begins with **Emporio Armani,** at no. 1. And **Lucky Brand Jeans** has just opened at no. 222. The numbering system is odd, but the stores are not.

Union Square is bordered by **Powell Street** on the Westin St. Francis side of the square; this street reaches to Market

Street—the distance of two large city blocks. Powell is an excellent retail strip, with a mix of stores you might not know about (such as **Lush,** the bath source from London), stores you already know and love (**Urban Outfitters,** this one more like Anthropologie than others), and big Euro chains, such as **Sephora,** the French beauty supermarket. You'll be passing this way anyway, so leave enough time to slowly make your way from Union Square to Market Street on Powell Street.

There's many a hidden resource in the Union Square area, so don't think of it as one giant generic mall. You'll note that the "Bay Area Resources A to Z" chapter of this book, beginning on p. 119, includes many, many listings in this area.

GETTING THERE

You can easily walk to Union Square from Market Street, which has its own BART and Muni stops, as well as scads of bus and streetcar routes. From Fisherman's Wharf, you can hop the Powell-Hyde cable car and get off at Union Square.

COFFEE, SNACKS & LUNCH

All of the department stores near Union Square have at least one restaurant; some have a serious restaurant as well as a cafe. Born to Shop news director Sarah Lahey likes the cafe at **Neiman Marcus** for a quick curried-chicken salad. Salads, sandwiches, and light entrees are mostly under $10.

CAFFE ARMANI
Emporio Armani, 1 Grant Ave., at Market St.

Don't snicker like that—it just so happens that the food here is great. This isn't your average cafe-in-a-store scene, and it's one of my favorite spots in San Francisco (though once you're inside, the place feels so swank and European that you could be in any big city). Furthermore, the landmark building itself is incredible. The location is good—right on Market Street, across from the Four Seasons Hotel—and convenient for the start or finish to a stroll among the fashion mavens and Euro-brand giants on Grant Avenue. Prices are in the moderate range: You can eat well for $20 per person. The food is, duh, Italian. For reservations, call © 415/677-9400.

DON'T MISS

BABETTE
361 Sutter St., near Stockton St.

Babette is representative of the movement in local designers. She began in an outer burb, moved to upper Grant Avenue, and is now situated in high-priced real estate right near Union Square. Why? Because she's not only good, but also offers a vision. Babette's clothes are made for easy living and for travel—they are often prewrinkled or crinkled so you don't have to worry about ironing. Some are plissé pleated, much like the Pleats Please line by Issey Miyake. The clothes have both droop and drape, are easy to wear for all figure types, and, while a tad pricey, are worth it for their versatility. Expect to pay $200 to $400 for a dress. There are sales though (phew!). © 415/837-1442. www.babettesf.com.

DIPTYQUE
171 Maiden Lane.

First, breathe deeply. Smell the air. I doubt you will sneeze—this is no head shop. It is, in fact, one of the few U.S. stores for this French fragrance brand that's most famous for its candles. These fancy candles, in glass jars featuring a label of jumbled alphabet soup, have become famous for their chic. Diptyque also manufactures soaps and colognes in the same famous scents as the candles. In addition, there's a line of designer scents specially created just for Diptyque, such as one by John Galliano and a few by Eskandar, the French designer of cult fame and expensive drapey clothes for the Neiman's set.

Scent is fashion these days, so some whiffs are more "in" than others (although the fashion set has been swearing by fig for years). I happen to love the scent that smells like a wood fireplace. Last spring, the hot new thing was called "sweet pea"—not like the flower, but the green pea. If you're a Diptyque regular, you can ask for what's new. The cult-favorite candles cost about $40, and, if you're willing to spend that much, are one of the all-time great gift items. © **415/402-0600**. www. diptyque.tm.fr.

GUMP'S
135 Post St., between Grant Ave. and Kearny St.

Call it a ritual, call it a celebration: Stand on tiptoe and shout hallelujah! Gump's is the stuff of legends. When I was a teenager, my mother and I had a regular San Francisco ritual—first we went to Gump's, and then to the ladies' room at I. Magnin. Both were already icons in San Francisco. I. Magnin has not survived (RIP), but Gump's just keeps getting better.

Gump's is simply, classically, what retail is all about. The store has—and has always had—a very specific focus, which is something lacking in most stores nowadays. That focus is a Western eye toward the East, which suits the San Francisco environment in particular but also serves the universal shopper, as Zen notions and Asian influences are felt in all walks of design these days.

Now, the reason all this works is that Gump's offers very sophisticated looks and merchandise that successfully integrate international style. This is not some version of the Chinese arts-and-crafts store. In fact, it feels more like a museum than anything else. Displays are sublime. Merchandise is hand-picked. A bevy of international—and local—designers is represented, so we're not talking "what I brought back from my trip to Vietnam" here. Rather, think the best jade selection in the city. Think hand-crafted necklaces that cost thousands of dollars. Think Agraria scent, home fragrance from a local firm made good with a cult standing.

Whether you buy anything or not is secondary to the importance of absorbing all that Gump's has to offer. This is what you came to San Francisco to see, to feel, to experience. © **415/ 982-1616**. www.gumps.com.

Mix
309 Sutter St., near Stockton St.

This store is just a few doors down from Babette and is geared toward the same shopper, although the merchandise is (as they say in show business) the same, but different. Mix carries a mix of designers, mostly European names that you probably haven't heard of. The overall look is sleek, a tad droopy or drapey, and much in the hand-crafted, *artiste* flavor. To sum up, they make a statement without being overly bold. Prices tend to be very high. I was tempted here, but didn't really have $1,000 to spend on a suit, no matter how chic or timeless. Sarah, Born to Shop news director, almost bought the perfect black cotton skirt (sans price tag), until she discovered it was $850—and that's without sales tax. Still, if you have the money, they've got the goods. ✆ 415/392-1742.

KNOW ABOUT

Borders
400 Post St., at Powell St.

Everyone needs to know about a good bookstore with enormous selection; this one is right at the edge of Union Square. There is a secret to finding it, however: Look up! Yup, this Borders is upstairs (on what Americans call the second floor), without a storefront on the street. It took me forever to find it. (This is embarrassing to admit, but I hope to save you the aggravation.) Borders offers shipping, so you don't have to schlep your books around all day. This location is open until 11pm Sunday through Thursday, till midnight on Friday and Saturday. It's a great place to hang out; there's even a cafe. ✆ 415/399-1633. www.bordersstores.com.

Fisherman's Wharf

Perhaps even more famous than Union Square, Fisherman's Wharf is a no man's land unto itself, a war zone of tourism gone astray. Stop me before I freak out! Quick, taxi! Yo, cable

Fisherman's Wharf & SoMa

Alcatraz Store **4**
Barnes & Noble **3**
Basic Brown Bear Factory **2**
Bed Bath & Beyond **11**
Bell'occhio **6**
Cable Car Store **4**
The Cannery **2**
Cost Plus World Market **3**
Flax **5**

Ghirardelli Square **1**
Jeremy's **10**
Metreon **7**
Nordstrom Rack **11**
Pier 39 Mall **4**
REI **12**
San Francisco Museum of Modern Art **8**
Trader Joe's **11**
Whole Foods Market **9**

car! I'm outta here. Oops, is that a Cost Plus World Market I see? Well, let me reconsider my position for a second.

The Wharf was once the busy heart of the city's great harbor and waterfront industries. As far back as when I was 16 and a regular here (that being the '60s), the area was already touristy—the kind of place that sold tiny, live turtles with decals pasted on their shells. They even mailed the turtles out in little boxes for you. The very thought may make us wince today, but who knew about being ecologically correct in 1964?

Fisherman's Wharf has, alas, changed. But not for the better. Today, it is a tacky, tacky place that, when crowded, makes me want to run away . . . or hide in the **Cost Plus World Market** store. In fact, the Cost Plus is next to a **Barnes & Noble**, and this might very well comprise the best shopping in the area. But I digress. I regress.

There was a time when Fisherman's Wharf was touristy but charming. That time is long gone. Now it's touristy and more touristy, and then conventiony on top of that. Yes, many of the hotel chains here specialize in conferences. There are scads of hotels and motels—every major chain has a property here. Furthermore, cruise ships come to dock right at the edge (Pier 39), so you've got thousands of tourists wandering around before taking off for Vancouver or Alaska. Did I call for that taxi yet?

Still, you gotta do what ya gotta do. If you must visit Fisherman's Wharf, note some of these little details:

- North Beach (p. 94) is the neighborhood that runs into Fisherman's Wharf, so you can hit two touristy areas in the same time frame.
- If you have kids with you, there are some places of specific interest to children, including the chocolate factory at Ghirardelli and the bear-stuffing factory at the Cannery.
- If this is your time to "do" the cable car, you can get off 1 block from Ghirardelli Square to shop and browse this entire area.

There is, as can be expected, a fair amount of shopping here and around the multiblock area called The Wharf. The mall **Pier 39** has multiples and tourist shops to attract cruise passengers and those who really think they need to buy cable cars with barometers in them. In fact, there are several malls.

If you are a sophisticated shopper, you will not be amused. Besides Pier 39, there is another mall, smaller and closer to **Ghirardelli Square** (see below), called **The Cannery**. This one is so touristy that the only excuse you have to shop here is that you have a small child in tow and are about to make your own bear at the **Basic Brown Bear Factory**. Wait, I take that back—there are also **Fire Engine Tours** (© 415/333-7077) that I think are worth a giggle; the tour departs from The Cannery but actually takes you across the Golden Gate Bridge to Sausalito. If you prefer to get around by Segway, you can rent one for a tour as well—though this is not a great vehicle for shoppers. Fire trucks at least give you more space for your packages. (For more on Segway tours, see p. 32.)

In season, a **farmers' market** takes place every Friday and Saturday morning, beginning at 8am. Waterside vendors sell fresh seafood and shrimp or crab salads in paper cups (at outrageous prices). They claim their goods are freshly caught. Hmmmm. Do I look stupid? Still, it's an experience.

And before I totally diss the whole experience and turn you cold on Pier 39, do note that there is a good Internet cafe in the **California Welcome Center**, Pier 39, Upper Level, on Beach Street (© 415/296-3493).

GETTING THERE

Chances of finding a place to park your car here are small. Even if you find a space, note that none allow for more than 1 hour's worth of parking. There are a couple of lots and garages that charge outrageous prices and are usually full. Instead, either take the Powell-Hyde cable car to the end of the line and walk, or hop on the F streetcar line, which has a great route that links the Castro district to Fisherman's Wharf.

Know About

Alcatraz Store
Pier 39.

While you can find Alcatraz souvenirs just about anyplace in San Francisco (yes, even Walgreens), this store is pretty funny, especially if you're 10 years old. Souvenirs range from prison-stripe painter caps ($10) to coffee mugs with a prisoner at the bottom of the cup trying to scale the walls ($7). ✆ **415/421-0103.**

Cable Car Store
Pier 39.

What can I say? I thought you might want to know. Yeah, everything sold here is related to cable cars, which are an emotional subject for many visitors. You can buy anything from a 14-carat-gold cable-car charm for your charm bracelet to a small model of a cable car to posters and postcards and coasters, too. ✆ **415/989-2040.** www.cablecarstore.com.

Cost Plus World Market
2552 Taylor St., at N. Point St.

There is no question that Cost Plus is a multiple, not unique to San Francisco in any way. In fact, there are about 250 of 'em dotted around the U.S. You probably have one, or its sister store World Market, in your own neighborhood. (Point of reference: Sometimes this store is called by one or the other name—Cost Plus or World Market—and sometimes by both.) If you're a regular at this chain, perhaps you don't need to visit again while in San Francisco. If you don't have one at home, I suggest you might enjoy this store. I love it. It's not as great as it used to be, but then, none of us are.

I send you here for a great selection of international food products (this is where I buy my flavored coffee), cheap gift items, and home style. You can buy the exact same Ghirardelli chocolates sold around the corner, but for less money—and

Ghirardelli Square

This is actually a subset of Fisherman's Wharf, but many tourists don't know the two areas are adjacent, so I'm discussing them separately in case you're working off a checklist of must-do parts of town. Must you do it? Not for me.

Not to date myself more than I already have, but as luck would have it, I was at the opening of Ghirardelli Square, some, uh, well, about 40 years ago. It was remarkable then. Now it's very, very touristy and doesn't have much good shopping.

While the **Ghirardelli Chocolate Manufactory** itself has an enormous gift shop and sells lotsa edible souvenirs, such as candy bars in various sizes and bags of chocolates, you can buy many of these items for less money at **Cost Plus World Market** (there's one just a block away) or at a branch of **Walgreens.** Perhaps these alternate sources aren't as glamorous as a bona-fide chocolate factory, but they aren't as crowded, either.

Ghirardelli makes cooking chocolate as well as eating chocolate. Its cooking choc is better than the average grocerystore version, and if you aren't into imported French or Swiss baking chocolate, you may want to trade up here. There are also plenty of flavored chocolates; many come in wafers or small candy bars. Ghirardelli positions itself as more chic than Hershey but not as chic as Godiva. The powdered hot-chocolate mix ($4) makes a good gift item.

Ghirardelli Square itself is a three-tiered shopping complex created around a defunct chocolate factory. Thanks to its sublime location, it became an immediate success. Unfortunately, the retail-restaurant tenants change constantly, and the mall has gone from upmarket to seriously touristy and a little bit seedy. I know, the truth hurts.

in a larger package. This location also has a very good selection of local wines at excellent prices. Sometimes you'll find Niebaum-Coppola's four-can set of bubbly called Sofia Mini. It's $20 and makes an adorable gift.

The items sold here are imports and resemble merchandise available at Pier 1 Imports, but the store has a nice mix and may especially amuse international visitors. Prices are low, style quota is high, and the mixture of foodstuffs plus interior design is convenient. I'd plan to spend at least an hour here. That's easy to do, as this store is open Monday through Saturday from 9am to 9pm, Sunday from 10am to 8pm—which are much extended store hours for a Sunday. Is that great, or what? ✆ 415/928-6200. www.costplus.com.

Chinatown

Okay everybody, chorus line now, and hand motions, too: "Grant Avenue, San Francisco, California, USA . . ." yeah, it's a song from *Flower Drum Song,* and if you know it, you already know as much as you need to about Chinatown. That is, you know that Grant Avenue is the main street through the area and where it's all happening.

Of the major tourist neighborhoods, Chinatown is probably the most fun and the most worth shopping—it's just that I happen to go to Hong Kong and China frequently, so I know what this stuff really costs.

On the other hand, there is a lot of merchandise here that's specially made for American use, so you will see items that don't even exist in Hong Kong or China—that alone could be worth the visit. D'ya wanna hear about my old-fashioned, book-bag-style tote made from pink Chinese silk? For $13? Yeah, Chinatown isn't so bad.

Chinatown begins on Grant Avenue at Bush Street, north of Union Square. Beyond this boundary, to the north, lies a 24-block neighborhood with two main north-south streets (Grant and Stockton), a dozen cross streets, and, best yet, a lot of little alleys. There is charm beyond the tourists.

Note: Although you know Grant Avenue as the heart of Chinatown, in reality, Grant has several other lives; at its beginning, you have Market Street and a stream of very fancy designer boutiques that have nothing whatsoever to do with Chinatown.

Chinatown & North Beach

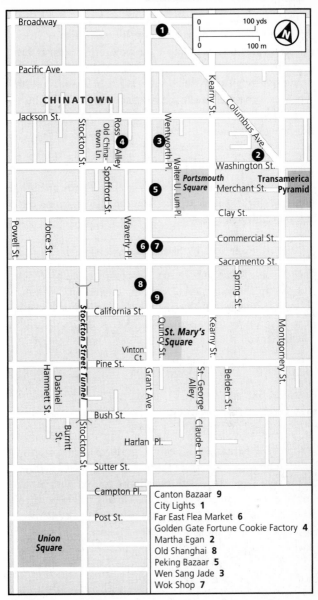

0   100 yds

0   100 m

Broadway

Pacific Ave.

CHINATOWN

Jackson St.

Kearny St.

Columbus Ave.

Stockton St.

Ross Alley

Old China-town Ln.

Spofford St.

Wentworth Pl.

Walter U. Lum Pl.

Washington St.

Portsmouth Square

Merchant St.

Transamerica Pyramid

Clay St.

Waverly Pl.

Commercial St.

Sacramento St.

Powell St.

Joice St.

Spring St.

Stockton Street Tunnel

California St.

Quincy St.

St. Mary's Square

Kearny St.

Montgomery St.

Vinton Ct.

Pine St.

Dashiell Hammett St.

Grant Ave.

St. George Alley

Belden St.

Bush St.

Burritt St.

Stockton St.

Claude Ln.

Harlan Pl.

Sutter St.

Campton Pl.

Post St.

Union Square

Canton Bazaar	**9**
City Lights	**1**
Far East Flea Market	**6**
Golden Gate Fortune Cookie Factory	**4**
Martha Egan	**2**
Old Shanghai	**8**
Peking Bazaar	**5**
Wen Sang Jade	**3**
Wok Shop	**7**

There's also, what locals call, Upper Grant, which is on the edge of North Beach. But the subject now is Chinatown.

Stores are open every day of the week. Some open at 9am, but only a few, so don't head over too early. Most keep more traditional retail hours and open at 10am. In season, they stay open into the night. The area is packed with TTs (tourist traps), but has a few stores that are enough fun to forgive them for being so obvious.

GETTING THERE

You can walk from Union Square—it's just slightly up the hill on, that's right, Grant Avenue. You can also arrive via cable car on California Street.

COFFEE, SNACKS & LUNCH

The Chinese restaurants I tested were touristy and/or terrible. I'd give up on the fantasy of a cheap, fun meal in Chinatown unless you're with a Chinese-speaking friend who knows the territory. Anyway, Chinatown is so close to the rest of downtown that you will not starve.

DON'T MISS

CANTON BAZAAR
616 Grant Ave., between California and Sacramento sts.

It's almost bizarre how many stores on Grant Avenue are named "Something Bazaar," so it's easy to get them all mixed up.

Canton Bazaar is perhaps the best of the TTs in Chinatown. It's a very large store with two floors packed with a huge range of every category of goods, including furniture. If you aren't careful, your eyes may glaze over and you could begin to think that everything in Chinatown's stores is the same. (It may be similar, but usually isn't the same.) This one-stop shopping mecca is like Ali Baba's cave gone Asian, with hints of what the Occidental market wants to buy.

One of the best things about Canton Bazaar is that a few of its items are made just for this store, so you can find things unavailable elsewhere in the world. The designers (or buyers) often take Western notions and have them translated into Chinese silks or satins; I went wild for the silk-brocade shoe bags for travel.

Prices are fair, but seem high to me since I'm used to bargains in China. On the other hand, I never saw some of this stuff in China, so it's a question of paying for it if you love it. ✆ 415/362-5750. cantonbazaar@aol.com.

GOLDEN GATE FORTUNE COOKIE FACTORY
56 Ross Alley, between Jackson and Washington sts.

Finding this place was fun, as Ross Alley is truly tiny and quaint and almost—if only for a second—puts you back in time, although it does not resemble a Chinese alley very much. That's all right, since they don't have fortune cookies in China anyway. The factory does have someone stamping out those cookies, and you will be given a free sample. The cookie you taste will be warm and delish. You will then buy bags of cookies, especially the chocolate variety since you have never seen them before. Later, you will discover the cookies taste awful. Oh yes, X-rated fortunes are available as well—these are marked and stored to one side. If you have curious children with you, beware. ✆ 415/781-3956. www.sanfranciscochinatown. com/attractions/ggfortunecookie.html.

KNOW ABOUT

OLD SHANGHAI
645 Grant Ave., between California and Sacramento sts.

Wait a second, first things first, and again, to repeat, do *not* get this store mixed up with Forgotten Shanghai (p. 126), which is not in Chinatown.

That understood, this is a fairly good store, rivaling Canton Bazaar as the best in Chinatown. Furthermore, it is right

Kristie Says

Kristie is a young Asian-American design student I met in San Francisco. Because she hangs out in Chinatown, I asked her to give us some insider tips. Here's her report:

Far East Flea Market, 729 Grant Ave., between Sacramento and Clay streets (© 415/989-8588), has a hodgepodge of stuff, but it's particularly good for families with young boys. There's a vast quantity of cheap and weird toys that only boys can appreciate. My 10-year-old cousin, Philip, went crazy here trying to figure out how to spend the money his mom had given him. The toy-car selection is pretty fantastic: There are little copies of everything from Porsches to Mini Coopers. Now I buy Christmas presents for all the boys in my family here.

Downstairs at **Peking Bazaar,** 826 Grant Ave., between Clay and Washington streets (© 415/982-9847), there's a huge selection of pottery, from tea sets to little bowls. A lot seems Japanese, but some are distinctly Chinese. Many shops in Chinatown sell this kind of pottery, but I think the overall selection here is pretty good, and the store is neat and clean, not dusty like other places. (*Note:* This is not the same store that Suzy raves about, which is listed on p. 76 and is called Canton Bazaar.)

Wen Sang Jade, Wentworth Alley, is not a jade shop that caters to tourists—you'll understand this the minute you step inside. It has the usual jade donuts and dragons and tigers, but also features cool jade pendants, such as a tiny wide-tooth comb, about a half an inch long. Really cute. I also like the fact that there's just about every color of silk string available behind the counter, so you can walk out of the store with a customized necklace. *Note:* The store keeps strange hours—it opens around 11am and closes at 5:15pm. Yeah, that's right, 5:15pm.

across the street, so you can get to the best spots in one big shopping spree. The place is a little more funky and less touristy, and it has more antiques (or old-looking items), especially in home style. © 415/986-1222.

Wok Shop
718 Grant Ave., between Sacramento and Clay sts.

There are more cleavers than Beaver ever imagined, as well as woks ranging in price from $20 to $200. The owner matches the wok with your personality and cooking style. Then you can get into flat-bottom vs. round-bottom and how to season your wok. © **415/989-3797.** www.wokshop.com.

Haight-Ashbury

Remember when you were cool and called this part of San Francisco by its hip name, "The Haight"? Yeah, man, that's tight. And while many will tell you the Haight has had a resurgence, I can't help but confess that I hate it. Except for two fabrics/crafts stores, I would never, ever (ever) return. It's both touristy and expensive.

I took Aaron and Jenny, our 20-something reporters, but they hated it, too. However, I've had local teens and 'tweens tell me how much they like the area and consider it one of their favorite places to shop. Peace and love, man. Make peace, not war. Hair piece.

Getting There

I took a taxi from Union Square and was shocked at how far away the area seemed to be. The meter read $11 and I gave a $2 tip; this is my idea of expensive. Especially since the entire area bored me to tears . . . and I still had to get back to downtown. If there is public transportation to the Haight, I couldn't make it work for me.

Coffee, Snacks & Lunch

As far as I'm concerned, the best thing about this area is the chance to eat. There are tons of cafes, bistros, diners, and holes-in-the-wall that beckon. You can try ethnic eats, foreign foods (crepes are foreign?), or old-fashioned American treats like omelets and grilled cheese. *Tip:* Try to eat at an odd hour, when the places are less jam-packed.

PEOPLE'S CAFE
1419 Haight St., at Masonic Ave.

Power to the People's all-American basics. Breakfast is served all day—the usual eggs, omelets, and French toast. Sandwiches are on homemade bread right out of the oven, thick and light and fluffy. The lemonade is homemade, too. Service can be slow if the place is busy, but it's worth the wait. © 415/553-8842.

TAQUERIA EL BALAZO
1654 Haight St., between Clayton and Belvedere sts.

Design your own taco or burrito here. Join the assembly line in this cafeteria-style eatery, and point to what you want (heartburn not included). © 415/864-2140.

CHECK OUT

AMBIANCE
1458 Haight St., between Masonic Ave. and Ashbury St.

If there were more stores like this in the Haight, I'd be over the moon. This is simply a funky shop with an overall look of layers and vintage, even though the clothes are mostly new. It looks and feels like vintage, so let's call it "antimacassar chic." Ambiance is somewhat on the same wavelength as Anthropologie. It is so mobbed on Saturdays that you may as well leave your claustrophobia at home. © 415/552-5095. www. ambiancesf.com.

Other branches are located at 3985 and 3989 24th St. (© 415/647-7144), and at 1858 and 1864 Union St. (© 415/923-9796).

AMERICAN APPAREL
1615 Haight St., between Belvedere and Clayton sts.

Before you write this line off as something more boring than the Gap, understand the politics behind the clothes. American Apparel uses only pure cotton; it has 20 different styles of simple T-shirts for humans, and even one for dogs; and all items are sweatshop-free. The store was founded in Los Angeles, but has become the rage of ecokids. Prices are low; colors are great. © 415/431-4038. www.americanapparel.net.

There are other locations at 2174 Union St. (© 415/440-3220), and in Berkeley at 2301 Telegraph Ave. (© 510/981-1641). A new store is coming soon to 363 Grant Ave., between Bush and Sutter streets.

DISCOUNT FABRICS
1432 Haight St., between Masonic Ave. and Ashbury St.

This is my kind of place, and I'd seek it out in any neighborhood; for me, it makes the Haight worth not hating. But I digress. This is a store filled with bolts and bolts of fabrics—home and clothing fabrics with dyes, trims, threads, sewing supplies, everything you need. Prices range from a tad high to nicely low, with an average of "fair." Hours are a bit unusual: Monday through Saturday from 10am to 6:45pm, Sunday from 11am to 5:45pm. © 415/621-5584.

MENDEL'S/FAR OUT FABRICS
1556 Haight St., between Ashbury and Clayton sts.

Mendel's stocks art supplies up front, then crafts supplies and fabrics in the rear. Mexican vinyl is also in the rear. In keeping with the neighborhood esprit, the store claims to sell "Far Out Fabrics." Cool, man. And if you think alternative retail keeps alternative hours, you'd be correct. Get this: Monday through Friday from 10am to 5:50pm, Saturday from 10am to 5:20pm, and Sunday from noon to 4:50pm. Could I make up those hours? © 415/621-1287. www.mendels.com.

YAK PAK
1474 Haight St., between Masonic Ave. and Ashbury St.

These totes are interesting enough for you to stop in and take a look. Check out the guitar-shaped bag as well as the many styles of messenger bags that are great for guys. © 415/241-0885. www.yakpak.com.

KNOW ABOUT

WASTELAND
1660 Haight St., between Clayton and Cole sts.

Vintage, and I don't mean wine. There are a handful of vintage-clothing shops on the street, and all are similar and overly pricey. Most of them have branches in other parts of town; some have branches in Los Angeles as well. ✆ **415/863-3150**.

Cow Hollow

In the cobwebs of my mind, Cow Hollow was one of the most adorable parts of San Francisco, all painted Victorian houses filled with cutie-pie boutiques and yuppie enterprise, brimming with love, sex, energy, and shopping smarts. On my most recent visit, I couldn't wait to rush over there to show it off to my 20-something kids, who also report for these pages. The adventure was a little bit embarrassing. What a difference a decade makes.

While Cow Hollow may think it's still cute, I'd suggest you forget it. To me, the Hollow is over the hill.

Located on Union Street west of Van Ness Avenue, between Russian Hill and the Presidio, this neighborhood once supported 30 dairy farms—hence the name. About 20 years ago, it became enormously trendy for retail, with its several blocks of Painted Ladies (Victorian houses in dreamy colors) turned into boutiques and a careful mix of funky national brands and local merchants.

Most of the good stuff has moved on; my feeling is that a **Noah's Bagels,** a **Starbucks,** a **Chico's,** and a **L'Occitane** simply do not a good shopping district make. I do like the store **Ambiance,** at 1858 and 1864 Union St., but there's a better location on Haight Street (p. 80). These days, there's just no there there.

My advice? Forget it and go to Fillmore Street instead (see p. 91).

Liz's Turn

Since Aaron and Jenny, Born to Shop's regular 20-something reporters, weren't that keen on Haight Street, I wanted someone who was.

Liz Lahey is 23. She grew up in Marin County, but now lives in Florida. When she comes back to town, Haight-Ashbury is the first stop on her shopping hit parade. Here's her report:

Amoeba Music, 1885 Haight St., at Stanyon (© **415/831-1200;** www.amoebamusic.com), is rightfully known as the best music store in the city. It's got a big selection of vinyl, as well as newer technology, and carries all types of music—from Christian to New Orleans jazz. There are also movie posters and a large listening area. Great scene.

Cheap Thrills, 1324 Haight St., between Masonic and Central (© **415/252-5687),** and 1687 Haight St., at Cole Street (© **415/252-8395),** are two separate storefronts, so don't get confused. One sells party favors and joke gifts. The other has Goth and dog-collar clothes. Woof, woof, woof. Down, boy.

It's BYOB (in this case, Bring Your Own Bong) at **Golden Triangle,** 1334 Haight St., between Masonic and Central (no phone). You'll see every color and price, going all the way up to $500. Talk about pipe dreams. And don't be square about it: If you use the word *bong,* you'll be thrown out of the store. The proper term these days is "water pipe." Can't take you anywhere, Mom.

Tattoos and piercings, anyone? What else can we say? Head to **Mom's,** 1408 Haight St., between Masonic and Ashbury (© **415/864-6667;** www.momsbodyshop.com), where you can choose your body art, ready to wear for the rest of your life. What will Mom say?

Piedmont, 1452 Haight St., between Masonic and Ashbury (© **415/864-8075;** www.piedmontsf.com), is drag-queen heaven for gals of all ages and sexes. There are walls of earrings and accessories, cute little hot pants and boas, and many wigs. If you're shy, you can shop online.

GETTING THERE

A taxi from Union Square will cost you $8 to $10.

COFFEE, SNACKS & LUNCH

As mentioned, there's a branch of **Noah's Bagels** (there's one everywhere in San Francisco) and, of course, **Starbucks**. The big brunch scene is at **Perry's**, 1944 Union St. (© 415/922-9022).

MODERATELY TOURISTY NEIGHBORHOODS

··

North Beach

While North Beach has an old and rather touristy reputation, it was full but not unpleasantly swarming with tourists when I visited, hence its position in this neighborhood category. The Italian quarter, which stretches from Montgomery and Jackson streets to Bay Street, has an easy-to-get-to location in its favor, as well as the famous **City Lights,** which, despite all the hype, is a darn good bookstore (see below).

There's a quasi-Euro feel to some of the area, although by the time you get to Washington Square on the far side, it's more of a village atmosphere than an Italian feel. Still, you can get a strong coffee without walking into a branch of Starbucks. The nightlife is equally swingy. Does anyone besides me even remember Carol Doda?

The main artery to North Beach is Columbus between Fisherman's Wharf and the Financial District. In this part of town, Grant Avenue is called Upper Grant by locals (though it's still marked "Grant Avenue" on street signs), to make sure everyone knows you aren't talking about Chinatown. The French boutique Lilith was once located in this area on Grant, but has since moved on to more chic pastures in Berkeley. Many of the other up-and-coming have also come up and left, but new little funky boutiques always replace them. For those who want cutting-edge shopping, Upper Grant is the best part of this area. There's also a slew of nail bars here if you feel like getting a manicure.

See p. 75 to review the "Chinatown & North Beach" map.

GETTING THERE

You can walk here from Union Square.

COFFEE, SNACKS & LUNCH

CAFE NIEBAUM-COPPOLA
916 Kearny St., at Columbus Ave.

If you can't get to nearby wine country but want a taste of Francis Ford Coppola's contribution to wine and food, pop into this popular bistro, where you can eat and sip and maybe even get a look at the Wizard of Oz. For reservations, call © **415/ 291-1700**. www.cafecoppola.com.

CAFFE TRIESTE
609 Vallejo St., at Grant Ave.

This is on Upper Grant, an area discussed in previous parts of this book that should not be confused with Chinatown. It's one of the iconic coffeehouses right in the heart of North Beach, with adorable stores around the corner. Next door, Caffe Trieste's own little shop sells coffee beans as well as coffee-making accessories. You can also buy the coffee in many area supermarkets. No credit cards. © **415/392-6739**. www.caffe trieste.com.

WASHINGTON SQUARE BAR & GRILL
1707 Powell St., at Union St.

What locals call the Washbag is one of two prominent cafes located on Washington Square Park (the other is Moose's). By walking through North Beach to the far side, you'll have explored the neighborhood yet settled down in a far less touristy area. The menu offers solid bistro basics with a French twist, as well as American classics (I had fried chicken). For reservations, call © 415/982-8123. www.wsbg.citysearch.com.

DON'T MISS

CITY LIGHTS
261 Columbus Ave., at Broadway.

I fell in love with my husband over a line from a Lawrence Ferlinghetti poem. What's important is not the personal love story, but the fact that City Lights, Ferlinghetti's iconic bookstore, is still here—and still one of the best independent bookstores in the country. In the 1960s, there was a sign here that said "Fuck Communism," which was considered totally outrageous. On my most recent visit, I noticed a button for sale at the cash register that said FUCK ART, LET'S DANCE. The more things change, the more they stay the same. And, in the morning, you find out she has bad breath and hates poetry. © 415/362-8193. www.citylights.com.

MARTHA EGAN
1 Columbus Ave., near Washington and Montgomery sts.

Just as Columbus veers off and leads to North Beach, you'll find this small shop that specializes in inventive clothing made from vintage fabrics. To illustrate just how clever the store is: When it's not open, there is a sign on the door that does not say CLOSED, but rather CLOTHED. The one-of-a-kind knits and stitched goods are just as cute. There's a funky blend of totes, handbags, sweaters, jackets, and even lampshades. © 415/397-5451. www.marthaegan.com.

SoMa

What city doesn't have an alphabet soup of acronyms to designate the newly hot parts of town? SoMa (South of Market) is not the SoHo of San Francisco, but it has been affected by recent development and is the so-called hot neighborhood of the moment. Originally, the area was largely rehabbed with dot.com money. It's anchored by the San Francisco Museum of Modern Art, Yerba Buena Gardens, Sony's Metreon, and a slew of big-bucks hotels. This neighborhood, which actually borders the Four Seasons Hotel and sits alongside the Marriott and the Moscone Center, is totally mainstream now, not even the slightest bit scuzzy.

However, there's more to SoMa further, uh, south. And yes, there are still some scuzzy parts—but they are quite a bit farther south. Tourists rarely venture past the core area around the Moscone Center, but the curious can easily explore for some genuine shopping ops. Watch your handbag.

See p. 69 to review the "Fisherman's Wharf & SoMa" map.

GETTING THERE

Since Market Street is one of the main thoroughfares right through downtown San Francisco, it hosts all major forms of transportation. The most touristy parts of SoMa are easily walkable from Union Square or reached via public transportation. To get deeper into SoMa, you will need a car or taxi.

COFFEE, SNACKS & LUNCH

Along with rapid growth comes quick turnover, and restaurants in this area come and go like fog on the bay. There are, however, a few spots that have stood the test of time and continue to serve great food. Born to Shop news director Sarah Lahey recommends the following in particular:

LULU
816 Folsom St., at Fourth St.

This iconic local restaurant serves comfort food with a touch of Provence. At lunchtime, you'll find excellent salads, tapas, and pizza; for a heartier meal, try the oven-roasted salmon or rosemary rotisserie chicken—and, if they're available, opt for the olive-oil mashed potatoes. Iron-skillet mussels arrive sizzling with a cup of drawn butter for dipping. Don't even think

about it (especially at lunchtime) without reservations. © 415/
495-5775. www.restaurantlulu.com.

YANK SING
49 Stevenson St., between First and Second sts.

San Francisco magazine continually rates this one of the best
Chinese restaurants in San Francisco. It does only dim sum—
you can nibble your way through more than 80 selections. Be
sure to try the "Creative Collection," which can include chicken
curry with avocado or lamb dumplings with mint. © 415/541-
4949.

There's a second location at 101 Spear St., near Mission Street
(© 415/957-9300).

DON'T MISS

METREON
101 Fourth St., at Mission St.

A mixed-use entertainment complex, this building contains several movie screens as well as the **Sony** store and some retail
opportunities in kiosks and small, open-store formats. The candy
vendor for the movie theater sells 50 different flavors of **Jelly
Belly** jelly beans. Even **Microsoft** has its own store here. Yes,
that Microsoft. © 415/369-6000. www.metreon.com.

NORDSTROM RACK
555 Ninth St., at Brannan St.

Okay, so the neighborhood ain't charming, and yeah, this is
almost warehouse space. On the other hand, ooh-la-la, is it
well hung.

Whatever Nordstrom doesn't sell on the floor of its department stores gets sent to its markdown distribution centers, of
which this is one. Let's call it two floors of fun. The designer
clothes are in a small corner of the store; the rest of the space
is a jumble of clothes, accessories, some home style, and shoes,
shoes, shoes. There is also a men's department.

In my humble opinion, this tiny strip center with Nordstrom Rack, Trader Joe's, Pier 1 Imports, and more is worth several hours of shopping delight—and cab fare. Just remember that this is far from chic and may not be any version of the San Francisco you think you've come to witness. © 415/934-1211. www.nordstrom.com.

TRADER JOE'S
555 Ninth St., at Brannan St.

Even if you have Trader Joe's in your hometown, you might want to visit at least one or two California branches, as they may be slightly different. Weekends, of course, are jam-packed, so you'll be not only shopping for food and wine but also busy staring at a variety of local types. The Trader Joe's concept is a sort of souk of gourmet foodstuffs and wine at the best possible prices. One of my stock-up items is Soy Vay, sauce for making Chinese chicken salad. This location is next door to the Nordstrom Rack, in a small strip of fun stores. © 415/863-1292. www.traderjoes.com.

There are additional locations at 3 Masonic Ave., near Geary Boulevard (© 415/346-9964), and 401 Bay St., at Mason Street (© 415/351-1013).

KNOW ABOUT

SAN FRANCISCO MUSEUM OF MODERN ART MUSEUMSTORE
151 Third St.

This museum gift shop offers a great selection of contemporary art books, as well as innovative design objects and furniture, contemporary jewelry and apparel, educational children's books and toys, posters and stationery, and an exclusive line of SFMOMA signature products. All proceeds support the exhibitions, educational programs, and artistic preservation efforts of the museum. © 415/357-4000. www.sfmoma.org.

Japantown

Japantown is touristy, but seemingly only filled with Japanese tourists, so it still feels authentic and is great fun to visit (and shop).

Bounded by Octavia Street, Fillmore Street, California Street, and Geary Boulevard, Japantown is most easily discovered through a single starting point: the **Peace Plaza,** which includes a hotel (the Radisson Miyako), mall, community center, and the Japan Center. Nearby, the **Kinokuniya Building,** 1581 Webster St., has the rest of what you want to see.

GETTING THERE

A taxi from Union Square will run you about $10.

COFFEE, SNACKS & LUNCH

The mall around the Peace Plaza is chockablock with eateries. **Mifune,** 1737 Post Street (© 415/922-0337), is a noodle bar in the Japan Center.

DON'T MISS

GENJI
Japan Center, 22 Peace Plaza.

The good news: This is a great source. The bad news: I could have saved $150 if I had just waited until I got here.

Genji, the anchor store to the Peace Plaza shopping mall, sells traditional Japanese furniture—new and old—along with some used kimonos. The short kimonos (which I like to wear with jeans and a turtleneck) cost $45 to $80 here; I paid $185 in Berkeley for virtually the same thing. Aside from furniture and kimonos, there are ceramics and small pieces as well. Genji also does custom work. © 415/931-1616. www.genjiantiques.com.

KNOW ABOUT

ICHIBAN KAN GROCERY STORE
Japan Center, 22 Peace Plaza.

This is not just a Japanese-products grocery store, but one that also has Pan-Asian cooking supplies and a small assortment of other items, all at good prices. Most of the things here can be found at other ethnic Asian markets in the Bay Area, but this makes a convenient and fun stop while you're exploring the neighborhood. ✆ **415/409-0472.**

NOT (YET) TOURISTY NEIGHBORHOODS

Fillmore Street

This is my favorite part of San Francisco, the neighborhood I suggest you explore in order to get the feel of the cute village street—and to have some fun shopping along the way. It's basically what you want San Francisco to be. The shopping ops are between Sutter and Jackson streets. Part of the fun, other than the sublime feel of the area, is the mix of resale and thrift shops, beauty sources (**Kiehl's, Benefit, Jurlique, MAC**), and finds. Real-people needs can be met at **Walgreens** (on Bush St.) and **Mollie Stone's,** which is enough of a gourmet supermarket to make grocery shopping fun. There's a **Starbucks** inside the supermarket and another one on Fillmore. There are also branches of the other big coffee brands nearby (see below).

GETTING THERE

A taxi from Union Square will run you about $13.

COFFEE, SNACKS & LUNCH

Of course there's a **Starbucks** and a **Noah's Bagels,** as well as a **Coffee Bean & Tea Tree,** where they make an iced coffee-chocolate drink that is to die for. You'll find a second Starbucks inside the **Mollie Stone's** grocery store.

CHEZ NOUS
1911 Fillmore St., between Pine and Bush sts.

This cozy restaurant is popular with the neighborhood residents. The Mediterranean-style menu focuses on tapas—choose from over 20, including phyllo dumplings filled with spinach and feta, calamari salad, and baked goat cheese with oven-roasted tomatoes. If available, try the Kobe beef or the grilled lamb chops with lavender sea salt. © 415/441-8044.

DON'T MISS

HYDRA
1919 Fillmore St., near Pine St.

You may peer in the windows of this bath and body shop, shrug, and feel like you've already seen all the shops like this that you care to see. That would be a big mistake. While the selection of bath bombs, soap slices, bath salts, and other body treats is similar to what you can find in other sources, the wide selection of rubber duckies is not.

These duckies come in two different types. The dressed-up version, like a duckie in bridal clothes, makes an adorable gift. The really interesting variety, however, goes by the name Devil Duck. There are perhaps a dozen different Devil Ducks, all different in terms of design. Just whaaaat is a Devil Duck? The tag reads: "Have a hot time in the tub." Translation: Devil Duck is a sex toy for women. It's the new and improved version of Rice-A-Roni, the San Francisco treat. For the shy or the technically inept: Take a look at the duck's tail. It has been modified to meet your personal needs. If you're really shy, you can order online. © 415/474-9372. www.hydrasoap.com.

PAPER SOURCE
1925 Fillmore St., near Pine St.

This store's motto is "Do something creative every day." To help you toward this goal, it sells various paper supplies, crafts items, and art papers; it also offers lessons and group classes. Don't miss the far rear of the store, where there is a huge collection of colored papers and envelopes in a variety of sizes—you can mix and match and go wild. ✆ **415/409-7710**. www.paper-source.com.

KNOW ABOUT

D&M WINE & LIQUOR
2200 Fillmore St., at Sacramento St.

California wines. Duh. Booze, too. ✆ **415/346-1325**. www.dandm.com.

MIO
2035 Fillmore St., between California and Pine sts.

This clothing store has a nice jumble of ethnic, funky, and easy-to-wear apparel. It's not the kind of source that immediately wows you, but rather the type of place where you look through the racks and realize that these are wearable clothes that make sense and have some creative spark. ✆ **415/931-5620**.

SHABBY CHIC
2185 Fillmore St., at Sacramento St.

This is the San Francisco branch of the SoHo (New York) concept store that promotes overstuffed furniture in comfy styles that could have been stored in the attic, but now have a delicious lived-in feel without being shabby at all. Not that you're probably shopping for furniture while visiting San Francisco—but the books and home style are worth investigating if you're looking for decorating ideas. ✆ **415/771-3881**. www.shabbychic.com.

Chestnut Street & the Marina District

One of the longest streets in San Francisco, Chestnut Street wanders in and out of cute zones. Therefore, it's most easily "done" by car first, so you can see the length and breadth and then decide where and if you want to stop . . . where and if you can get a parking space. The main shopping part of Chestnut is between Franklin and Lyon streets, which abounds with shops, cafes, boutiques, and cute. (Check out the 2000–2200 blocks.) This area is often referred to by locals as the Marina district.

Note: Some of the stores here have additional branches in other "cute" parts of town.

GETTING THERE

Chestnut runs parallel to Lombard Street (1 block away), which is convenient if you're driving towards the Golden Gate Bridge. Any of the Muni buses that go along Lombard will get you here.

COFFEE, SNACKS & LUNCH

JOHNNY ROCKETS
2201 Chestnut St., at Pierce St.

Come here for hot dogs, burgers, tuna melts, onion rings, and the best shakes in town. The table-side mini jukeboxes have all the sounds of the '50s and '60s. ☎ 415/931-6258. www.johnny rockets.com.

DON'T MISS

AMA
2276 Chestnut St., at Scott St.

Mamma mia, Ama mia, this store imports a hot-to-trot Italian look in clothes and accessories. Be forewarned: It sometimes falls into the category of fun to look at, but not to be worn in public. ☎ 415/345-1090.

BARE ESCENTUALS
2101 Chestnut St., at Steiner St.

Bare Escentuals is a makeup and skin-care line sold on QVC as well as in its own freestanding shops. The success of this Bay Area company is a local-gal-makes-good kind of story. Note the products created for problem skin and various medical conditions. © 415/441-8348. www.bareescentuals.com.

CATNIP & BONES
2220 Chestnut St., near Pierce St.

Clothes and accessories for dogs and cats. No relationship with Skull & Bones. © 415/359-9100.

PAPER SOURCE
2061 Chestnut St., between Fillmore and Steiner sts.

This is a terrific store for those addicted to colors, papers, cards, crafts, covered boxes, doodads, and touch-me, feel-me wrappings. © 415/614-1585. www.paper-source.com.

Hayes Street

Hayes Street is funky and has the feel of raw talent beginning to explode. This area is also called the Hayes Valley and has been coming along for about 30 years without dramatic results. In fact, the stores change around a lot; most of the fun stuff is in the 500 block. (The shopkeepers and bistros have wisely banded together within 2 blocks or so to make it easy for the consumer to shop.) This area isn't too far from the Moscone Center and is a fun way to see someplace small and edgy.

There are a few galleries here; if you love Mexican art and crafts and folk items, you will adore **Polanco**, 393 Hayes St. (© 415/252-5753; www.polancogallery.com). You'll also see some furniture design places, many that specialize in ethnic sleek, similar to Philippe Starck's designs or imports from Scandinavia. The neighborhood design gurus allow you to browse and will do up your home for you if you simply ask. There are also several shoe stores in the area.

As funky as Hayes Street is, don't expect total urbanism. There is a nearby Walgreens, but it's hidden away on Gough Street. Otherwise, you'll see no chain stores; no Starbucks. Phew. Is it worth a special trip? Well, that depends on how much you need a burger.

COFFEE, SNACKS & LUNCH

Count on **Flippers**, 482 Hayes St. (℗ 415/552-8880), one of the best hamburger dives in town, to stay constant. The Sunday-brunch crowd likes **Absinthe**, 398 Hayes St., at Gough St. (℗ 415/551-1590).

CHECK OUT

FLIGHT 001
525 Hayes St., between Laguna and Octavia sts.

The San Francisco branch of a Greenwich Village (New York) shop, Flight 001 has the same great mix of travel essentials and gimmick inventions meant to enhance travel, or just make you smile. It's a great source for gifts for people who have it all—or for just finding a few little luxuries to make your next long haul a bit easier. The store also carries some luggage and totes. ℗ 415/487-1001. www.flight001.com.

NOMADS
556 Hayes St., between Laguna and Octavia sts.

This men's store sells simple, postpreppy, international chic for metrosexuals. ℗ 415/864-5692.

TRUE SAKE
560 Hayes St., between Laguna and Octavia sts.

This is what you came to San Francisco to find—an original concept, and yet one that's related to the local geography. This store sells only sake. You can sake to me. ℗ 415/355-9555. www.truesake.com.

KNOW ABOUT

ALABASTER
597 Hayes St., at Laguna St.

This began as a garden-furniture, Italian-folksy, artsy-rustic kind of store and has since added pieces from Europe and New

England that have that covered-in-moss, rusty, or chipped-wood, dear-to-the-heart feel to them. Some of the items are new but just look rugged. It's the mélange that wins local hearts and minds, making you want to simply move in. © **415/558-0482.** www.alabastersf.com.

Friend
401 Hayes St., at Gough St.

Philippe Starck meets Alessi here, with glass tube bracelets and neon and every hot, contempo-design toy from the big Euro names. © **415/552-1717.** www.friend-sf.com.

Sacramento Street

Another long street in town, with nuggets of good shopping stretches. The area that's coming of age for shoppers is in Presidio Heights, between Lyon and Spruce streets. There are a number of nice antiques stores here.

Getting There

A taxi from Union Square should cost about $12.

Don't Miss

Designer Consigner
3525 Sacramento St., between Laurel and Locust sts.

The name says it all. This is a resale shop where a lot of Laurel Heights ladies who lunch on salads bring their gently worn clothes. Because they eat greens, sizes tend to be small. © **415/440-8664.**

Forrest Jones
3274 Sacramento St., between Presidio Ave. and Lyon St.

From the name of this store, you'd perhaps expect a haberdashery—certainly not a hardware store. And a very fancy hardware store at that. Forrest Jones carries many European items and brands, hard-to-find hardware and finials, and a good collection of dishes, baskets, gadgets, and fun stuff. © 415/567-2483.

THE GROCERY STORE
3625 Sacramento St., between Spruce and Locust sts.

Despite its name, this boutique is not a grocer at all. It's actually one of the chic-est stores in San Francisco and sells very high-end designer clothing for women. © 415/928-3615.

SUE FISHER KING
3067 Sacramento St., between Baker and Broderick sts.

This home-style store is known mostly for the good eye of its owner/creator and her ability to mix up a variety of merchandise. You can find anything you need for your home or to give as a housewarming gift here, but the store's reputation relies on that multicultural, casual-rich-girl look. © 415/922-7276. www.suefisherking.com.

California Street & Laurel Village

This is one of the city's main drags—it chugs through various parts of town. In one particular spot, the area is known as Laurel Village. This is as far from a touristy area as you can get, but it's fun to know about because of its yuppie feel, laced with the charm of a real village and the stores that you want to shop, including one of the last five-and-dimes in America. *Warning:* Prices at the dime store are much higher than at any Walgreens (of which there are many). Certainly this area isn't what you've come all the way to San Francisco to see, or to shop, but absorbing it will make you feel like a local and let you know what it's like to really live in the City. And who knows? Maybe you'll rent a house here, swap apartments, or end up nearby on your next trip.

GETTING THERE

You can get here on the bus, but the area is not at all for tourists; so, the only real reason you'd end up here is because you are living nearby or driving past. Don't even think about making a special trip.

CHECK OUT

BOOKS INC.
3515 California St., at Locust St.

This full-service bookstore has a renowned children's section. ✆ **415/221-3666.** www.booksinc.net.

CAL-MART
3585 California St., at Spruce St.

Check out this old-line San Francisco supermarket with a branch of Sweet Things bakery inside. ✆ **415/751-3516.**

STANDARD 5 & 10
3545 California St., between Locust and Spruce sts.

For those of you who remember what Woolworth's was like, this is not Woolworth's or even a Woolworth's wannabe. This is, without doubt, a relic, a dinosaur. It is an old-fashioned dime store, sans soda fountain, that sells a little of everything; the nostalgia is biting. So are the prices. (A Jiffy mailing envelope here was $1.85, compared to $1.50 at Walgreens.) ✆ **415/751-5767.**

VIKING HOMECHEF
3527 California St., between Locust and Spruce sts.

Viking HomeChef is not only a leading source for appliances, cookware, and cookbooks, but also a place for classes and hanging out. Viking is known for its own brand of kitchen equipment and professional gear, but carries other brands as well. ✆ **415/668-3191.** www.vikingculinary.com.

Valencia Street & the Mission District

The Mission district is an area that is truly wild. I immediately rolled up the car windows and locked the doors, but also began making notes of the gorgeous houses here, and realized this is a great area to buy real estate. If I were looking for commercial real estate, I think I'd latch onto any of the six movie theaters from the 1960s that have been all but abandoned. The Mission has thrift shops, fortune tellers, junk stores, funky markets, ethnic everything, and more than a handful of stores that are constantly going out of business.

The neighborhood also has a lot of famous restaurants; many visiting celebs and dignitaries hang here. Some of the more mainstream restaurants in San Francisco, such as the Slanted Door, actually got their start in the Mission.

Mexican and Latin American immigrants live here, although the yuppies have been arriving in droves. Ethnic cuisine, traditions, and art make the Mission district a hot neighborhood to visit. In a recent drive-by, I jotted down this small list of storefronts in a single block: Roberto's Tax Service, Dragon City Bakery, Pandaria Caballo de Oro, Out of the Closet Thrift Shop, Senegal Cuisine, and Goodwill. I think that says it all.

Although locals say the area begins at Valencia and 16th, the real charm is centered on 23rd and 24th streets. I use the word *charm* loosely; blue bloods need not apply.

GETTING THERE

There's a BART stop at 24th Street.

COFFEE, SNACKS & LUNCH

This part of town is known for emerging restaurants and taste combos that will someday make its chefs or owners famous. There are also numerous places for takeout and snacks.

LUCCA RAVIOLI COMPANY
1100 Valencia St., at 22nd St.

Lucca, Lucca, terrific Italian deli. © 415/647-5581.

TARTINE
600 Guerrero St., at 18th St.

This local bakery with cafe is the talk of many foodies who head here from all over. ✆ **415/487-2600.** www.tartinebakery. com.

CHECK OUT

BOTANIC YORUBA
998 Valencia St., at 21st St.

C'mon baby, light my candle. There are also plenty of supplies for Caribbean religions and cults. ✆ **415/826-4967.**

GOOD VIBRATIONS
603 Valencia St., at 17th St.

Browse all sorts of sex toys along with some books and videos. This is a store owned by women, created by women, for women. Now, just where did I put my G-spot? ✆ **415/522-5460.** www.goodvibes.com.

    There are other locations at 1620 Polk St., at Sacramento Street (✆ **415/345-0400**), and at 2504 San Pablo Ave., at Dwight Way, in Berkeley (✆ **510/841-8987**).

LAKU
1069 Valencia St., between 21st and 22nd sts.

Laku features hats as art, although the homemade slippers are just as creative. There are all sorts of accessories here, including some items for kids. It's mostly knits—this is not the time for Ascot. ✆ **415/695-1462.**

The Castro

Actually, this area is pretty touristy, so perhaps it doesn't belong in this part of the chapter. Maybe it all depends on your orientation. Baddah boom!

It doesn't take much awareness to figure out that the Castro stands for gay. You get not only gay tourists who are attracted to the gay retail, but also straights who want to either stare at gay men holding hands or gawk at some of the merchandise that certainly isn't like anything you'll find at the mall back home.

Castro Street itself is just a short block or two, but it has a wonderful village feeling, or a Village People feel, anyway. Market Street, which is the cross street and the gateway to the area, handles the retail overflow. Note the rainbow flags and banners flying from the street poles.

Most of the gay-oriented retail is directed toward gay men, although some stores, especially bookstores, feature merchandise for both gays and lesbians. Market Street is home to a lot of mainstream retail—including **Tower Records, Safeway** (said to be a major pickup spot), **Pottery Barn, Walgreens, L'Occitane, Body Shop, Peet's Coffee,** and so on. Even **Crossroads Trading,** a small chain of recycled-clothing shops, seems like a San Francisco brand rather than any kind of alternative retail source. For designer tushes, there's a **Diesel** for trendy denim. Church Street, a branch street located alongside the Safeway, is an extension of the area.

GETTING THERE

The Castro centers on the end of Market Street, between 17th and 18th streets. A fair amount of retail is on Market Street itself, so consider taking the F streetcar to the end of the line there, and then walking.

COFFEE, SNACKS & LUNCH

TWIN PEAKS TAVERN
401 Castro St., at Market and 17th sts.

One of the oldest bars and gay meeting places in the area, Twin Peaks is a long-established part of making the scene. ✆ 415/864-9470. www.twinpeakstavern.com.

CHECK OUT

A DIFFERENT LIGHT
489 Castro St., at 18th St.

This bookstore for gays and lesbians also carries a good selection of guidebooks. ✆ **415/431-0891.** www.adlbooks.com.

BEAD STORE
417 Castro St., at Market St.

To my understanding, beads do not have any sexuality, so it's a mere coincidence that one of San Francisco's best bead stores is in the Castro. ✆ **415/861-7332.**

CROSSROADS TRADING COMPANY
2123 Market St., at Church St.

This clothing-store chain sells used and vintage apparel. ✆ **415/552-8743.** www.crossroadstrading.com.

DOES YOUR FATHER KNOW?
548 Castro St., between 18th and 19th sts.

Different from the following store—and much more racy. I guess Dad's made of stiffer stuff. ✆ **415/241-9865.**

DOES YOUR MOTHER KNOW?
4079 18th St., between Noe and Castro sts.

The usual shtick you'd expect to find in a touristy area, ranging from greeting cards to refrigerator magnets—for gays and lesbians. ✆ **415/864-3160.**

NANCY BOY
2319 Market St., at Noe St.

This store makes me wonder if the British expression for a gigolo is "fancy boy," and for a gay man, "nancy boy." It's one of the many stores in the area with a clever name that draws you in just because it sounds like fun. It sells scent and beauty treatments to avid gay and straight shoppers alike. ©️ 415/626-5021. www.nancyboy.com.

Potrero Hill

Heretofore a more or less residential area for those who couldn't afford more chic real estate . . . but guess what? It's hot! It's happening! You can buy a fixer-upper for less than a million dollars!

Restaurants and bars have arrived, along with the inevitable takeout gourmet shops, and now the retail scene is just beginning. This particular San Francisco hill is just beyond the new Design District (p. 109); to be at the heart of the neighborhood action, head for the intersection of 18th and Connecticut streets. Frankly, there's not a lot happening quite yet, although if you go for a look-see, you might want to check out **Goat Hill Pizza,** one of the anchors to the 'hood. There's also **Chez Papa,** for casual French food, and the usual village necessities—an ice-cream shop, florist, **Christopher's Books,** and so on. The cross streets in this area are named for states, so check out the action on Texas, too.

Nearby, in what is also known as Potrero Hill, there's a small mall called the **Potrero Center,** at 16th and Bryant streets, that has all the basics one needs to live happily ever after: **Ross Dress for Less, Old Navy, Sally Beauty Supply, Petco, Safeway, Peet's Coffee,** and **Noah's Bagels.**

Not far away (and within walking distance if you don't mind a hill or two) is the Design District, as well as the store **Dandelion,** 55 Potrero Ave., one of the best gift shops in town. "Gift shop" barely suffices as a description; see p. 153 to read all about it. If you can handle the trek, there is a cache of excellent stores between Ross Dress for Less and Dandelion; they are listed below in the Design District section, since they are not really up Potrero Hill. They are hill adjacent, for you mountain goats out there.

GETTING THERE

You can take a taxi to Potrero Hill, or simply drive around in your big rental car. The area isn't so developed for shoppers that it warrants the price of cab fare on its own. Do note, however, that this part of town adjoins the Design District, allowing you to easily combine the two areas in one outing.

Clement Street

This district is possibly only for students of urban architecture and retail or for those interested in the sociology of changing neighborhoods. For the most part, Clement is a long street, reached by an obscure bus, with a long commercial zone that serves the immigrant population. The area is somewhat like Valencia Street in the Mission district, but cleaner. It's not at all frightening. The 500 block is all noodles; by the 800 block, you'll find Walgreens and Goodwill, as well as the Russian Bear Restaurant in the heart of a Russian retail block.

Here's all you need to know: One block has begun to gentrify. Hip new stores are clearly going to conquer the others. The cute stuff is in the block below the 100s and begins where Clement Street starts at Arguello Boulevard. Note that most of the stores in the cutie-pie part are closed on Mondays, but open on Sundays.

GETTING THERE

Oh, boy. Here's a choice for you: D'ya wanna spend $20 on a taxi from Union Square or take a bus for a very long time?

CHECK OUT

APRIL IN PARIS
55 Clement St., between Arguello Blvd. and Second Ave.

The owner of this handbag shop worked for Hermès for years, and therefore gets tons of notice and press and attention from people who act like she is what neighborhood retail is all about. Conceptually, of course, she is. Did I see any handbags I would kill to own? Actually, no. She does custom work, too. © 415/750-9910. www.aprilinparis.us.

SATIN MOON FABRICS
32 Clement St., between Arguello Blvd. and Second Ave.

This shop is worth the trip, if you're into funky stores selling antiques and repro vintage fabrics, many with Oriental prints from the 1930s. The owners are just as much fun to look at as the fabrics. © 415/668-1623.

South Park

This is a really hidden neighborhood, rarely frequented by locals who aren't cool—let alone tourists. It's also called China Basin, and you would have done well to have bought real estate here 5 years ago. The first coming of this area was the dot.com boom, but then there was the dot.com bust. Now this part of town has a cross section of adorable residential nuggets as well as rehabbed warehouses for business and residence. I dare you to not fall in love with the townhouses around the small park called South Park.

Nearby, there's the beautiful home of the San Francisco Giants, **SBC Park,** which opened in 2000; a fabulous designer discount store; and plenty of places for coffee or lunch. Obviously, parking is hard to come by when there's a ballgame. Directly across the street from the ballpark is a huge **Borders.** My bet is that the whole area will get mall-ified within 10 years.

GETTING THERE

You're going to need a taxi; take one straight to Jeremy's (see below). This will cost about $8 from Union Square.

COFFEE, SNACKS & LUNCH

ACME CHOPHOUSE
24 Willie Mays Plaza.

In a town that takes its chefs almost as seriously as Paris, Acme's managing chef, Traci Des Jardins, is a local heroine. The restaurant, directly across from the ballpark, is a great place for grills or sandwiches. © **415/644-0240**. www.acmechophouse.com.

DON'T MISS

JEREMY'S
2 South Park.

Oh me, oh my, where to start? Jeremy's is one of the most unusual designer discount outlets in the world because it has great stuff, big names, and everything you want at fair prices. But, and yes, there is a but: This store specializes in damaged merchandise. That doesn't mean the clothes are in shreds, but there may be flaws like straggling threads or sagging hooks. I bought an Armani skirt for $13! And yes, thank you, it was even in my size. The problem with the skirt is that some of the embroidery is coming unraveled, although at that price, who cares?. Will anyone ever notice? Naw. © **415/882-4929**. www. jeremys.com.

Mid-Market SoMa

Market Street, west of the most well-known SoMa district, does not even have the feel of an up-and-coming area. There's nary a vibe of adventure or coming gentrification. Nonetheless, there are enough good stores (and restaurants) to draw regular repeat visits from locals, especially those in the design trade.

GETTING THERE

Taxi fare from Union Square will run you about $5.

COFFEE, SNACKS & LUNCH

ZUNI CAFE
1658 Market St., between Franklin and Gough sts.

The open kitchen, the Med-style cooking, the menu of roast chicken and burgers—it's still trendy after all these years.

Reservations: still imperative. Parking: impossible to find. This is one of the "in" spots that locals and visitors alike strive to visit. The burgers have been voted top of the mark. The restaurant is sort of in the middle-of-nowhere part of Market Street, but it's convenient to a little shop called Bell'occhio (see below). ✆ 415/552-2522.

CHECK OUT

BELL'OCCHIO
8 Brady St.

When I die and go to retail heaven, I will own this store, or one just like it. A hole-in-the-wall right off Market Street, Bell'occhio is just about the size of a small bedroom. It sells ribbons and treasures and soaps and stuff. The European-made plastic containers in the shape of birds and bees (or flowers or ants or apples) would make a creative person wild with the desire to turn them into centerpieces or decorative art-work. A feast for the senses. ✆ 415/864-4048.

FLAX
1699 Market St., at Valencia St.

Flax has art supplies and enough fun stuff to make you want to paint the Golden Gate Bridge, your own way. If you are in a car and driving to various parts of town, you will pass directly by this store en route to the Mission district and/or the Castro. ✆ 415/552-2355. www.flaxart.com.

Design District

Before you skip over this section with a shrug, saying you aren't a designer or aren't interested in showrooms, places to the trade, home style, or anything else, let me explain that for anyone with a good eye, this is a must-do district. And believe me—it's open enough to the public to be worth your while.

The Design District has no Painted Ladies or gorgeous architectural landmarks. The adjacent Potrero Hill area has some nice-enough houses; the residential areas are being renovated and no doubt will soon be a rainbow of sophisticated colors. But for now, you don't come for the architecture, or even the residential parts.

You come here to shop. Duh.

The design buildings are what you would expect, although there are also services that specialize in taking civilians into trade-only showrooms. So much of this area is regular retail that unless you are redoing your home and in need of an expert, you won't even miss the wholesale ops. Some of the best stores in town are in this district.

GETTING THERE

Take a taxi to Henry Adams Street and the San Francisco Design Center, which should cost about $8 from Union Square. If you don't have a car, there is an amazing amount to see within walking distance. There are some hills, though, so wear sensible shoes.

COFFEE, SNACKS & LUNCH

SALLY'S
300 De Haro St., at 16th St.

Not to be confused with the Sally Beauty Supply chain, this is a restaurant, a cafe, a dive, a treat. You stand in line, cafeteria style, and then sit down, family style. It's sort of California-style, truck-driver gourmet—many things have a Mexican or fusion twist. Breakfast is served all day; I always have "green eggs and ham" (the eggs are green because they're mixed with a Mexican verde sauce). © 415/626-6006.

DON'T MISS

FORGOTTEN SHANGHAI
245 Kansas St., between 15th and 16th sts.

Be still, my Chinese heart. Carry me away, oh ye who have forgotten Shanghai, and shame on any of you who think this is a Chinatown tourist trap. Forgotten Shanghai is not only the store of your dreams, but one you would never have found without me. And frankly, I wouldn't have found it without Wendy and Karen. It's on my "10 Best Stores in San Francisco" list; see p. 2 for details. ☎ **415/701-7707.** www.forgotten shanghai.com.

SILK TRADING CO.
1616-A 16th St., at Rhode Island St.

You may already be familiar with this firm, as it has various stores dotted around the country. Silk Trading also does business via its catalog and website. Stop by in person, though: Essentially, the store is a great visual treat, with walls hung with various silks from all over the world. There's even a bargain niche in the rear and some accessories already made up from the fabrics. If you love textiles and color, you will go wild. Prices vary enough to give you choices for just about any budget, from midrange to high-end. ☎ **415/282-5574.** www.silktrading.com.

CHECK OUT

DANDELION
55 Portero Ave., off Division St.

This is more like a specialty store or small department store than a gift shop—it's two stories high and features everything from greeting cards and jewelry to novelty items and tabletop to books on all subjects, including travel, art, and gay interests. Take plenty of time to browse here—the store is crammed with stuff. ☎ **415/436-9500.** www.tampopo.com.

SAN FRANCISCO DESIGN CENTER
2 Henry Adams St.

While most design centers are closed to the trade, this one is not closed tightly. You can walk in, grab a nibble at the open-air cafe in the atrium, and use your cellphone to call any of several services that will take you to the trade-only showrooms.

Or book ahead and then "do" the 'hood. © 415/490-5800. www. sfdesigncenter.com.

OUT OF TOWN

Sausalito

Oh dear. How to be honest here, without being rude? Let me see. Well, Sausalito, standing on a reputation for charm that is over 30 years old, is across the bay—a pleasant ferry ride away. It's not for serious shoppers. Sarah and I went over for an afternoon, had great fish and chips, poked in the stores, and sighed over the loss of innocence. There was a time, back when we were girls, when Sausalito was magic. Now—big sigh—it's one giant tourist trap without many redeeming factors.

GETTING THERE

The easiest, most fun method of transportation from San Francisco is by ferry, which leaves from—how perfect!—the Ferry Building. This way, you can shop and eat your way through the Ferry Building's stores and stalls. If you are disappointed in Sausalito, fret not—you can just head right back to the wonderful Ferry Building.

CHECK OUT

ENG'S DESIGN
763 Bridgeway, Sausalito.

Eng's carries cards, wrapping paper, diaries, pillows, gifts for the home, and items of Zen-like handcrafted beauty. © 415/331-0377. www.engsdesign.com.

HEATH FACTORY AND FACTORY STORE
Liberty Shipyards, 400 Gate Five Rd., Sausalito.

This is not within walking distance of the touristy part of town—you will need a car to get here. It might also help if you call ahead, as first-timers may have trouble finding anything in this warehouse district. That said, the factory is very much worth seeking out if you like stoneware. The two-part store has new merchandise as well as markdowns, which include boxes of tiles. The stuff is totally stunning, but not inexpensive. The regular-price coffee mugs are around $15, while sale items go for $7.50. A gorgeous coffeepot costs over $100. This stoneware can go in the microwave and does not burn your fingers when you retrieve it (I use this line and have tested it). If you aren't into stoneware, however, forget the whole thing. ✆ 415/332-3732. www.heathceramics.com.

Tiburon

—by Sarah Lahey

There's no place like home, that's for sure—especially when your home is right outside San Francisco. I'm partial to the Marin County burbs of Tiburon and Mill Valley (see below) because I've lived here for 30 years. We have just about everything here, except for Saks and Neiman's. All the shopping is great, even the supermarket. But, of course, I do have a few faves to pass on. Welcome to my 'hood.

GETTING THERE

Tiburon is a quick 15-minute ferry ride from the Ferry Building. You'll get great views of the San Francisco skyline and Alcatraz, but ferry schedules are more convenient for commuters than visitors—so check www.blueandgoldfleet.com before embarking. Also note that Tiburon shopping is a whole lot more fun than Sausalito's, so if you're looking for a day out and some time on the water, this could be the choice.

If you're driving from San Francisco, head north on Highway 101 and take the Tiburon Boulevard/East Blithedale Avenue (Hwy. 131) exit. Then go east on Tiburon Boulevard and you'll reach downtown Tiburon in about 5 minutes.

COFFEE, SNACKS & LUNCH

ROONEY'S CAFE & GRILL
38 Main St., Tiburon.

If the fog is in and you can't see two feet in front of you, or if you want to blend in with the locals, walk across the street to Rooney's, where you'll get the best sandwiches and salads in town. You may also overhear the latest gossip from my friends. We all agree that Rooney's has the best Reuben on the planet (and we frequently travel to New York). My favorite salads are the curried chicken and, in season, the fresh Dungeness crab stack with avocado—it makes my mouth water just thinking about it. ✆ **415/435-1911.**

SAM'S ANCHOR CAFÉ
27 Main St., Tiburon.

Voted the Bay Area's "Best Outdoor Restaurant" by the *San Francisco Chronicle,* Sam's is a favorite with both visitors and locals. If it's a nice day, sit out on the deck and take in the killer views while seagulls fly down and steal your fries. My husband and I went to Sam's on our first date, 30 years ago, and we're still regulars for Sunday brunch. Do try one of the famous Ramos Fizzes; you'll order another and another and, well, shopping will be a breeze. ✆ **415/-435-4527.** www.samscafe.com.

CHECK OUT

CITRUS
13 Main St., Tiburon.

Inexpensive designer-inspired handbags and shoes at fab prices are what you'll buy at this trendy boutique. Most of the bags are faux leather, but they look great and come in all the "in" colors. Same thing with the shoes—if you need sage kitten heels to wear to a wedding, this is the place to look. There's also a good selection of gift items for home and baby. *Note:* No refunds (only store credit), so be sure when you buy. ✆ **415/435-1321.**

The Custom House
Boardwalk Shopping Center, 1550 Tiburon Blvd., Tiburon.

I found my dining table, an old Gump's design, at this large consignment shop years ago. It features high-end antiques and home style (no clothing), accepting only the best merchandise. Consigners and buyers come from all over the Bay Area—it's that good. On my last visit, I saw English silver, Waterford crystal, Imari-style china, and a beautiful Baccarat vase. Prices are reasonable, but they're not giving it away. ✆ 415/435-5350.

Le Sportif
Boardwalk Shopping Center, 1550 Tiburon Blvd., Tiburon.

This small shop has been a local favorite for as long as I can remember. Classic trousers, suits, contemporary sportswear— it's all here. It sells Kinross cashmere and has a trunk show in August, when you can order this fabulous line at a discount. ✆ 415/435-2220.

Old Gold Jewelry
17 Main St., Tiburon.

Contemporary, brushed-gold designs are the specialty of this shop. The local designers work in 18-carat gold and platinum to create jewelry that is understated yet ultrachic. Their stacking rings are the best I've seen, but you need lots for the right look, and they're not inexpensive. If I were looking for a wedding ring and marrying someone rich, this would be my first stop. ✆ 415/789-9583.

Paparazzi
31 Main St., Tiburon.

This popular boutique carries everything from beachwear to evening gowns. It doesn't stock high-end designer goods, but rather moderately priced, contemporary classics with European influences. There are lots of mix-and-match possibilities. I found a gorgeous aquamarine lace top to go with jeans or a suit—wore it twice before my 24-year-old daughter permanently "borrowed" it. It's also a great source for handbags and accessories; you'll find high-quality styles here that you won't see at Union Square, and prices are a fraction of what you'd pay for a designer bag. The straw totes are fabulous. ✆ **415/435-2622.**

TAILS OF TIBURON
34 Main St., Tiburon.

This shop carries everything your dog or cat needs, including Marc Jacobs and quilted, Chanel-inspired travel bags. You'll find toys, clothes, healthy treats, and a good selection of books. My Scottish terrier, Bentley, gives the dog bed a four-paws rating. ✆ **415/789-1301.**

KNOW ABOUT

DIANA'S OF TIBURON
Boardwalk Shopping Center, 1550 Tiburon Blvd., Tiburon.

Tiburon used to have a five-and-dime where we went for pantyhose, gift wrap, toys, greeting cards, and the like. Well, that store closed, and along came Diana, who has the best real-people shop in town. It's much more posh than the dime store, and she doesn't sell panty hose, but we all shop here for stationery, children's gifts, Christmas cards, cocktail napkins, and on and on. ✆ **415/435-7448.**

Mill Valley

—by Sarah Lahey

This cutie-pie village is just 5 minutes from my home, so I go to Mill Valley all the time. I hope you love it as much as I do. Like Tiburon, it has oodles of charm with unique upscale boutiques, no multiples (well, a couple, but they're small), and lots of one-of-a-kind shopping opportunities.

GETTING THERE

Heading north on Highway 101 from San Francisco, take the Tiburon Boulevard/East Blithedale Avenue (Hwy. 131) exit. Then go west to Mill Valley. A 5-minute drive on East Blithedale will take you right to the middle of the downtown area.

COFFEE, SNACKS & LUNCH

PEARL'S PHAT BURGER
8 E. Blithedale Ave., Mill Valley.

Pearl's is an all-American diner serving "phat" burgers (½ lb.) or minis (¼ lb.). It also has hot dogs, onion rings, garlic fries, shakes, and salads. ✆ 415/381-6010. www.pearlsdiner.com.

DON'T MISS

MAISON REVE
11 Throckmorton Ave., Mill Valley.

This is one of my favorite shops anywhere; it could easily be in St. Remy. Maison Rêve translates as "dream house," and that's exactly what you'll have if you outfit your home here. You'll find furniture and decorative objects, linens straight from Provence markets, and French-country antiques for house and garden. The old paned windows framing botanical prints are so chic—and well priced. The owner travels to France frequently, so the inventory is always fresh. She offers interior-design

---

Fills & Fine Art

For a great manicure, stop by **At the Top Salon**, 10 E. Blithedale Ave., Mill Valley (✆ **415/381-3707** or 415/381-3708; www.atthetopsalon.com), right next door to Pearl's Phat Burger. Book with Cherie—and while you're here, browse the artwork on display at this hair salon–cum–art gallery.

services and container parties as well. I could be very happy living in this store. © 415/383-9700. www.maisonreve.com.

CHECK OUT

ALPHA DOG
6 Miller Ave., Mill Valley.

Dogs born with silver bones in their mouths shop here. I bought Suzy's new puppy a "Chewy Vuitton" handbag; he takes it with him everywhere. © 415/389-6500. www.alphadog.com.

CANVAS
77 Throckmorton Ave., Mill Valley.

This is one of the best boutiques in town, if you're young or young at heart and wear a size 12 or under. The clothing is one-of-a-kind, with European labels such as Juliet Dunn London. The jeans selection is incredible—the store stocks nearly 10 lines, including Seven for All Mankind, and the staff is trained to help you find the perfect fit. I wanted to buy one of the metallic woven-leather handbags, but $650 was over my budget. © 415/383-0520.

L'ATELIER REBECCA BRUCE
23 Sunnyside Ave., Mill Valley.

Over the past 20 years, Rebecca Bruce's work has been featured in *W, Elle,* and *Essence,* as well as in film and on CNN. Eclectic and minimalist in design, her elegant pieces are perfect for travel. Each collection features mix-and-match separates, which run the gamut from casual to very dressy; with a change of accessories, you can go straight from Saks to the opera. Prices are moderately high, but the designs are timeless—so think of this as investment buying. © 415/388-8090. www. rebeccabruce.com.

MILL VALLEY HAT BOX
118 Throckmorton Ave., Mill Valley.

I've walked by this shop many times, but, since I'm not a hat person, never gone in. Big mistake. After seeing some great-looking travel makeup bags in the window, I strolled in and was so impressed, I may start wearing hats. There were froufrou numbers appropriate for an English wedding, crushable travel styles, and everything in between. Labels include Helen Kaminski and Erica Javits. The store even sells old-fashioned round hatboxes in all sizes—and those travel kits by Susan Spicer could double as evening bags. ℭ **415/383-2757.**

PULLMAN & CO.
108 Throckmorton Ave., Mill Valley.

This home store may at first look like many others, but pay attention and you'll see some good buys. It stocks some furniture, but the real finds are in accessories and bath items. The style has Asian influence, but this isn't the ho-hum import stuff seen elsewhere. Prices are very reasonable; I've bought lamps, wastebaskets, throw pillows, and even a door mat. I like to pick up hostess gifts in the bath department—English scents and potions are well priced, and I swear by the Harmonie Blanche hand lotion. There's usually a sale table with enough bath linens to put together a full set or two. ℭ **415/383-0847.**

WILKESSPORT
57 Throckmorton Ave., Mill Valley.

This is the less expensive, less formal, but still chic division of San Francisco's famed icon store Wilkes Bashford. It's one of the few worthwhile men's shops around, carrying mostly casual wear and a good selection of shoes. ℭ **415/381-5183.** www.wilkessport.com.

Chapter Six

....

BAY AREA RESOURCES A TO Z

Shop 'til you drop! Drop acid in the Haight! (Oops, we don't do that sort of thing!) Go boppety-bop on a cable car, and hang tight to those packages. Load up on Southern pecan–flavored coffee beans from Cost Plus World Market. Sing back to Tony Bennett. And tell me everything, because though San Francisco is not the greatest shopping city in the world, it does have a little of everything—and combined with the adjoining areas, it offers a chock-full visit, vacation, or convention-going experience with plenty of things to see and buy.

The greater San Francisco area is enormous, so you'll have plenty of ops to shop. Shopping within the City itself tends to be more sophisticated than in the burbs, but you have some rather wealthy burbs here, so the pickings are good. Three chapters in this book are devoted to out-of-town resources; the listings in this chapter are mainly in the City, unless there is a significant piece of the scene to be noted elsewhere or I am trying to make a point of balancing out the choices.

Downtown San Francisco—handily accessible to visitors—has a very wide range of types of shopping. Contrary to the rules of urbanization, San Francisco has a fair number of traditionally suburban, so-called big-box stores in the downtown area. Not that you've come to town to shop at Costco, but it happens to be rather easy to get to the Costco warehouse in the SoMa area. San Francisco also has a large selection of national department stores, many international designer brands, a lot of discounters and off-pricers, and wonderful pockets of mom-and-pop shops that are also explored in chapter 5, "Shopping Neighborhoods."

If you're in a hurry or looking for quick hits, be sure to see chapter 1, which contains my "best of" listings.

ACTIVE SPORTSWEAR

NIKETOWN
278 Post St., at Stockton St.

Located right on the edge of Union Square, Niketown isn't certain if it's a tourist attraction, an entertainment facility, or a store for the community. With the usual Nike flair, the building has all the wallop you've come to expect from this new breed of retail. Just do it. Also just note that as far as these types of places go, this one is not so big that you will lose your mind. It's entertainment and shoe business rolled into one, but it's not overwhelming. ℭ 415/392-6453. www.nike.com.

NORTH FACE
180 Post St., at Grant Ave.

Another popular brand for the outdoorsy, ski-crazy, and outward-bound shopper, the line is best known for its use of high-tech, fleece, and lightweight but warming fabrics. Besides clothing, there's also gear. Note that there is an outlet store in Berkeley, at 1238 Fifth St., that's open daily. ℭ 415/433-3223. www.thenorthface.com.

ORVIS
248 Sutter St., off Kearny St.

Fishing is the house specialty here, but there's plenty of gear—and clothing—for other sports, for both men and women. ℭ 415/392-1600. www.orvis.com.

Bay Area

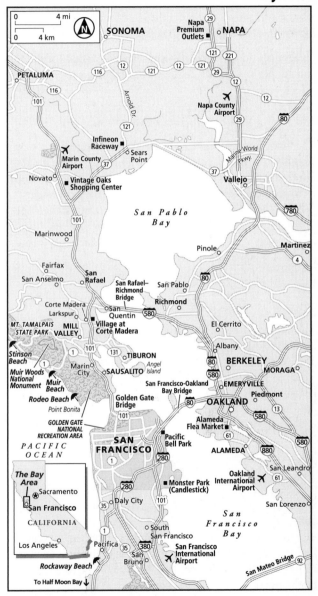

SONOMA

Napa Premium Outlets

NAPA

(29)

(121) (221)

PETALUMA

(116)

(116)

(101)

(12)

(121) (12) (121)

Arnold Dr.

(121)

(29)

(12)

(12)

(80)

Napa County Airport

(29)

Infineon Raceway

Sears Point

Marin County Airport

(37)

Marine World Pkwy.

Vallejo

(37)

Novato

Vintage Oaks Shopping Center

(780)

San Pablo Bay

(101)

Marinwood

Pinole

Martinez

(4)

Fairfax

San Anselmo

San Rafael

San Rafael–Richmond Bridge

San Pablo

Richmond

(80)

Corte Madera

Larkspur

San Quentin

(580)

El Cerrito

MT. TAMALPAIS STATE PARK

Village at Corte Madera

MILL VALLEY

(1)

(101)

Albany

BERKELEY

Stinson Beach

(131)

TIBURON

(80)

(580)

MORAGA

Muir Woods National Monument

Marin City

SAUSALITO

Angel Island

EMERYVILLE

Piedmont

Muir Beach

Rodeo Beach

Point Bonita

Golden Gate Bridge

San Francisco–Oakland Bay Bridge

OAKLAND

(13)

GOLDEN GATE NATIONAL RECREATION AREA

(101)

(80)

Alameda Flea Market

(580)

PACIFIC OCEAN

SAN FRANCISCO

(1)

(280)

Pacific Bell Park

ALAMEDA

(61)

(880)

The Bay Area

Sacramento

San Francisco

CALIFORNIA

Los Angeles

(280)

Monster Park (Candlestick)

Oakland International Airport

San Leandro

(61)

Daly City

(101)

(35)

San Lorenzo

San Francisco Bay

(280)

South San Francisco

(1)

Pacifica

(35)

(380)

San Bruno

San Francisco International Airport

Rockaway Beach

To Half Moon Bay ↓

San Mateo Bridge

(92)

PATAGONIA
Fisherman's Wharf, 770 N. Point St.

Patagonia's outdoor active wear is especially good for skiing and hiking. ✆ 415/771-2050. www.patagonia.com.

PUMA
856 Market St., between Fourth and Fifth sts.

The Puma brand is back from the dead and enjoying a new storefront in San Francisco. Along with Adidas, these are the hot German brands to buy into. The store isn't huge, but stop by to peruse the shoes, the fashion, and the in-the-know clientele who have brought this brand back into cult status. The unusual color combinations are part of the line's success. Prices are also less than astronomical, unlike at some other brand stores. ✆ 415/788-9880. www.puma.com.

REI
840 Brannan St., between Seventh and Eighth sts.

This Seattle-based mountain- and outdoor-sports firm carries gear and clothing for very, very active types. Note that this is near several of my listings in the SoMa area and just a block from Nordstrom Rack. The reason the store is slightly off the beaten track is that it's simply huge—this kind of space can't be found in too many downtown areas. ✆ 415/934-1938. www.rei.com.

ANTIQUES

Stores that specialize in the Asian look, some of them selling antiques, are listed on p. 125.

There's a strong auction scene in San Francisco, especially for antiques—you might want to check with **Bonhams & Butterfields**, 220 San Bruno Ave. (✆ 415/861-7500; www.bonhams.com), to see what's coming up on the calendar.

If you like to call your choice of merchandise "antique" but are really talking about "junk" or "stuff"—well, fret not, the best flea market in the area is a doozy. The **Alameda Point Antiques & Collectibles Faire** is held the first Sunday of the month in Alameda, in the East Bay (p. 10).

There are a lot of other antiques shows in the various communities around San Francisco, many of them vetted and considered important. For a list of what's on, ask your hotel concierge. You will probably need a car.

Likewise, there is a history of recycling in this area—you'll find scores of Goodwill locations all over town, many thrift shops (some of them quite fancy), and of course, stores and stores galore selling used or recycled clothes, a few of which I have listed in this chapter under "Vintage" (p. 167).

Otherwise, the districts housing bona-fide antiques stores are widespread, as are the opportunities to see (and buy) all sorts of stuff. There's a very, very *(very)* fancy grouping of old-money–style antiques stores around **Jackson Square,** at the edge of the Financial District. Obviously, you have to have cashed out of your dot.com before it crashed to be able to afford this merchandise. As intimidating as these shops may appear, the dealers will welcome you, educate you, and, of course, sell you incredible items for your home. Born to Shop news director Sarah Lahey, who also sells English antiques, advises you to dress well and stop by the following shops:

HUNT ANTIQUES
478 Jackson St., between Sansome and Montgomery sts.

Specializing in furniture, fine art, and accessories from the 18th and 19th centuries, this showroom overflows with style and substance. You'll find long case clocks and barometers, Welsh dressers, and plenty of friendly advice here. Brian helped research a china pattern that had stumped me for weeks; within 5 minutes, I had my answer. ✆ **415/989-9531.**

KATHLEEN TAYLOR–THE LOTUS COLLECTION
445 Jackson St., between Sansome and Montgomery sts.

If you love fine fabrics and tapestries, stop in here and prepare to drool (but not on the pillows, please). Kathleen sells European, Asian, and other ethnic textiles, tapestries, and wall hangings, along with throw pillows starting at $2,000 (and no, that's not a typo). ℂ 415/398-8115. www.ktaylor-lotus.com.

JOHN DOUGHTY ANTIQUES
619 Sansome St., near Washington St.

John has one of the largest shops in Jackson Square as well as some of the most reasonable prices. He stocks 18th- and 19th-century English and French antiques, although English wares dominate this showroom. This is one of the few shops with a good collection of small items, including candlesticks and boxes. In addition to country-style furniture, you'll find fireplace accessories, porcelain, and a friendly staff ready to help you pull together the perfect look. ℂ 415/398-6849.

ART SUPPLIES

Arch 99 missouri – 17th (handwritten annotation)

Maybe all the acid graffiti of the '60s rubbed off on the retail population. Art supplies, crafts supplies, and all sorts of stuff to play with seem to be an area specialty. If you get to my favorite mall in Marin County, the Vintage Oaks Shopping Center (p. 157), there's a large crafts store, **Ben Franklin,** where you can lose yourself for days.

FLAX
1699 Market St., at Valencia St.

New Yorkers have known the name Sam Flax for generations; this outpost of the old Flax business serves both the design community and the artsy-craftsy folk who appreciate the wide selection. ℂ 415/552-2355. www.flaxart.com.

MICHAEL'S
590 Sutter St., at Mason St.

This store is not related to the national chain of crafts and art supplies by the same name, but is rather a small store that leans toward the drawing and painting arts. It's about 2 blocks from Union Square. © 415/421-1576.

PEARL
969 Market St., between Fifth and Sixth sts.

Pearl is considered the competition to Flax, with a slightly less commercial undertone. The merchandise is more oriented toward serious art than hobbies. During the week, the store opens at 9am, so morning birds can start shopping early. © 415/357-1400. www.pearlpaint.com.

ASIAN INSPIRATIONS

Thanks to its proximity to Asia and to the large and varied Asian communities in San Francisco and the Bay Area, you will find a wide choice of goods—both fashions and furnishings—with an Asian touch, be they a somewhat Zen statement at **Armani** or the luxe mode and mood of **Gump's.** You can also visit Chinatown and Japantown for a chance to wander and be surrounded by Asian inspirations.

BIG PAGODA
310 Sutter St., near Grant Ave.

This home style is modern, sleek, and often imported from Vietnam or made new from Asian shapes and styles. The acid-green crackle ginger jars stay fixed in my mind as a must-have. The store features mostly lamps, jars, bowls, and adornments. © 415/296-8881. www.bigpagoda.com

ENG'S DESIGN
763 Bridgeway, Sausalito.

This is a paper store with home design and accessories from Japan and Vietnam. It's the best store in the touristy shopping district of Sausalito. The handmade papers—especially wrapping papers—are too sublime to throw away once the gift has been unwrapped. ✆ 415/331-0377. www.engsdesign.com.

E&O TRADING
314 Sutter St., near Grant Ave.

E&O is actually a restaurant and microbrewery, not a shop—but it feels like an Asian furniture warehouse, so I've included it here. It is, after all, a visual inspiration. ✆ 415/693-0303. www.eotrading.com.

FORGOTTEN SHANGHAI
245 Kansas St., between 15th and 16th sts.

Forgotten Shanghai isn't an Asian inspiration; it's the real thing—but many Chinese touches have been modified into wearable and usable modern lifestyle items. A Chinese diaper bag? This store is so sensational that I can't help but mention it throughout this guide, so you'll find tidbits elsewhere as well. ✆ 415/701-7707. www.forgottenshanghai.com.

GENJI
Japan Center, 22 Peace Plaza.

Genji trades in Japanese antiques, reproductions, Asian furniture, and some tabletop, as well as used kimonos. It's located in the mall in central Japantown. ✆ 415/931-1616. www.genji antiques.com.

KOZO
1969 Union St., between Buchanan and Laguna sts.

Stop by to browse the Japanese paper goods, photo albums, and gift items—they're all sleek, gorgeous, refined, and often expensive. The store's name comes from a type of rare, hand-made Japanese paper. ✆ 415/351-2114. www.kozoarts.com.

THOUSAND CRANES
1803 Fourth St., Berkeley.

Part of the distinctive shopping style of Berkeley's best shopping street, Thousand Cranes has a strong mix of futons, everyday wares, paper goods, and clothing. The kimonos are expensive when compared to those at Genji (see above); some have been remade into apron styles with front buttons for a twist on the traditional style. ✆ 510/849-0501.

BATH & BEAUTY

BARE ESCENTUALS
2101 Chestnut St., at Steiner St.; Pier 39, Beach St. and the Embarcadero; Stonestown Galleria, 3251 20th Ave.; 1795 Fourth St., Berkeley.

Bare Escentuals is a local line made with natural ingredients, much of it meant to be therapeutic. The color cosmetics, treatments, and bath products are sold through stores and on TV. The brand has divided its products into various groupings, so there's bath and body; a spa line; the **i.d. bareMinerals** line of makeup made with minerals (www.bareMinerals.com); and finally **md formulations,** made with dermatological and aging problems in mind.

Of the color cosmetics, there are many products and a wide range of shades. The line stresses the fact that all products in all groups are made without preservatives. Perhaps most exciting is that the prices are not in the Neiman Marcus stratosphere, but rather in the $25-to-$50 range, considered quite reasonable for skincare these days. ✆ 800/227-3990. www.bare escentuals.com.

BENEFIT
2117 Fillmore St., at California St.; 2219 Chestnut St., between Scott and Pierce sts.; 685 Market St., between Kearny and Montgomery sts.; 1831 Fourth St., Berkeley; 35 Throckmorton, Mill Valley.

Headline: Local Marin County girls make good with line of color cosmetics and treatments that are a must-have for young area socialites. The company began in Mill Valley under the name Face Place, but became Benefit in 1990, leading to its present-day celebrity cult status. The humor in the brand and the packaging has helped propel certain products off the pages of the catalogs—such as Boo Boo Zap, for instance. How could anyone resist a name like that? The fun, unique packaging practically jumps off the shelves, too—it's sort of frilly and silly and girly and retro. While there is some European and Asian distribution, this line still makes a good gift for international shoppers to take home. It's sold in Benefit boutiques as well as at department stores and Sephora.

The line is extensive in both color cosmetics and treatment products. It has a devoted following, partly because the community support from the Benefit team has been so great that locals want to buy the products in order to return the favor. Giveaways at charity events often start trends. If you stop by one of the boutiques, expect a free consultation and even makeup application. ✆ 800/781-2336. www.benefitcosmetics.com.

CASWELL-MASSEY
370 Sutter St., off Stockton St.

Caswell-Massey has that old-fashioned apothecary feel and sells soaps and other bath luxuries. ✆ 415/296-1054. www.caswell masseyltd.com.

DIPTYQUE
171 Maiden Lane.

The famed French cult brand is best known for its candles, but also makes scented soaps and colognes. ✆ 415/402-0600. www.diptyque.tm.fr.

ELIZABETH ARDEN OUTLET
1222 Sutter St., near Polk St.

The magic number here is 80%. Yes, believe it or not—that's the savings you'll get off the retail price on perfumes and beauty products that have been discontinued or have aged past their shelf lives. Open Tuesday through Saturday from 11am to 6pm. ✆ 415/346-7144.

If you're in the East Bay, there's an Elizabeth Arden Warehouse at 4550 San Pablo Ave., Emeryville (✆ 510/601-1251); it's open Thursday through Sunday from 11am to 6pm.

H2O PLUS
174 Geary St., off Stockton St.

This mass-market line from Chicago is sold only through its own stores and website; there's a very wide range of products, including bath and bathing accessories, healthcare and treatments, and skincare. It's an excellent gift source for men, women, and children, especially if you don't have this store back home.

H2O Plus is one of those rare brands that doesn't cost too much, yet makes high-quality products that are packaged well and fun to use. It also launches new products that follow or make fashion trends, so you can often find a great and unusual gift item here for the person who has everything. ✆ 415/956-0545. www.H2Oplus.com.

KIEHL'S
2360 Fillmore St., between Clay and Washington sts.

Kiehl's is a centuries-old firm with simple packaging and fine ingredients (excellent for sensitive skin). It recently passed out of the founding family and into the hands of big business, resulting in national expansion and new stores popping up. The skin-care, hair-care, and bath items are cult must-haves. Though considered a luxury line, Kiehl's presents itself as a somewhat no-nonsense brand without a lot of hype. Prices are not low, but you get the idea that you are paying for quality. There's no advertising campaign, no superstar models—just the goods, the brand, and the good word of mouth. © 415/359-9260. www.kiehls.com.

L'OCCITANE
2207 Fillmore St., at Sacramento St.

The French brand has gone worldwide and mass market, spreading a touch of Provence into everything it makes: soaps, shampoos, skin care, bath and body products, color cosmetics, and men's products. There's even room spray for your home. Although this may be the last place on earth you'd think to buy a lipstick, L'Occitane's lippy-sticky is actually long-lasting without added chemicals. © 415/563-6600. www.loccitane.com.

LUSH
240 Powell St., off Geary St.

If you stand downwind at Union Square on a breezy day, you just might get a whiff of London's Lush store, the first one in the U.S. For Lush fanatics, note that this is a division of the Canadian branch of the company, so all products meet requirements of the F.D.A. (Some of the European-made products are different.) The prices are high, and once the novelty has worn off, you may not be so smitten.

But if you don't know the brand yet, this is a must-must-must-do. Lush is a sort of modern version of the Body Shop gone deli, with wheels of cheese that turn out to be soaps, Chinese takeout cartons of face scrub, and the brand's most famous gimmick of all, the bath bomb. Since bath bombs now cost about $5 each, you might want to bathe with a lot of people or someone you really, really care about. Still, it's a great novelty gift for a shower or a love affair.

Once you've tried it, you may be ready for something else. Bath bombs are high on novelty, but at that price, forgive me— I'll just steal the little soap amenities from my hotel, thank you. Instead, I go for my favorite soap: Red Rooster (orange and cinnamon glycerin). *Tip:* Watch out for the way the price tags read—the products are priced by the pound, and no one buys a pound of soap. So if it says $25.99, don't freak. © 415/693-9633. www.lush.com.

There's another location at 2116 Union St., between Webster and Fillmore streets (© 415/921-5874).

M.A.C.
1833 Union St., between Laguna and Octavia sts.; 2011 Fillmore St., at Pine St.; 1850 Fourth St., Berkeley.

M.A.C. came to fame as a Canadian makeup house providing an unusually wide range of colors that are long-lasting, pure, and sold at fair prices. The brand was bought by Estée Lauder and has expanded into major cities all over the world, including San Francisco; it's also sold in department stores. M.A.C. is a great find for international shoppers because of its decent prices, high quality, and enormous variety of shades and choices. Word is that M.A.C. uses more pigment in its colors than other brands, which explains the density, the wearing time, and its popularity in the professional world of makeup artists. © 800/588-0070. www.maccosmetics.com.

PURE BEAUTY
3600 16th St., at Noe and Market sts.; 1560 Haight St., between Clayton and Ashbury sts.; 4 Embarcadero Center; 2124 Fillmore St., at California St.; 756 Irving St., at Ninth Ave.; 3535 California St., between Spruce and Locust sts.; 2085 Chestnut St., off Steiner St.; Stonestown Galleria, 3251 20th Ave.

This chain looks at first like a beauty-supply store, which it is not. Rather, it sells the full range of various treatment brands and specializes in hair and skin products. I am mad for the

Dermalogica skincare line, a Los Angeles brand that is not too easy to find in department stores. There is a branch of Pure Beauty in nearly every major trading area. www.purebeauty.com.

SEPHORA
33 Powell St., at Market St.; 2083 Union St., at Webster St.; SFO International Terminal, Level 3.

I say tomato, you say tomahto; I say *Seph*-o-rah, you say Seph-*or*-ah. Tomato, tomahto, let's go shopping now. Indeed, Americans seem to pronounce the name of this store as Seph-*or*-ah even though it's a French chain of beauty supermarkets for fragrance, skin care, bath, and cosmetics.

But wait, let's get small and talk about some trade secrets. What makes Sephora work so well in the international environment is that the stores adapt to the local culture. In the San Francisco flagship store, on Powell Street, you'll see a wide range of never-before-heard-of U.S. and California brands along with all sorts of funny and funky products. Although I live in France and, thus, have Sephora stores coming out my ears and toes, I dream of returning to this particular store just so I can replenish the stash of brands I've never seen elsewhere. Yeah, even the Jessica Simpson line is funny and right there in your face. My favorite product is an eye pencil made in Germany by the Sue Dewitt Studio brand; my color is Kenya, a deepest darkest African brown. ✆ 877/**SEPHORA**. www.sephora.com.

BIG NAMES (AMERICAN)

The big-name designer stores are mostly around Union Square, so you can get off BART at Market and Powell, or else take the cable car or bus to Union Square.

BCBG MAX AZRIA
331 Powell St., at Geary St.
✆ 415/362-7360. www.bcbg.com.

MARC JACOBS
125 Maiden Lane.
℡ 415/362-6500. www.marcjacobs.com.

RALPH LAUREN
Crocker Galleria, 90 Post St., between Kearny and Montgomery sts.
℡ 415/788-7656. www.polo.com.

ST. JOHN
Four Seasons Hotel, 767-A Market St., at Fourth St.
℡ 415/856-0420. www.stjohnknits.com.

BIG NAMES (INTERNATIONAL)

Most of the big-name international boutiques are also located around Union Square.

AGNES B.
33 Grant Ave., off Geary St.
℡ 415/772-9995. www.agnesb.com.

BOTTEGA VENETA
108 Geary St., at Grant Ave.
℡ 415/981-1700. www.bottegaveneta.com.

BURBERRY
250 Post St., between Stockton St. and Grant Ave.
℡ 415/392-2200. www.burberry.com.

CHANEL
155 Maiden Lane.
℡ 415/981-1550. www.chanel.com.

CHRISTIAN DIOR
216 Stockton St., off Geary St.
℡ 415/544-0394. www.dior.com.

EMPORIO ARMANI
1 Grant Ave., at O'Farrell St.
© 415/677-9400. www.emporioarmani.com.

GIORGIO ARMANI
278 Post St., off Stockton St.
© 415/434-2500. www.giorgioarmani.com.

GUCCI
200 Stockton St., at Geary St.
© 415/392-2808. www.gucci.com.

HERMES
125 Grant Ave.
© 415/391-7200. www.hermes.com.

LORO PIANA
212 Stockton St., off Geary St.
© 415/593-3303. www.loropiana.com.

LOUIS VUITTON
233 Geary St., off Stockton St.
© 415/391-6200. www.vuitton.com.

MAX MARA
175 Post St., off Grant Ave.
© 415/981-0900.

PRADA
140 Geary St., between Stockton St. and Grant Ave.
© 415/391-8844. www.prada.com.

SALVATORE FERRAGAMO
233 Geary St., between Stockton and Powell sts.
© 415/391-6565. www.ferragamo.com.

TSE CASHMERE
60 Maiden Lane.
© 415/391-1112. www.tsecashmere.com.

WOLFORD
115 Maiden Lane.
© 415/391-6727. www.wolford.com.

YVES SAINT LAURENT
166 Maiden Lane.
✆ 415/837-1211. www.ysl.com.

BOOKS

BORDERS
400 Post St., at Powell St.

Perhaps the largest of the downtown bookstores, the Post Street Borders is located upstairs on a Union Square corner, right across from Saks. I mention this because I had a horrible time finding the place, since I was looking for a street-level storefront. This branch is huge, has a cafe, sells music and movies, and will ship. ✆ 415/399-1633. www.borders.com.

There are other branches at 200 King St., near SBC Park (✆ 415/357-9931), and in Stonestown Galleria, 3251 20th Ave. (✆ 415/731-0665).

CITY LIGHTS
261 Columbus Ave., at Broadway.

One of the most famous stores in San Francisco—and perhaps in the U.S. if you ever followed the Beat scene—City Lights offers a huge selection of well-chosen titles that often reflect the political consciousness of a lost generation. And it's open until midnight, too. ✆ 415/362-8193. www.citylights.com.

VIRGIN MEGASTORE
2 Stockton St., at Market St.

This store is an amazing part of the Virgin empire, with listening stations that go on forever and a chance to really look into the scene in both music and people-watching. Aside from the music, there are multimedia sections, a cafe, and a ticket kiosk. Open until midnight on Friday and Saturday. ✆ 415/397-4525. www.virgin.com.

CALIFORNIA CASUAL FASHION

While there are a number of California big names who have made it in the fashion world, in this section I am referring to a very specific look, which I call "California casual." There are other American designers who do this look, and they are not necessarily from California nor do they sell specifically in California (such as Eileen Fisher), but the style is especially prevalent in Northern California.

Clothes in this category are for women, have some Asian droop to them, and are usually wide and not at all tight to the form. Most are made of natural fabrics such as cotton and linen and employ a soft color palette. This design statement is especially good for large and/or tall women; the clothes often have elastic waists or drawstrings and are sold in layers, so you can complete the look in your own style.

BRYN WALKER
1799 Fourth St., Berkeley.

A slightly better-made, more chic, and more expensive version of the CP Shades styles, without as many pieces nor as many colors. Bryn Walker does have more knits, though. The store is in a small strip center running parallel to the realities of Fourth Street, just a few hundred feet from CP Shades. ✆ 510/525-9418.

CP SHADES
1829 Fourth St., Berkeley.

CP Shades is one of my favorite brands in the whole world; I just wish it had more stores around the U.S. and doubly wish it hadn't given up its Cow Hollow location in San Francisco. Alas, this store is reason enough to visit Berkeley's famed Fourth Street.

Now then, the clothes are as described above. The colors are very Armani—soft, dusty, often the colors of leaves and buds in spring or winter. They use linen, cotton, and hopsack to provide texture, wrinkle, and detail. Skirts are mostly wraparound,

Catalog Stores

Several firms that began life as catalog businesses have gone into bricks-and-mortar retail—just think of J. Crew. In a handful of cases, these catalog brands do not have stores all over the country and are therefore of some interest to the visitor.

J. Jill, in the San Francisco Shopping Centre, 865 Market St., at Fifth Street (© **415/541-9223**; www.jjill.com), has very slowly—but actively in California—entered the mall scene with its own stores. The Bay Area suburbs also have branch locations of this mail-order business, which specializes in classic looks with enough of a fashionable touch to keep them from being boring. Think J. Crew and Ann Taylor—in a range of sizes and moderate prices.

Smith & Hawken, 2040 Fillmore St., between California and Pine streets (© **415/776-3424**. www.smithandhawken. com), began life as a luxe gardening and outdoor-lifestyle catalog and has now morphed into a group of stores in major U.S. cities and wealthy ZIP codes. If you haven't visited the store before, stop by to check out its nice ambience.

---

elastic, or drawstring style. Prices are moderate; they seem to top off between $75 and $100, with many items costing around $25 to $35. When there are sales, you can buy one of everything. © **510/204-9022**. www.cpshades.com.

EMILY LEE
3509 California St., at Locust St.

This store specializes in the look I have dubbed "California casual," although many of the designers represented here come from outside the state. Shop for Flax, Eileen Fisher, and other brands. If you don't like baggy chic, don't freak—this store also has tight, tight, tight jeans and plenty of young looks. © **415/ 751-3443**.

JOSHUA SIMON
3915 24th St., between Noe and Sanchez sts.

This Mission District shop features droopy droopy from all over the world, meaning there's a slightly ethnic touch. ✆ 415/821-1068.

DEPARTMENT STORES

BLOOMINGDALE'S
Market St., between Fourth and Fifth sts., adjacent to the San Francisco Shopping Centre (not yet open at press time).

As we go to press, Bloomingdale's is not yet open. I mention this specifically because the opening has been delayed so many times that no one seems to know when the store really will open, although this one is now scheduled for autumn of 2006. I've also never seen a really good Bloomie's branch store—it's the Manhattan mother ship for me or nothing at all. Still, the store is expected to find a niche because its merchandise tends to be higher-end than Macy's. (And while Nordstrom does have big brands, it's more of a specialty store and doesn't have that much stock.) To add a little sizzle to the pot, the newly renovated Neiman's is nothing to write home about, which gives Bloomie's a chance to really serve the local market. ✆ 866/593-2540. www.bloomingdales.com.

MACY'S
170 O'Farrell St.

The Union Square Macy's is headquarters for everything. Note that the men's store is around the corner. Also note that there are phenomenal sales and promotions and deals where you sometimes get to take 20% off the already marked-down price. Also note that Macy's really wants the tourist shopping business, so there's a visitor center and something called the Macy's Savings Pass, which can be used for a flat 10% discount on just about everything in the store. There is also an

International Savings Pass for those who do not hold U.S. passports (for more information, call © **415/954-6271**). © **415/397-3333**. www.macys.com.

NEIMAN MARCUS
150 Stockton St.

Although I'm from Texas and try to be loyal (Hook 'em, Horns!), I gotta tell you that I am not impressed with the Union Square branch of Neiman Marcus. If you are into obscure and expensive designer brands—Eskandar, for example—you will find them here. The store does strive to find lines that no one else carries, especially in the upper price ranges. It also does an excellent business with its newsletter, advising local patrons on what's new in the store and what they need to load up on to be properly dressed for the season. Otherwise, I find the place to be a great big yawn. © **415/362-3900**. www.neimanmarcus.com.

NORDSTROM
San Francisco Shopping Centre, 865 Market St., at Fifth St.

The Seattle-based department store famous for its customer-service policies is located on the upper floors of this vertical mall. The piano player is here, as are the salespersons who will help you, keep your home phone number, and take care of you as no one ever has before. The store has a good handbag and shoe department, along with very good menswear. © **415/243-8500**. www.nordstrom.com.

SAKS FIFTH AVENUE
384 Post St.

I have a very simple motto about shopping at this store: "If you need something, go to Saks." Saks is, among all other things, dependable. One of the local specialties is the wedding department, as well as the evening attire, which is ordered to match up with the local opera, charity ball, and social season. There is a separate men's store at 220 Stockton St. © **415/986-4300**. www.saksfifthavenue.com.

DISCOUNTERS & OFF-PRICERS

LOEHMANN'S
222 Sutter St., between Kearny St. and Grant Ave.

Here's a destination the size of a small department store, with floors and floors crammed with stuff, much of it divided into categories of use (office, weekend), age, lifestyle, or body type—e.g., one floor is devoted to young women. There is a separate shoe store across the street. Petites and plus sizes are represented, too. ℭ 415/982-3215. www.loehmanns.com.

MARSHALLS
901 Market St., at Fifth St.

Marshalls and TJ Maxx are owned by the same New England firm. There do not seem to be any TJ Maxx stores in the Bay Area, but never mind. This is a conveniently located (close to the San Francisco Shopping Centre), basement-level, off-price store that is always worth a browse—and becomes even more fun when you find a serious bargain. This branch is a fairly ordinary Marshalls, but if, for some reason, you've never been to one before (you're from France, right?), it's nice to know that alternative retail is this close to the big-time shopping. The merchandise includes men's, women's, and children's clothing; some luggage; housewares and home style; and a small selection of beauty products and fragrance. ℭ 415/974-5368. www. marshallsonline.com.

NORDSTROM RACK
555 Ninth St., at Brannan St.

You have to be a devoted shopper to get to this outlet store— it will most likely cost you $7 in taxi fare each way (from the Union Square area). The neighborhood is somewhat seedy; there are no charms here. Instead, you get a real warehouse crammed with merchandise, including everything from designer clothes to shoes (and shoes and shoes) to housewares. ℭ 415/934-1211. www.nordstrom.com.

ROSS DRESS FOR LESS
799 Market St., at Fourth St.; 2300 16th St., between Bryant St. and Potrero Ave.; 5200 Geary Blvd., between 16th and 17th aves.

Ross Dress for Less is a California discounter that has changed a lot in recent years and now seems indistinguishable from Marshalls or TJ Maxx. There is a store right at the corner of Market and Fourth streets, in the heart of downtown San Francisco shopping, so you shouldn't miss it. This is also the place to go if you need something for your trip—more underwear, a bathing suit, luggage, and so on. I found the housewares department to be heart-stoppingly good. *Note:* The Market Street branch of Ross is only a block from Marshalls, described above. ℂ 800/945-7677. www.rossstores.com.

FABRICS & NOTIONS

BELL'OCCHIO
8 Brady St.

Bell'occhio is a strangely delish little shop that I came quite close to naming as one of the best stores in town. I didn't do it because the store is hard to get to and doesn't carry that much merchandise—rather, it sort of specializes in casting a spell. There are some ribbons, candles and teas, and this-and-thats, all worth touching and glowing over. The location is right off Market Street, not far from the art-supply store Flax and across from the famous Zuni Cafe. ℂ 415/864-4045.

BRITEX FABRICS
146 Geary St., between Stockton St. and Grant Ave.

This townhouse space has been turned into a fabric treasure-house of designer silks, Asian prints, crafts supplies, and more ideas than you could ever run through your Singer. Take the elevator to the top floor and then touch everything in sight as you walk downstairs. *Note:* While most stores in San Francisco

are open on Sundays, this one is not. ✆ 415/392-2910. www.
britexfabrics.com.

MENDEL'S/FAR OUT FABRICS
1556 Haight St., between Ashbury and Clayton sts.

Mendel's is good for both crafts and fabrics, with an emphasis on funky textiles—be they novelty patterned flannels or Mex-
ican-print vinyls. ✆ 415/621-1287. www.mendels.com.

PIERRE DEUX
134 Maiden Lane.

Yards and yards of the famous French Provençal *tissus Indiennes* here, as well as furniture, gifts, and much to covet if you
like the style. ✆ 415/296-9940. www.pierredeux.com.

RIBBONERIE
191 Potrero Ave., at 15th St.

Located near the new Design District, this store is—as you would
guess from its name—crammed with ribbons. There are also
other trims, along with a few buttons and pieces of vintage jewelry. The trims and ribbons vary in style, from the really expensive French stuff to the many novelty items that reflect a sense
of whimsy and a fair pricing policy. ✆ 415/626-6184. www.
theribbonerie.com.

SATIN MOON FABRICS

32 Clement St., between Arguello Blvd. and Second Ave.

It's worth coming here just to meet the owners of this funky
fabric house that specializes in vintage (and reproduction vintage), Asian-inspired home-style fabrics. There are a few other
cute stores across the street, making a trip out here an adventure if you are a fabric maven or love Asian looks from the
1930s and '40s. ✆ 415/668-1623.

SILK TRADING CO.
1616-A 16th St., at Rhode Island St.

This is a branch store of the national company and mail-order business, which has the best selection of silks in town—all pedigrees and all prices. There is a bargain area, as well as a few fashion accessories already made up from the fabrics. Mostly, customers look at yard goods on boards. It feels like a to-the-trade source, but is definitely open to the public. © 415/282-5574. www.silktrading.com.

FASHION BASICS

ANNE FONTAINE
118 Grant Ave.

This Union Square boutique is a French brand with stores in most major U.S. shopping cities. The house specialty has always been the basic, classic white shirt; in the last few years, black has been added. The shirts and blouses and tops vary from casual to dressy to even very dressy—they prove that "black + white = easy dressing" is the most fundamental French lesson. If the prices strike you as high, steal the looks and ideas. © 415/677-0920. www.annefontaine.com.

CHICO'S
San Francisco Shopping Centre, 865 Market St., at Fifth St.

I have listed Chico's in the "Multiples" section, later in this chapter, but mention the store here as well because it has become such an important factor in the current retail scene, with an especially strong presence in the Bay Area. Chico's also has a large online and catalog business, as well as locations all over the U.S. If you don't already know the line, you might want to have a look-see. I haven't been crazy about the recent thrust into prints, colors, or attempts at fashion, and prefer the brand for solids and classics. The prices are fair, the size range is wide, and the clothes are great for travel. This is one of the best-selling brands in America these days, so by all means, have a look. ℗ **415/495-2748**. www.chicos.com.

HENRY COTTON'S
105 Grant Ave., at Geary St.

Henry Cotton's is an Italian firm known for the quality of its cottons (hence the name), which are milled in northern Italy. The sportswear looks are classics, with more men's than women's wear—but the five floors of fashion means you'll find enough to outfit the whole family in the kind of clothes that always look good and always make you feel rich and well dressed. ℗ **415/391-5557**. www.henrycotton.co.kr.

FOODSTUFFS

Many cities are identified with a particular taste. San Francisco is especially known for its food scene because of the number of famous chefs here and the interest in local produce, but also because there are so many brands, flavors, and foodstuffs that are specific to this destination. The fusion choices are enormous—markets sell products from all over Asia alone. But there are also some local flavors to be snatched right off the shelves or from behind the counters.

BOUDIN BAKERY
Multiple locations, including 2890 Taylor St. and 156 Jefferson St., both near Fisherman's Wharf; Ghirardelli Square, 900 N. Point St.; Pier 39; 619 Market St., near Montgomery St.; 4 Embarcadero Center.

Boudin is the most famous of the local bakeries doing sourdough bread. There are locations all over town, including two near Fisherman's Wharf. (If you need a last-minute souvenir or gift loaf to bring home, note that sourdough bread—albeit a different brand, from the mass-market bakery La Parisien—is

sold at all area airports.) ✆ **800/992-1855**. www.boudin
bakery.com.

COST PLUS WORLD MARKET
2552 Taylor St., at N. Point St.

This is a national chain, so you possibly have a branch in your
hometown and already know that it has good prices on wine,
Ghirardelli chocolates, and various gourmet foodstuffs. I buy
my flavored coffee here. ✆ **415/928-6200**. www.costplus.com.

FERRY BUILDING MARKETPLACE AND FARMERS' MARKET
Market St. and Embarcadero.

First, you have to understand the historical relationship between
San Francisco, its love affair with chefs, and their interest in
locally grown ingredients. Add to that the renovation of the
Ferry Building, a landmark site right on the water (as you might
imagine from its name). What you get is one of the most exciting shopping and eating experiences in America. The interior
of the building contains some food stalls, restaurants, and
stores selling food-related merchandise, such as a branch of
Sur La Table (p. 154). While the indoor vendors and restaurants are open throughout the week, the place really pops on
weekends with the outdoor market, chef tours, cooking classes,
and a circus of food-related events. The granola guy (at Galaxy
Granola) is said to be fabulous. In good weather, you'll start
to think the five people you meet in heaven will all be farmers. ✆ **415/693-0996**. www.ferrybuildingmarketplace.com.

GHIRARDELLI CHOCOLATE MANUFACTORY
Ghirardelli Square, 900 N. Point St.

Ghirardelli chocolate is a local brand that is actually sold all
over the United States, but it has excellent distribution in San
Francisco—you can buy bonbons, chocolate bars, chocolate
wafers, hot-chocolate mix, and a variety of other products. Back
in the mid-1960s, the company opened Ghirardelli Square as
a tourist center, mall, and showcase for its retail operations.

You can take a chocolate tour, eat at the soda fountain, or buy products. In other parts of this book, I have mentioned that you can get much of the same products at Cost Plus World Market for less money—and less ambience. It's your choice. *Note:* This place is a zoo on weekends and in the summer season. © 415/775-0102. www.ghirardelli.com.

HARRY & DAVID
Westin St. Francis, 335 Powell St.

Although known for its fruit-of-the-month mailings and fruit catalogs, this company also runs a nice little business in giftable foodstuffs and food-related products. © 415/296-9233. www. harryanddavid.com.

IMPERIAL TEA COURT
1411 Powell St., at Broadway.

We're not talking Lipton here, and certainly not Boston Tea Party. Some of the more esoteric teas cost $400 a pound. You can browse and buy, or call ahead for a tasting appointment. © 415/788-6080. www.imperialtea.com.

LIGURIA BAKERY
1700 Stockton St., at Filbert St.

Get here early (it opens at 8am and closes by 4pm), stand in line, and be prepared for the most flavorful and original tastes to be sold out—like the homemade focaccia. © 415/421-3786.

SEE'S CANDIES
Multiple locations, including 350 Powell St., between Geary and Post sts.; 3 Embarcadero Center; 542 Market St., at Sutter St.; Stonestown Galleria, 3251 20th Ave.; and all area airports.

While See's is a somewhat traditional candy maker doing a range of filled chocolates, it's most famous for its lollipops (called See's Suckers) and its brittle. In recent times, the company has expanded the sucker flavors to be a little more "with it." I vote for the original three flavors (chocolate, vanilla, butterscotch). They make a great gift to take home. © 800/347-7337. www. seescandies.com.

TRADER JOE'S
555 Ninth St., at Brannan St.

Yes, it's a grocery store, but if you don't have a Trader Joe's in your hometown, you might want to stop in—especially if you're a foodie. You'll see wine and all kinds of nibbles. © 415/ 863-1292. www.traderjoes.com.

There are additional locations at 3 Masonic Ave., near Geary Boulevard (© 415/346-9964), and 401 Bay St., at Mason Street (© 415/351-1013).

WHOLE FOODS MARKET
1765 California St., at Franklin St.

I think you'll want to have a car with you to shop here—it's sort of out there and not in the thick of the tourist scene. Indeed, what tourist hangs out at an organic and gourmet grocery store? Well, I get a kick out of it. This is a very California kind of sightseeing attraction. Of course, you must visit the salad bar. And have a nice day. © 415/674-0500. www.wholefoods.com.

There are additional locations in SoMa at 399 Fourth St., at Harrison Street (© 415/618-0066), and in Berkeley at 3000 Telegraph Ave., at Ashby Avenue (© 510/649-1333).

XOX TRUFFLES
754 Columbus Ave., between Filbert and Greenwich sts.

I've written an entire section on chocolate in chapter 8, starting on p. 228, since most of the chocolate makers are in the East Bay. XOX Truffles has a branch in its home town of Oakland, but it is best known for its small shop here in North Beach. And yes, there are cabernet truffles. © 415/421-4814. www.xox truffles.com.

GIFTS & SOUVENIRS

I don't want to strike you as a low-class bozo, but I tend to look for area gifts at **Walgreens,** of which there are millions of branches all over the Bay Area, and at **Cost Plus World Market,** which sells bags of Ghirardelli chocolates at prices lower than in Ghirardelli's own store. You can also buy a large, discounted bag of chocolates and divide it up for several people—put a handful of candies into an Alcatraz coffee mug, wrap it in cellophane, and say "voilà!"

Most of the big hotels have gift shops, as you would expect. The best (and largest) is at the **Westin St. Francis,** which is also convenient since it's right on Union Square. But I am not beyond buying foodstuffs (bread! suckers!) at the airport . . . or heading to the grocery store for some locally made coffee (**Caffe Trieste** is sold in grocery stores as well as in its own coffee shop). As far as I am concerned, you can get all the gifts you will ever need on one visit to **Trader Joe's** (see above). Below, more traditional addresses for gifts.

CITY LIGHTS
261 Columbus Ave., at Broadway.

Forgive me, but the best gift I've given anyone cost $2 and came from City Lights: a button that I bought at the front cash register bearing the slogan FUCK ART, LET'S DANCE. ✆ 415/362-8193. www.citylights.com.

DISNEY STORE
400 Post St.

Hey, I'm just the messenger; don't shoot me. ✆ 415/391-6866. www.disneystore.com.

GHIRARDELLI CHOCOLATE MANUFACTORY
Ghirardelli Square, 900 N. Point St.

See the listing under "Foodstuffs," on p. 144. ✆ 415/775-0102. www.ghirardelli.com.

HYDRA
1919 Fillmore St., near Pine St.; 1710 Fourth St., Berkeley; Village at Corte Madera, 1618 Redwood Hwy., Corte Madera, Marin County.

As mentioned many times in this book, that Devil Duck sex toy makes a great gift. And it costs well under $10. See p. 92 for the whole scoop. Hydra also carries soaps and bath gimmicks for those who don't want to be ducked. www.hydra soap.com.

PIER 39
Pier 39.

A touristy mall filled—just jam-packed—with TTs (tourist traps) and the chance to buy souvenirs depicting Alcatraz, cable cars, Keane paintings, and everything else. Well, come to think of it, those Keane paintings are pretty much out of style and you may not even remember those urchins with enormous eyes. But I date myself. Oh dear. www.pier39.com.

WALGREENS
Multiple locations throughout San Francisco and the Bay Area.

This ubiquitous drugstore chain has a good-enough selection of postcards, Alcatraz stuff, and Ghirardelli chocolates to keep anyone amused. © 800/289-2273. www.walgreens.com.

HAIR & NAILS

CARLTON HAIR
San Francisco Shopping Centre, 865 Market St., at Fifth St., basement level.

This is one of those nothing-to-look-at, nothing-to-remember places that is very good to know about because it sells professional beauty supplies, does nails, has stylists, and is not very expensive—nor do you need an appointment. A variety of beauty services, hair treatments, color possibilities, and price ranges are available. Call for information or an appointment, or just stop in. ✆ 415/495-8300.

GINA KHAN SALON/YOSH FOR HAIR
173 Maiden Lane.

This salon, formerly known as just Yosh for Hair, is still one of the most famous in town. Semiretired, Yosh is still available for bookings on a limited basis. I've been having my hair done here for over 30 years. ✆ 415/989-7704. www.ginakhan.com.

TEASHI
2340 Polk St., between Union and Green sts.

Manicures begin at $15 and pedicures at $30, but prices go up depending on what sort of exotics you may opt for—such as the Hawaiian Hang Ten, a pedicure that includes a soak in coconut milk, a papaya-oil cuticle treatment, pineapple-sugar exfoliation, and a 10-minute massage. To book ahead, call ✆ 415/749-0990. www.teashi.com.

UNION NAIL
310 Sutter St., at Grant Ave.

Head upstairs for a drop-in manicure or pedicure in chic surroundings. I had a manicure with fills, a pedicure, and an extra foot massage—the total was just $50 (and I tipped well). The crowd is a mix of local businesswomen, Chinese yuppies, and middle-aged women eagerly eavesdropping on the other conversations. ✆ 415/544-0414.

HANDBAGS

While there are several specialty stores known for their handbags, the local department stores all do a good business in small leather goods and work especially hard to find brands that no one else has.

If you have the money to spend, **Neiman Marcus** has the best selection of unusual bags, especially when it comes to the funky kind that are almost craft or art pieces. You may also get a good deal on a major handbag at the Neiman's sales.

Nordstrom is strong in the midpriced and moderate brands—the store often has looks that are inspired by those bags that sell for $1,000 elsewhere.

The discount and off-price stores all sell handbags and small leather goods as well.

The big-name European leather-goods firms are listed under "Big Names (International)," on p. 133.

APRIL IN PARIS
55 Clement St., between Arguello Blvd. and Second Ave.

× navy?

Hmmm, I'm on shaky ground here, feeling somewhat ambivalent about this place. The designer has a lot of talent and makes a good product. But her boutique is also far from downtown, her prices are very high, and she seems to be dining out on the hype originating from the fact that she once worked for Hermès. Still, her bags are very well made, no question about it; she does custom work, too. Serious handbag ladies will find it worthwhile; casual shoppers can give it a miss. ✆ 415/750-9910. www.aprilinparis.us.

COACH
190 Post St., at Grant Ave.

I find it strange that Coach has changed so much recently and is now trying to make it as an international brand, which seems a bit presumptuous. In the good old days, Coach meant a distinctive bag crafted out of belt leather—well made and moderately priced, offered in seasonal colors. Now, there's logo fabric with leather trim, styles that have been inspired by other design firms, and nothing that speaks of the firm's heritage based in American culture. ✆ 415/392-1772. www.coach.com.

COLE HAAN
324 Stockton St., between Sutter and Post sts.

While this source should be listed under shoes, it has, in recent years, begun to make such stylish and chic handbags that you need to know about it. And the Union Square store is huge. © 415/391-1760. www.colehaan.com.

GHURKA
170 Post St., between Grant Ave. and Kearny St.

With stores only in New York and San Francisco, this might be a brand you aren't familiar with. The look is canvas or linen trimmed with excellent-quality leather; the line includes bags, accessories, totes, and luggage. It's all very preppy without looking L.L.Bean, sort of Old World British. © 415/392-7267. www. ghurka.com.

LONGCHAMP
114 Grant Ave., between Geary and Post sts.

This French brand bridges the gap between status and price; most of its handbags cost $150 to $300, yet come in styles and colors that make them a smart accessory without being over the top. There are also small leather goods, totes, and umbrellas, plus an entire line of folding nylon totes and backpacks that are perfect for travel. The logo is not intrusive, but is still familiar to those who care. © 415/362-7971. www.longchamp.com.

HOME STYLE & TABLETOP

CRATE & BARREL
55 Stockton St., at O'Farrell St.

I, too, get mixed up on the differences between Crate & Barrel and Pottery Barn. The way I remember it is simply this: Crate & Barrel is bigger and better. (It also has an outlet store in Berkeley; see p. 220 for details.) The range of goods is a little less

hot-off-the-catalog page than at other sources. ℃ **415/982-5200.**
www.crateandbarrel.com.

DANDELION
55 Portero Ave., off Division St.

This is essentially a gift and lifestyle store that mostly sells table-top, with some emphasis on paper goods, including a book section upstairs that even has gay literature. Conveniently located right near the Design District, the store has a chic clientele and specializes in "the perfect little" anything—be it a picture frame, table setting, ash tray, or whatever. ℃ **415/436-9500.**
www.tampopo.com.

FORREST JONES
3274 Sacramento St., between Presidio Ave. and Lyon St.

Yeah, okay, I get it—this is a hardware store. So what? It's the fanciest and most complete hardware store you've ever seen, and get this—it has Asian hardware! This European-style store is crammed floor to ceiling with housewares: dishes from France, cookware from Italy, and, yes, hardware from Vietnam. ℃ **415/567-2483.**

GUMP'S
135 Post St., between Grant Ave. and Kearny St.

A mesmerizing selection of home style, jewelry, scent, and wow-me items. Don't miss it for the world. And no, everything here is not Asian. I saw some incredible Scandinavian glass work last time I was in the store. ℃ **415/982-1616.** www.gumps.com.

NEST
2300 Fillmore St., at Clay St.

It's impossible not to love a store that looks like your own home—this one filled with finds from French flea markets, housewares, things to cuddle with, house gifts for others, and comfort treasures. ℃ **415/292-6199.**

SCHEUER LINENS
340 Sutter St., between Grant Ave. and Stockton St.

A mélange of sheets, bedding, towels, bathroom accessories, and astrology soaps. ✆ 415/392-2813. www.scheuerlinens.com.

SUE FISHER KING
3067 Sacramento St., between Baker and Broderick sts.

You pays your money for what you sees—and it's very artistic in a cozy way. King's eye and choice of merchandise are what bring shoppers here; her room sets and arrangements have that ready-to-move-in feel. It's an eclectic look with many small and gift items. ✆ 415/922-7276. www.suefisherking.com.

SUR LA TABLE
77 Maiden Lane; Ferry Building Marketplace, Market St. and Embarcadero; 1806 Fourth St., Berkeley.

This Seattle-based store is one of the most important resources in town, and a breakthrough retailer in terms of bringing French imports (dishes, tools, equipment, cookbooks) to the table, bringing cooking classes to the storefront, and making expensive brands accessible to all. The store in the Ferry Building is not as good as the mother ship on Maiden Lane. There are locations in other cities as well, but a browse through the main store will make you feel as though you've discovered the real magic in Ali Baba's kitchen. ✆ 866/328-5412. www.surlatable.com.

WILLIAMS-SONOMA
340 Post St., between Stockton and Powell sts.; 2 Embarcadero Center; 2000 Chestnut St., at Fillmore St.; Stonestown Galleria, 3251 20th Ave.

Originally created in San Francisco, this chain of stores saves the best for the home market at the flagship on Union Square. While it has recently moved into a furniture line, Williams-Sonoma is best known for foodstuffs, cookware, tabletop, and cookbooks. It also follows trends, so when *Sex and the*

City was the hot TV show, you could buy the ready-to-make mix for the perfect Cosmopolitan. There's even a line of soaps and hand-care items made from fresh lettuce. ✆ 877/812-6235. www.williamssonoma.com.

JEANS

Although the fabric from which jeans are made, denim, is from France (de Nîmes) and was originally worn by sailors, most fashion historians credit the California Gold Rush and the city of San Francisco as the originators of the American blue jean. Levi Strauss is headquartered in town, and many European brands have shops to show just how much the basic has changed.

DIESEL
101 Post St., at Kearny St.

Diesel is an Italian firm that sells fashion jeans known for their tight fit—or it can custom-make jeans just for you. ✆ 415/982-7077. www.diesel.com.

LEVI'S STORE
300 Post St., at Stockton St.

Levi Strauss, a brand known throughout the world simply as Levi's, is the original denim from the Gold Rush days and the firm that started it all. The flagship store on Union Square displays historic garments, all the lines, vintage, and made-to-measure jeans. ✆ 415/501-0100. www.levi.com.

LUCKY BRAND JEANS
San Francisco Shopping Centre, 865 Market St., at Fifth St.; 2301 Chestnut St., at Scott St.

The L.A. answer to Diesel, this fashion brand of blue jeans is particularly popular with young women who are into fit, fit,

fit. It has cute retro ads and appeals to teenage girls. ✆ 800/964-5777. www.luckybrandjeans.com.

MALLS

....

CROCKER GALLERIA
50 Post St., at Montgomery St.

Not a large mall, but it has an excellent Polo store, along with Gianni Versace and a few other upmarket brands. ✆ 415/393-1505. www.shopatgalleria.com.

EMBARCADERO CENTER
Battery St. to Justin Herman Plaza, Sacramento to Clay sts.

Created specifically for those who work in the area, this nothing-special mall has all the big brands you have at home (Ann Taylor, Banana Republic, Gap). Yawn. ✆ 415/772-0700. www.embarcaderocenter.com.

SAN FRANCISCO SHOPPING CENTRE
865 Market St., at Fifth St.

Find every major brand in the known world here—it's also very convenient for visitors. Even though it is, indeed, a mall, it's got everything and, thus, is worth your time because it will help you save time. The anchor store here is Nordstrom; tenants range from American Eagle to Kenneth Cole, Origins to L'Occitane, Brookstone to Tumi. ✆ 415/495-5656. www.westfield.com.

STANFORD SHOPPING CENTER
680 Stanford Shopping Center, at El Camino Real and Sand Hill Rd., Palo Alto.

This mall caters to affluent Silicon Valley shoppers, with anchor tenants of Bloomingdale's, Macy's, Neiman Marcus, and Nordstrom. See p. 139 for more information. ✆ 650/617-8200. www.stanfordshop.com.

STONESTOWN GALLERIA
3251 20th Ave., at Winston Dr.

Stonestown is not so convenient for travelers, yet it's crammed with national brands and big-name department store anchors (Macy's and Nordstrom). Yes, there's even a See's Candies. © 415/759-2626. www.shopstonestown.com.

VILLAGE AT CORTE MADERA
1618 Redwood Hwy., Corte Madera, Marin County.

How ya gonna get them out of the burbs and into the City? No problem, all the big stores have come to the big money. Every major multiple is at this upscale mall in Marin. The anchor stores are Nordstrom and Macy's. Chains represented include Banana Republic, Bebe, J. Crew, L'Occitane, Max Studio, Restoration Hardware, and Williams-Sonoma. Check out Hydra (of Devil Duck fame) and Papyrus, an upscale paper-goods source. And go to Phyllis's for fabulous burgers. © 415/924-8557. www.villageatcortemadera.com.

VINTAGE OAKS SHOPPING CENTER
140 Vintage Way, at Hwy. 101/Rowland Blvd., Novato, Marin County.

This is my favorite mall in Marin County. It has more than 50 stores ranging from real-people places, such as Costco and Target, to clothing discounters, such as Marshalls and Ross Dress for Less—not to mention Ben Franklin Crafts, where artsy types can entertain themselves for hours. See p. 174 for more information. © 415/897-9999.

MENSWEAR

The major department stores surrounding Union Square have menswear departments or even stores of their own. The discount and off-price stores, such as **Marshalls** and **Ross Dress**

for Less, as well as **Nordstrom Rack,** also sell men's shoes, clothing, and accessories—even suits.

Most of the big-name designer stores carry menswear, and
you'll also want to check such sources as **Henry Cotton's** (p. 144)
and **Jeremy's** (p. 227). The Castro (p. 101) is filled with stores
that cater to male shoppers. The major multiples also have
plenty to offer, and the selection in San Francisco may be larger
than at your mall back home; see p. 160 for addresses of **Abercrombie & Fitch, Banana Republic, Old Navy,** and the like.

BILLYBLUE
54 Geary St., between Grant Ave. and Kearny St.

BillyBlue carries mostly expensive and chic Italian brands for
men who know the difference. ✆ **415/781-2111.** www.billy
blue.com.

BROOKS BROTHERS
150 Post St., between Grant Ave. and Kearny St.

The line here has a boxy cut and a slightly updated, preppy,
yet still conservative look. It fits large American men well, but
may not work for Asian or European body types. ✆ **415/397-
4500.** www.brooksbrothers.com.

BULLOCK & JONES
272 Post St., between Stockton St. and Grant Ave.

A preppy haberdashery as befits the mostly conservative business bunch. ✆ **415/392-4243.** www.bullockandjones.com.

MEN'S WEARHOUSE
601 Market St., at Second St.; 17 Stockton St., at Ellis St.

Here's an off-price source you should know about if you need
something in a pinch but are loath to pay full price. ✆ **415/
544-0627.** www.menswearhouse.com.

ROCHESTER BIG & TALL
700 Mission St., at Third St.

Conveniently located at the edge of the Financial District, this store specializes in large sizes and offers both casual and business attire; there's also some dress-up and formal. © 415/982-6455. www.rochesterclothing.com.

ROLO
2351 Market St., between Castro and Noe sts.; 1235 Howard St., between Eighth and Ninth sts.; 1301 Howard St., at Ninth St.

Rolo's three stores have been important to the local scene for bringing cutting-edge fashion into the mainstream community. You've got everything from your big Italian brands to Paper Denim & Cloth jeans to men's skin care. There are also clothes for women. The store at 1301 Howard St. is an outlet where unsold merchandise from previous seasons is marked down. © 415/861-4862. www.rolo.com.

SELIX
123 Kearny St., between Post and Sutter sts.

Forgot the tux for the convention's big to-do? Fret not—you can buy or rent here. © 415/362-1133. www.selix.com

THOMAS PINK
252 Post St., between Stockton St. and Grant Ave.

The British shirt maker is known for bold stripes and hot colors—shirts that exhibit a touch of humor while still being basic enough for a banker. Each shirt has an extra-long tail and a square of pink fabric that serves as a logo. © 415/421-2022. www.thomaspink.com.

VAN HEUSEN FACTORY OUTLET
601 Mission St., at Second St.

Van Heusen still sells a quality dress shirt, made even better if you get a good price. ✆ 415/243-0750. www.pvh.com.

WILKES BASHFORD
375 Sutter St., between Stockton St. and Grant Ave.

The man who brought dressing well to San Francisco is still a better source for men's clothing than women's. Your object of desire here is likely to be expensive, European, and in good taste, though slightly unusual and singing of sophistication. The store does alterations. You will look like Prince Charming for the rest of your life. ✆ 415/986-4380. www.wilkesbashford.com.

MULTIPLES
....

You probably won't find any surprises at the following chain stores—but then again, you never know. The San Francisco locations may carry a larger selection and more varied merchandise than what you'll find back home.

ABERCROMBIE & FITCH
San Francisco Shopping Centre, 865 Market St., at Fifth St.; Stonestown Galleria, 3251 20th Ave.
www.abercrombie.com.

AMERICAN EAGLE OUTFITTERS
San Francisco Shopping Centre, 865 Market St., at Fifth St.; Stonestown Galleria, 3251 20th Ave.
www.ae.com.

ANN TAYLOR
San Francisco Shopping Centre, 865 Market St., at Fifth St.; 240 Post St., between Stockton St. and Grant Ave.; 3 Embarcadero Center; Ghirardelli Square, 900 N. Point St.; Stonestown Galleria, 3251 20th Ave.
www.anntaylor.com.

ANN TAYLOR LOFT
246 Sutter St., between Grant Ave. and Kearny St.
www.anntaylorloft.com.

BANANA REPUBLIC
256 Grant Ave., at Sutter St.; Embarcadero Center, 2 Sacra-
mento St.; Stonestown Galleria, 3251 20th Ave.
www.bananarepublic.com.

BEBE
San Francisco Shopping Centre, 865 Market St., at Fifth St.;
21 Grant Ave., off O'Farrell St.; Stonestown Galleria, 3251
20th Ave.; 2095 Union St., at Webster St.
www.bebe.com.

BENETTON
San Francisco Shopping Centre, 865 Market St., at Fifth St.;
39 Stockton St., between Market and O'Farrell sts.; Anchor-
age Square, 2800 Leavenworth St., at Beach St.
www.benetton.com.

CASUAL CORNER
301 Geary St., at Powell St.
www.casualcorner.com.

CHICO'S
San Francisco Shopping Centre, 865 Market St., at Fifth St.;
Stonestown Galleria, 3251 20th Ave.; 3505 California St.,
at Locust St.; 1974 Union St., between Buchanan and
Laguna sts.
www.chicos.com.

CLUB MONACO
San Francisco Shopping Centre, 865 Market St., at Fifth St.
www.clubmonaco.com.

EDDIE BAUER
Stonestown Galleria, 3251 20th Ave.
www.eddiebauer.com.

EXPRESS
San Francisco Shopping Centre, 865 Market St., at Fifth St.;
Stonestown Galleria, 3251 20th Ave.
www.expressfashion.com.

GAP
Multiple locations, including 100 Post St.; 890 Market St.;
Stonestown Galleria, 3251 20th Ave.; 1485 Haight St.;
Embarcadero Center, 3 Sacramento St.; 2040 Chestnut St.
www.gap.com.

J. CREW
San Francisco Shopping Centre, 865 Market St., at Fifth St.;
Stonestown Galleria, 3251 20th Ave.
www.jcrew.com.

OLD NAVY
801 Market St., at Fourth St.; 2300 16th St., between
Bryant St. and Potrero Ave.
www.oldnavy.com.

TALBOTS
128 Post St., between Grant Ave. and Kearny St.; Ston-
estown Galleria, 3251 20th Ave.
www.talbots.com.

PETS

GEORGE
2411 California St., at Fillmore St.; 1844 Fourth St., at
Hearst St., Berkeley.

Nothing could be finer than the made-to-order pet collars
here, which feature your pet's name and your phone number
embroidered right into the warp and weft. You pick the colors. Yes, George is the name of the dog. www.georgesf.com.

SEX TOYS

GOOD VIBRATIONS
603 Valencia St., at 17th St.; 1620 Polk St., at Sacramento St.; 2504 San Pablo Ave., at Dwight Way, Berkeley.

Created by women, for women. Peruse the films, toys, and more. www.goodvibes.com.

HYDRA
1919 Fillmore St., near Pine St.; 1710 Fourth St., Berkeley; Village at Corte Madera, 1618 Redwood Hwy., Corte Madera, Marin County.

This bath and soap store has a large selection of very playful Devil Ducks. They come in two sizes, both priced well under $10, and various colors. For girls only. See p. 92 for the whole scoop.

SHOES

ARTHUR BEREN
222 Stockton St., between Geary and Post sts.

This is the fancy specialty shoe shop in town, the one that carries all of the upmarket brands—including the hard-to-find Taryn Rose line, created by a foot doctor for hard-to-fit feet. © 415/397-8900. www.berenshoes.com.

DSW WAREHOUSE
111 Powell St., at Ellis St.

The large DSW store, right in the thick of tourist shopping, features everything from dress-up shoes and designer name brands to athletic, men's, and women's footwear. There's even a birthday club so you can buy more shoes. Some items are discounted, but some of these babies can still cost over $200 a pair. The shoes I bought for $29.99, however, were one of the triumphs of my trip. ☎ 415/445-9511. www.dswshoe.com.

Laku
1069 Valencia St., between 21st and 22nd sts.

Ooh and aah over the handmade slippers in a store that is mostly known for its handmade caps. This is extraordinary work. ☎ 415/695-1462. www.lakuyaeko.com.

Loehmann's Shoes
211 Sutter St., at Kearny St.

Across the street from the Loehmann's off-price clothing store (p. 140) is this mini department store with several stories of just shoes, for both men and women. ☎ 415/399-9208. www.loehmanns.com.

Rockport
165 Post St., between Grant Ave. and Kearny St.

These are serious shoes for people who care about fit and comfort. Products include sports shoes, dress shoes, and some clothes. The comfort-as-a-lifestyle thing edges up on fashion victims and winks. ☎ 415/951-4801. www.rockport.com.

Shoe Biz
1420, 1422, and 1446 Haight St., between Masonic Ave. and Ashbury St.

Shoe Biz is a small local chain that specializes in copies of the big-name, big-money styles at very reasonable prices. It's great for throwaway must-have looks that update any outfit and put you onto the catwalk of life. If you prefer comfort shoes to pointy toes, don't fret—there's athletic footwear, as well as the popular Vans brand, too. ☎ 415/861-1674. www.shoebizsf.com.

SPAS

Most of the hotels and department stores now have spas, as do many of the bigger and better health clubs. The most famous spas are actually in Napa and Sonoma, covered in chapter 7. Nonetheless, there are some San Francisco day spas that offer special services and that are especially well known for their California-style fusion treatments and natural products.

CHAKRA
256 Sutter St., between Grant Ave. and Kearny St.

The Chakra salon uses Aveda products exclusively. This seemingly California brand was actually created by an Austrian man, Horst Rechelbacher, who is into well-being and natural products as a lifestyle choice. Chakra offers products and treatments (including massages, manicures, makeup application, salon services, and more) as well as classes in breathing and yoga. © 415/398-5173. www.chakrasalonspa.com.

TRU SPA
750 Kearny St., between Washington and Clay sts.

It's a rain forest in this spa's Tropical Rainforest Room, but beauty services such as facials and manicures are also available. For appointments, call © 415/399-9700. www.truspa.com.

SPECIAL SIZES

HARPER GREER
580 Fourth St., at Brannan St.; 1799 Fourth St., Berkeley.

Harper Greer carries clothing for plus-size women; see p. 12 for a full review. © 800/578-4066. www.harpergreer.com.

ROCHESTER BIG & TALL
700 Mission St., at Third St.

See the listing under "Menswear" (p. 159) for details. ℭ 415/ 982-6455. www.rochesterclothing.com.

TEENS & 'TWEENS

....

ANTHROPOLOGIE
880 Market St., between Fourth and Fifth sts.; 750 Hearst Ave., Berkeley.

When I grow up and leave France, I will work for this chain of stores that sells the look I adore—a hodgepodge of French country, Americana, vintage, homemade, granny chic, and ethnic Asian. Anthropologie markets a look and a feel, as well as women's clothing (for everyone from teens to the young at heart), gifts, books, housewares, lingerie, soaps, and bath items. Touch everything; take no prisoners. www.anthropologie.com.

BETSEY JOHNSON
160 Geary St., between Stockton St. and Grant Ave.

The world's oldest teenager actually shares the designing these days with her daughter, who is also older than a teenager. Nonetheless, the clothes are still hip and hot and young and with it. ℭ 415/398-2516. www.betseyjohnson.com.

MARGARET O'LEARY
1 Claude Lane, near Union Square; 2400 Fillmore St., at Washington St.; 1832 Fourth St., Berkeley.

This store isn't just for teens, but the look is so gamine, I thought it was nicely placed in this part of the book. O'Leary is originally Irish but is now considered a local designer. The look at her boutiques is flirty and soft; she mixes her own stuff with well-known alternative brands, such as Dosa, which is one of my favorites. www.margaretoleary.com.

Urban Outfitters
80 Powell St., at Ellis St.; 2590 Bancroft Way, Berkeley.

The younger and hipper version of Anthropologie, from the same family of lifestyle stores. The Union Square branch is a very large outpost in the heart of everything, with clothes for all, home style, books, novelty items, and stuff that's just fun to look. *Note:* It's not for travelers with disabilities; the store is on many levels. www.urbanoutfitters.com.

THRIFT

Designer Consigner
3525 Sacramento St., between Laurel and Locust sts.; 563 Sutter St., between Powell and Mason sts.

The name says it all.

Junior League Next-to-New Shop
2226 Fillmore St., between Sacramento and Clay sts.

You'll find an excellent selection of furniture, housewares, books, and clothes that you might actually want to wear. No vintage looks, though—this is usually designer stuff or classics. ✆ 415/567-1627.

VINTAGE

Aardvark's Odd Ark
1501 Haight St., at Ashbury St.

Made famous 30 years ago when Robin Williams admitted that he bought his clothes—and Mork's—at Aardvark's, this L.A. store opened a branch in San Francisco about 25 years ago and is considered the granny of the vintage look. Like most of the stores in this area, Aardvark's opens at 11am daily. ✆ 415/621-3141.

BUFFALO EXCHANGE
*1555 Haight St., between Clayton and Ashbury sts.; 1210
Valencia St., at 23rd St.; 1800 Polk St., at Washington St.;
2585 Telegraph Ave., Berkeley.*

Buffalo's good for basics like jeans and bowling shirts. The prices
are high, though—to me, anyway. www.buffaloexchange.com.

CROSSROADS TRADING COMPANY
*1519 Haight St., between Ashbury and Clayton sts.; 2123
Market St., between 14th and 15th sts.; 1901 Fillmore St.,
at Bush St.; 555 Irving St., between Sixth and Seventh aves.;
2338 Shattuck Ave., Berkeley.*

It's recycled everything here. There are some labels and a few
vintage items, but mostly this is meat and potatoes for kids
who can't afford regular retail or for those smart enough to
buy used blue jeans. www.crossroadstrading.com.

WINE
....

Look for California vintages at the following wine shops, as
well as sources like **Cost Plus World Market**, 2552 Taylor St.,
at North Point (© **415/928-6200**; www.costplus.com), and
Trader Joe's, 555 Ninth St., at Brannan Street (© **415/863-1292**;
www.traderjoes.com).

CALIFORNIA WINE MERCHANT
4121 19th St., at Castro St.
© **415/864-4411.**

D&M WINE & LIQUOR
2200 Fillmore St., at Sacramento St.
© **415/346-1325.** www.dandm.com.

PLUMPJACK WINES
3201 Fillmore St., at Greenwich St.
© **415/346-9870.** www.plumpjack.com.

Chapter Seven

....

NAPA & SONOMA VALLEYS

Just as there are Nantucket people and Martha's Vineyard people, those who strongly prefer one to the other, I find there are Sonoma people and Napa people. The areas have both developed lately, but Sonoma remains a little funkier than Napa. And Santa Rosa, which was once a real city serving a suburban public of escapees from San Francisco, is now adding on the cute.

Real-estate fever took hold ages ago, spas multiply in the night, and everyone here knows that Sofia is a wine, not a movie director. (Although in real life, she's both.) And no, no one thinks Sofia is a big city in Bulgaria. The only nearby big city is the City itself, San Francisco, and people escape it in such a hurry that holiday and weekend traffic is bumper to bumper.

Putting aside the traffic, note that it's not feasible to do both Napa and Sonoma in a day trip. You can speed through on an overnighter, but you will enjoy yourself far more if you take some time and spend a few nights, or limit your explorations to one or two neighborhoods in one of the two valleys.

Finally, don't drink and drive. (See below for how to accomplish this.)

AREA ATTITUDE

....

Before you head out on your Napa and/or Sonoma adventure, understand that this area has been honed, polished, and marketed into a destination just shy of a movie set. The very whisper of the name Napa brings with it immediate and strong associations—of wine, food, luxury hotels and spas, and, yes, shopping.

The shopping ops you will encounter fall into some very specific areas of merchandise and themes—and they'll just keep coming at you. Thankfully, there's enough variety in the goods and possibilities to keep you somewhat amused, but count on everything costing top dollar, and count on the feeling of being taken, at least some of the time . . . unless you hit one of the several outlet malls (Napa, St. Helena, Petaluma) or do some real-people shopping, as reported later in these pages.

Naturally, there are wines and wines and more wines to buy. Along with them are all the wine-related equipment, tools, amenities, and gift gadgets you can imagine: plates painted with grapes and grapevines, wine coasters and stoppers, wine spa cures. (More on that one later.)

Wine is useless without good food, so you will also find a stage that worships local chefs—and their cookbooks—as well as a number of farm stands, farmers' markets, and grocery stores that specialize in gourmet foodstuffs. Olives—and therefore olive oils—are grown, harvested, and often pressed on the same properties that grow grapes. You'll also find that grapes and olives are popular motifs as a design metaphor for the Napa/Sonoma lifestyle.

Because of Napa's affinity with the South of France, Napa merchants also push the French country look. You will find a lot of stores that specialize in French country–esque (it may or may not actually be from France) merchandise, be it linens, antiques, reproduction furniture, dishes, or even dish towels. In most cases, this will mean a French Provençal look, but a few stores offer French Basque traditions, which are more moderne and less fussy, usually in raw linen with colored stripes.

There's a somewhat funky esprit to this area outside of San Francisco—you'll see that locals are particularly interested in the arts and crafts and uncommon beauties of things that are not mass-marketed. And because the grapes and olives come

Napa & Sonoma

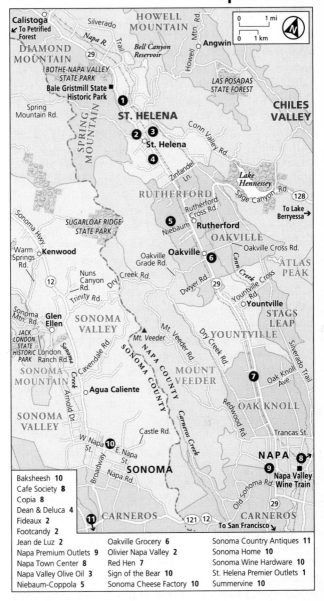

Calistoga
↙ To Petrified Forest

Silverado Trail

HOWELL MOUNTAIN

Howell Mtn. Rd.

Angwin

DIAMOND MOUNTAIN

Napa R.

(29)

Bell Canyon Reservoir

BOTHE-NAPA VALLEY STATE PARK

Bale Gristmill State Historic Park ❶

LAS POSADAS STATE FOREST

CHILES VALLEY

Spring Mountain Rd.

ST. HELENA

SPRING MOUNTAIN

❷ ❸

St. Helena

Conn Valley Rd.

❹

Zinfandel Ln.

Lake Hennessey

Sage Canyon Rd.

RUTHERFORD

SUGARLOAF RIDGE STATE PARK

Rutherford Cross Rd.

To Lake Berryessa →

(128)

Sonoma Hwy.

❺

Niebaum **Rutherford**

OAKVILLE

Oakville Cross Rd.

Warm Springs Rd.

Kenwood

Oakville Grade Rd.

Oakville ❻

ATLAS PEAK

Conn Creek

(12)

Nuns Canyon Rd.

Dry Creek Rd.

Dwyer Rd.

(29)

Yountville Cross

Trinity Rd.

Glen Ellen

SONOMA VALLEY

Yountville

STAGS LEAP

Sonoma Mtn. Rd.

JACK LONDON STATE HISTORIC PARK

London Ranch Rd.

Cavendale Rd.

Mt. Veeder

Mt. Veeder Rd.

MOUNT VEEDER

YOUNTVILLE

Dry Creek Rd.

❼

Oak Knoll Ave.

Silverado Trail Rd.

SONOMA MOUNTAIN

Sonoma Creek

NAPA COUNTY

SONOMA COUNTY

Carneros Creek

Redwood Rd.

OAK KNOLL

SONOMA VALLEY

Arnold Dr.

Agua Caliente

Castle Rd.

Trancas St.

❼

W. Napa St. ❿

E. Napa St.

NAPA ❽↗

Broadway

SONOMA

Napa Rd.

Napa St.

❾

Napa Valley Wine Train

❿

CARNEROS

⓫↓

(121)(12)

Old Sonoma Rd.

CARNEROS

To San Francisco ↘

(29)

Baksheesh **10**
Cafe Society **8**
Copia **8**
Dean & Deluca **4**
Fideaux **2**
Footcandy **2**
Jean de Luz **2**
Napa Premium Outlets **9**
Napa Town Center **8**
Napa Valley Olive Oil **3**
Niebaum-Coppola **5**

Oakville Grocery **6**
Olivier Napa Valley **2**
Red Hen **7**
Sign of the Bear **10**
Sonoma Cheese Factory **10**

Sonoma Country Antiques **11**
Sonoma Home **10**
Sonoma Wine Hardware **10**
St. Helena Premier Outlets **1**
Summervine **10**

0   1 mi
0   1 km

from the earth, that earth and all that can be crafted from it are exceptionally appreciated. A number of artisans base themselves throughout the area; handmade ceramics are the most popular products, in part because the motifs can be coordinated with the subject matter.

The locals are also uncommonly interested in well-being. Most of the hotels have spas; there's also the day-spa concept. Few visitors consider a trip to the area without trying the mud. Some of the best shopping finds are located in hotel gift shops or spa shops, where various muds, clays, ashes, and goops celebrate the local hot springs and the byproducts of grapes and grape-seed oil.

The intellectual appreciation of wine, the interest in food, and the good life pretty much define the kinds of shopping you'll find when driving through. Expect merchants to have an appreciation of the type of customer who has an interest in and the ability to pay for this sort of thing. Although the factory-outlet business has been created to capitalize on the upmarket audience who appreciates wine and food and has the money for a nice hotel and spa, there is a big difference between professional tourist traps and the stores that cater to a celebration of the lifestyle. The many mentions in this chapter of Costco, Cost Plus World Market, and Ross Dress for Less—all mass-market off-pricers or discounters—hopefully prove that you don't have to get stuck in a tourist trap if you don't want to.

NORTH VS. SOUTH

As you can tell from looking at a map, the Napa Valley area is linear, running along the famed Highway 29. Back in the early days of the area's growth, St. Helena was the heart of the cute and, for a while, was the most developed town. With the arrival of the big-name chefs farther south in Yountville, the areas around the towns of Yountville and Napa have become more popular. Businesses and restaurants in the northern portion often claim they're hurting—some are even closing.

There has been a small split, with high-end hotels, resorts, and spas moving into the north, and more real-people choices picking the area around the town of Napa, which is also easier to visit by day-trippers.

In either valley, remember that the farther north you go, the fewer tourists, the better the prices, and the more chance you have of some authentic vibes.

GETTING THERE

From San Francisco, there are assorted wine tours by bus, bike, motorcycle, and limo—you can go for a day, an overnight, or on a package. Or you can simply get into your big rental car and drive. The drink-and-drive issue becomes a concern later on (once you start drinking, to be exact), so see "Getting Around," below, for information on tours and drivers who keep you safe when you don't want to drive.

If you're driving out of San Francisco, follow signs to Highway 101 and the Golden Gate Bridge. Start singing "California, Here We Come." You are headed for Marin and Muir Woods. Mind the gap. No shoving, please.

After you pass Novato, you will have to choose between Napa and Sonoma. Then follow the appropriate signs. Some six million tourists a year come to the area; fall is high season. Expect traffic.

GETTING AROUND

As I keep saying: Don't drink and drive. Indeed, the local philosophy is that for day tastings and visits to multiple vineyards, you will use a designated driver. For evenings out, you will use a car and driver.

Car service is not very expensive, so everyone can take advantage of it. It's best to arrange it ahead of time, although your hotel concierge will invariably have some contacts or ways to rescue you. Try any of the following resources.

Drive-by Shopping

I know, I know: You're headed for Napa and/or Sonoma, you're on the road, and you don't want to waste time with piddling stops. But wait, before you get to either—don'tcha want to stop at a great mall?

You'll have to continue on Highway 101 past the Napa/Sonoma turnoff for about a half a mile. Then take the next exit, Rowland Boulevard, where you'll find the **Vintage Oaks Shopping Center**, 140 Vintage Way, Novato (℃ 415/897-9999). The mall is located right off the highway, so you really aren't going out of your way. Besides, aren't you dreaming of pancakes?

This place is one of my favorite destinations in the Bay Area—an old-fashioned, suburban-sprawl sort of mall filled with big-box stores and anchored by an **IHOP** (International House of Pancakes). There's a **Costco**, as well as various off-pricers, such as **Marshalls** and **Ross Dress for Less,** plus an excellent crafts store (**Ben Franklin**) and the discounter **Target.**

There are also many all-American multiples and chain stores: you know, the usual suspects, such as **Ann Taylor Loft, Old Navy, Sephora,** and **Petco.** When I realized that the spa I was headed to (Sonoma Mission Inn) required bathing suits, I made a dash into Marshalls!

Please don't forget that you will also drive by the **Village at Corte Madera**, 1618 Redwood Hwy., Corte Madera (℃ 415/924-8557; www.villageatcortemadera.com), while heading through Marin County. This is a very with-it shopping space created for moneyed Marin matrons so they don't have to go all the way into the City. The anchors here are **Nordstrom** and **Macy's;** other tenants include every multiple you can think of, from **Bebe** and **J. Crew** to **Aveda** and **L'Occitane** to **Restoration Hardware** and **Williams-Sonoma.** For a unique gift, stop by **Hydra** and check out those famous Devil Ducks.

Across the highway is **Corte Madera Town Center,** 770 Tamalpais Dr. (www.shoptowncenter.com), where you'll find stores like **Bare Escentuals,** the **Container Store, Marshalls,** and **REI.** If you do, indeed, get out this way, look for **West Elm** (℃ 415/927-0202; www.westelm.com), a furniture and home-style store based on the catalog of the same name. This place is enormous and more ethnic in choices than Ikea, but it's geared toward the same type of young, hip shopper and home-decor purposes.

Right down the road is a branch of **Cost Plus World Market**, 2040 Redwood Hwy. (© 415/924-7743; www.world market.com). Stock up on wine here—not at those fancy wineries you're about to visit! This is also a great shopping op, in general, with all sorts of imported foodstuffs and home decor. At the end of your Napa/Sonoma excursion, load up here on your way home.

These real-people choices are great to know about for those who love suburban big-box shopping. Also note that this is your last chance before Napa and Sonoma to buy anything at a reasonable price or in a non-touristy shopping atmosphere. Hmm, well, maybe that's not true—I suppose there are some stores in Santa Rosa for real people. And there are also factory outlets dotted here and there. But if you actually *need* something, or want to buy from stores or brands that you know well, these options provide a fun brush with a reality check.

AMERICAN LIMOUSINE WINE-TASTING TOURS
The specialty here is the day trip from San Francisco, which costs about $300. You and up to seven of your closest friends can pile into a biiiiig stretch. © 415/225-5110.

CALIFORNIA WINE TOURS
This firm offers a variety of tours and driving services, be it airport pickup or limo drivers who don't drink and drive. It has buses, vans, SUVs, and official and unofficial tours. © 800/294-6386. www.californiawinetours.com.

CELEBRITY LIMOUSINE
Celebrity is less of a tour business and more of a driving service, but its chauffeurs are flexible and knowledgeable if you're looking to do something different. A private wine tour for up

to eight passengers starts at around $300 for 5 hours. © 800/307-7974. www.celeblimo.com.

GROWING THERE

Californians are so familiar with their grapes that many of the varietals have nicknames, such as "cab" (cabernet) and "zin" (zinfandel). In California, the wines are known first by the name of the grape and then by the mix. In contrast, French wine is known by the region in which the grapes are grown; even the French may not know the names of the individual grapes or the blend of the grapes in a particular bottle.

The grapes grown in this area include cabernet, chardonnay, merlot, pinot noir, and zinfandel. Both still and sparkling wines are produced. Remember that sparkling wine made outside of the French province of Champagne cannot be called Champagne or even champagne.

Some specific parts of the valleys are known for their work with a certain type of grape. In the Russian River area, there is more pinot noir, while Rutherford is growing cabernet sauvignon. For a quickie overview at the relationships between region and varietal, look at it this way:

	REDS	WHITES
Bordeaux	cabernet sauvignon, merlot	sauvignon blanc, semillon
Burgundy	pinot noir	chardonnay
Rhône	syrah, grenache	viognier, roussanne, marsanne

TASTING AROUND

Most vineyards charge a fee for their tastings. Usually it's a flat fee—about $10 or $15 per person—and you get your choice of four tasting-size pours. This pour is not a full glass,

Wine Surfing

Drink no wine before its time—but surf as much as you want. In addition to the websites in the individual listings in this chapter, the following online sources may be helpful.

- www.epicurious.com is the website for *Gourmet* and *Bon Appétit* magazines.
- www.foodandwine.com will tell you how to match wine with meals. It also offers recipes, tips on serving wine, and a wine-related book list.
- www.napavintners.com covers the Napa Valley (duh) and its wineries.
- www.winebusiness.com is tied to the industry publication *Wine Business Monthly* and features a directory of other wine websites.
- www.wineinstitute.org is the official site of the San Francisco–based Wine Institute. It's primarily a trade and media organization, but anyone can log on and get the scoop on California wines. It doesn't recommend specific wineries, but does provide information on what to look for in each of the various wine-producing regions.
- www.wines.com features winery listings and reviews.
- www.winespectator.com is the website for the industry's most popular consumer magazine. It can be technical and somewhat complicated for the average consumer, but it's the most frequently quoted magazine in the trade. For most winemakers, a 90+ rating from *Wine Spectator* is to die for.

but it's not a teardrop, either. Rent the movie *Sideways* (which actually takes place in the wine country near Santa Barbara, not Napa) and you'll get the idea.

CARD ME

The drinking age in the state of California is 21. Expect to be carded if you're younger than 30. Foreign visitors, note this term of American slang: Being "carded" means you will be asked for an identification card with proof of age.

TALKING THE TALK

Boutique Wines: Small vineyards make only a few hundred (possibly a thousand or so) bottles of a particular wine, which has limited distribution and therefore sells on word of mouth (literally and figuratively).

Custom Crush: A blend made to your specs. If you talk about a vineyard "doin' a custom crush," this means it has a supply of certain grapes and will mix up a brew that is unique and will never happen again.

Garage Grapes: Forget the fake châteaux and big gift shops and acres of grapes. Why not grab a few grapes and make your own wine in the garage? And if you have more than you can consume, of course you can sell to friends, neighbors, or even passersby. This is enormously trendy in California as well as other wine-growing regions of the world.

Home Wine: Same idea as Garage Grapes—but this isn't as down-home as it sounds. For the last 20 years or so, there's been the Home Winemakers Classic, held at **St. Supéry Vineyards and Winery,** 8440 St. Helena Hwy., Rutherford (© 707/ 942-0809; www.stsupery.com), where homemade distillations are judged. There are usually about 100 entrants; winning is considered a big deal.

Lay Down: To store away in a wine cellar until the wine comes of age. For proper maturity, storage must offer a temperature-controlled environment.

Méthode Champenoise: Many years ago, the French province called Champagne won a very important lawsuit that made it illegal to call any sparkling wine Champagne if it was not grown in the French province of Champagne. Therefore, sparkling wines made outside this area of France either are called sparkling wine (duh) or are known by the way they are made, which is the *Méthode Champenoise,* a phrase that is usually marked on the label of any California sparkling wine. This is a pretty straightforward translation, so you get the drift. And for heaven's sake, when you're sipping it at a tasting, hold the glass by the stem. If you hold the bowl part, you will demonstrate that you are an idiot. (The warmth of your hand will make the bubbles go insane.)

Spaghetti Red: Back in the dark ages, we all drank an inexpensive chianti with Italian food, and nothing was considered more boho than a spaghetti dinner and a bottle of chianti. Now, cheap and cheery red wines that don't cost too much are referred to by the moniker Spaghetti Red. Two Buck Chuck, sold at Trader Joe's stores, is considered the top of this type of heap, but there are local labels as well—ask at any winery or wine store.

Warehouse Wines: This is similar to Garage Grapes, only unlike the garage vintner, who makes his wine at home, the warehouse vintner uses industrial space—usually a warehouse. Among the vintners, this is a snob issue because garage people are proud of their smaller efforts.

SHOPPING AT WINERIES

For Wine: Do not expect wine to cost less at the vineyard than at your neighborhood wine store, grocery store, or even warehouse club. Do expect a flat 10% discount on each case you buy, whether at a vineyard or a liquor store. Selection is the reason you shop at a vineyard to begin with. But if you want to have selection from a variety of labels, then you need a wine store, preferably one that specializes in the local grape (see below).

For Stuff: Since we live in the age of merchandising, it's normal that vineyards now sell all sorts of merchandise. Some of it is emblazoned with the winery logo, some of it is wine related, and much of it is stuff you might buy just because you are there. Very often, there are cookbooks from area chefs as well as other local foodstuffs; a big item is olive oil from locally grown olives.

SHOPPING AT WINE STORES

....

While you may have a great time shopping in the local vineyards, note that prices will be better at Costco and Cost Plus World Market, both of which are strategically situated so you can continue making purchases on your way back into San Francisco (see below).

Alas, part of the joy of driving and poking around the area is the local wine shops, so be sure to stop at any or all of the following.

In Napa Valley, try **Wine Garage,** 1020 Foothill Blvd. (Hwy. 29), Calistoga (© **707/942-5332;** www.winegarage.net), and **St. Helena Wine Merchants,** 699 St. Helena Hwy., St. Helena (© **707/963-7888**).

In Sonoma Valley, there's the **Wine Exchange of Sonoma,** 452 First St. E., Sonoma (© **707/938-1794;** www.wineex sonoma.com), right on the town's central plaza.

SHOPPING FOR WINE BARGAINS

....

For good prices on wines, make sure you shop around at my two favorite sources, Cost Plus World Market and Costco.

Cost Plus World Market has locations at 3934 Bel Aire Plaza, Napa (© **707/255-9755**); 2685 Santa Rosa Ave., Santa Rosa (© **707/526-0600**); 2040 Redwood Hwy., Greenbae, in Marin (© **415/924-7743**); and back in the Bay Area at 2552 Taylor St., San Francisco (© **415/928-6200**); and 101 Clay St., Oakland (© **510/834-4440**).

Costco has warehouses at 1900 Santa Rosa Ave., Santa Rosa (© **707/578-3775**); 5901 Redwood Dr., Rohnert Park (© **707/ 540-9113**); and 300 Vintage Way, Novato, in Marin County (© **415/899-1332**).

Note: Often, the prices at Costco are the same as at the vineyards, so don't "hold out" in order to save a buck and then find yourself high and very dry.

There are also several stores in San Francisco that specialize in area wines; see p. 168 for more information.

WINE AUCTIONS

The biggest auction of the year is held in May, but there are a series of local auctions to help raise money for local causes. Ask at area tourist offices for information, or stop into **Steve's Hardware,** 1370 Main St., St. Helena (© 707/963-3423), where local auction action is posted. Often the auctions take place at schools or churches and benefit community projects.

The biggest, **Auction Napa Valley** (© 707/963-3488; www.napavintners.com), is held at Meadowood every May or June. This event covers 4 days of wining and dining, with auction bids in the tens of thousands of dollars for single bottles. Always sold out (at over $1,200 per person for all events), this celebration attracts the Hollywood crowd as well as local celebrities.

Another popular auction is the **Sonoma County Showcase** (© 800/939-7666; www.sonomawine.com), held in mid-July. This one is less formal and features walk-around wine tastings with an on-the-green performance by the San Francisco Symphony. It costs around $800 per person for all events.

Also, check out the **Sonoma Valley Harvest Wine Auction** (© 707/935-0803; www.sonomavalleywine.com), held Labor Day weekend at the Sonoma Mission Inn's Golf Club. Event prices range from $75 to $600.

SHIPPING WINE

State laws regulate whether or not it is legal for wine to be shipped to your home. International shipping is legal, but too difficult to begin to contemplate (unless you are very drunk).

BOX N' MAIL
585 Fifth St. W., Sonoma.

This pack-and-send store offers wine shipping in addition to all of the standard services you'd expect (copying, faxing, notary public). © 707/939-7047.

STAGECOACH EXPRESS
3377 Solano Ave., Napa.

This shipping service is located in Redwood Plaza, a strip mall where many real-people services are offered. You pay for the box, the packing, and the shipping; the store will get the wine to you or yours if it's legal to do so. © 707/257-1888. www. stagecoachexpress.com.

GREAT GIFTS FROM THE AREA

You're probably planning to give wine or some form of bubbly as a gift to your friends back home—hopefully something unique to them and their palates. However, if you want to find gift items besides the usual bottles of wine, there are other options that celebrate the local lifestyle and let you bring wine country home with you.

To accompany all that wine you're lugging back, **gourmet foodstuffs** are always a hit. See "Fruits of the Earth," below, for information on olive oils and other delicious ideas.

Consider any of the zillions of **spa products** that can be found in bath-and-beauty shops, spas and salons, and hotel gift shops. These products can range from orange-and-rosemary-infused hand cream to an antioxidant sugar scrub with grapefruit; the options are limitless. See p. 185 for information on my favorite product discoveries.

Another idea is a **chocolate-covered wine bottle,** available only at **Goosecross Cellars,** 1119 State Lane, Yountville (© 800/276-9210; www.goosecross.com). I am not talking cutie-pie miniature anything here—this is a real bottle filled with real wine that has then been dipped in real chocolate!

Sofia Mini is a bubbly Blanc de Blancs packaged in a can similar to soda pop; it's available in a four-pack or gift box. The cans are small and chic, and the whole thing is so cute you could drink it with a straw! Available at **Niebaum-Coppola,** of course, at 1991 St. Helena Hwy., Rutherford (℃ **800/782-4266** or 707/968-1100; www.niebaum-coppola.com), but also at various wine stores and even, sometimes, at Cost Plus World Market. The price of a four-pack is invariably $20. Online, check out www.sofiamini.com.

FRUITS OF THE EARTH

....

Olive Oil

The similarity between olives and grapes is rather amazing. The surprise, however, is how long it took the vineyards to catch on. In the past few years, there's been a big push on locally made olive oils, and a small number of stores and farm stands are devoted just to the sale of the premium-grade stuff.

You want to look for oil from the first pressing—marked "extra virgin." The age (and ripeness) of the olives at the time of pressing is reflected in the flavor; some people like a fruity olive oil, while others like it sweet. In most cases, you will be invited to taste the oils (dip bread into the oil; don't slurp) before deciding which type you prefer. Fancy oils are usually used on salads or already-cooked foods, not for cooking or frying.

Area olive oils are for sale in specialty oil stores and small markets, as well as at the better-known gourmet grocery stores such as **Dean & Deluca,** in Napa Valley at 607 S. St. Helena Hwy., St. Helena (℃ 707/967-9980), and **Oakville Grocery,** in Napa at 7856 St. Helena Hwy., Oakville (℃ 707/944-8802), and in Sonoma at 124 Matheson St., Healdsburg (℃ 707/433-3200). Expect to pay anywhere from $15 to $50 for a bottle of good olive oil.

NAPA VALLEY OLIVE OIL MANUFACTURING
835 Charter Oak Ave., St. Helena.

This takes a little patience to find, but has a more authentic feel to it than Olivier Napa Valley, described below. While it specializes in making olive oil, this is actually a little deli. © 707/963-4173.

OLIVIER NAPA VALLEY
1375 Main St., St. Helena.

Looking a little too Provençal for my personal taste, this shop specializes in marketing cute, marketing Provence, and then marketing olives and olive products. The shoppers all seem to think it's adorable; forgive me if I sound rather jaded. © 707/967-8777. www.oliviernapavalley.com.

Cheese

While large commercial dairies have all but disappeared from the area, there are many small farmers with flocks of animals—particularly goats—who make cheese that's sold to local restaurants or at farmers' markets. The artisanal cheese scene began in the late 1970s and has grown enough to make a dent in the market scene.

Perhaps the most cheese-related fun involves a visit to the **Sonoma Cheese Factory,** in Sonoma Plaza, at 2 Spain St., Sonoma (© 707/996-1931; www.sonomajack.com). It specializes in its own hard-cheese creations, but also sells many other varieties.

Produce

ALL STAR ORGANICS
Tomales Bay Foods, 5300 Nicasio Valley Rd., Tomales.

Heirloom tomatoes are the specialty here, but other fruits and veggies are available in season. © 415/488-9464.

Farmers' Markets

- **Calistoga:** June through September, Saturday from 8:30am to 12:30pm at 1546 Lincoln Ave.
- **Healdsburg:** May through November, Saturday from 9am to noon at North and Vine streets; June through October, Tuesday from 4 to 6:30pm at Town Plaza, in the center of town.
- **Napa:** May through October, Tuesday from 7:30am to noon at Copia parking lot, 500 First St.
- **Sonoma:** Year-round, Friday from 9am to noon at Depot Park, Spain and First streets.
- **St. Helena:** May through October, Friday from 7:30am to noon at Crane Park, off Highway 29 near Crane and Grayson avenues.

LITTLE ORGANIC FARM
1855 Tomales Rd., Tomales.

This is not a farmers' market, as all the produce comes from one source, and it's not really a farm stand, either. It's basically a farm that happens to sell to the public, offering various fruits in season and the house specialty, potatoes, of which there are some 20 different varieties. If you've never made homemade french fries, ask here about the right potatoes, and go for it—a whole new world of tastes awaits. ℂ **707/773-1338.**

SPA LINES

The importance of the spa experience as part of the destination is another tribute to the land itself—these treatments in Napa and Sonoma are based on local mud baths and natural hot springs. Also lots of fun is testing out all the spa products available—whether it be the ones given as amenities in your hotel, sold in area gift shops, or found on your shopping explorations.

Sonoma Mission Inn & Spa, 100 Boyes Blvd., Sonoma
(© 707/938-9000; www.sonomamission inn.com), has a giant-
sized pump of its famous apricot lotion at the check-in desk
as well as at the concierge desk; there's more to come in your
room. MacArthur Place, 29 E. MacArthur St., Sonoma (© 707/
938-2929; www.macarthurplace.com), has grape-seed bath
soaking tea in its rooms, as well as a line of grape-seed bathing
amenities. Turndown service at Calistoga Ranch, 580 Lommel Rd., Calistoga (© 707/254-2800; www.calistogaranch.com),
even includes a small bottle of massage oil. Ooh-la-la.

The best product lines:

BODY TIME

Do not confuse this brand with the Body Shop, or its creators,
with locals—they are actually from Berkeley. Body Time looks
like an apothecary line, but features hundreds of products, from
aromatherapy to Otuke Shea Butter. Its philosophy is very green,
so you can buy small bottles to have filled or refill your own
containers. I splurged on the Orange Rosemary Hand & Foot
Care Cream. © 888/649-2639. www.bodytime.com.

KERSTIN FLORIAN

I found this total spa line in the gift shop at the Sonoma Mission Inn. While there is an anti-aging cream, I preferred Spa
Body, a lifestyle line created by using various products together
to reinforce your well-being habits. The line is from Hungary
and brings to mind the basic philosophy of a Beverly Hills skin-
care maven: clean and hydrate, clean and hydrate. There are
also numerous products you can bring back with you to create your own home spa. © 888/KERSTIN or 949/206-0175.
www.kerstinflorian.com.

OLAVIE

This firm is based in New York, but has good distribution in
Sonoma. It was possibly inspired by the Caudalíe range of
skin-care products from Bordeaux, France, but uses chardonnay grape-seed extract from Burgundy. My best buy was the

antioxidant sugar scrub with grapefruit. *C* **212/316-9828.** www.olavie.com.

SHOPPING EN ROUTE

....

Back near the fork in the road that determines whether you end up in Napa or Sonoma, you will pass various Marin County shopping attractions, such as those mentioned on p. 174. But once in Sonoma County, there's still a shopping op that pops up before the actual fork in the road.

SONOMA COUNTRY ANTIQUES
23999 Arnold Dr. (Hwy. 121), Sonoma.

Even though this store is on the "wrong" side of the road as you are leaving San Francisco and heading toward Napa and Sonoma, you should stop en route—since, on the way home, you will be preoccupied by the desire to stop at Costco and Cost Plus World Market for wine. Sonoma Country Antiques features a barnlike sprawl of furniture, much of it from France, with a real barn in the rear. It pays to track when the shipments arrive, as supplies can be depleted by the time you get yourself here. And there's nothing more pathetic than a barn that isn't packed to the rafters with furniture. Prices are high, but not totally outrageous. Open daily from 10am to 5:30pm. *C* **707/938-8315.** www.sonomacountryantiques.com.

NAPA VALLEY

....

Getting There

There are various day and even overnight wine tours that you can take from San Francisco (see p. 175 for options), although most people prefer to rent a car and head out on their own. From San Francisco, cross the Golden Gate Bridge, and head toward Marin County.

Information, Please

Many of the towns' visitor centers offer a free town map with hand-drawn details. These fall into the cutie-pie department as well as the mental category of "may be useful—why not?" *Note:* These maps usually have sponsors; firms that do not contribute are not covered.

The Lay of the Land

Highway 29 is the main drag of the Napa fork (if the bridge is behind you, this is the right-hand fork into the Napa Valley). Also sometimes called the **St. Helena Highway,** this road is about 35 miles long and leads from Carneros, at the base of the fork, right through a daisy chain of little villages. Note that this isn't a highway in the freeway sense of the word— it's really not any fancier than the Boston Post Road.

The **Silverado Trail,** which sounds very romantic and Old West and, maybe, a little like a movie title, runs parallel to Highway 29. It's the address for some of the luxury properties that are nestled more into the hills rather than along the main through street.

Sleeping in Napa Valley

AUBERGE DU SOLEIL
180 Rutherford Hill Rd., Rutherford.

Perhaps the most famous property in Napa Valley is the Auberge du Soleil, a celebration of food, wine, hospitality, and well-being that became so successful it spawned an entire group of luxury hotels. The Auberge Resorts group also owns the Calistoga Ranch (see below). In order to keep this 20-year-old property fresh, renovations are ongoing, and major additions have been made for the upcoming season.

Spa du Soleil has been redone, now offering six private treatment rooms (two designed for couples), each with its own garden, fountain, and outdoor shower or bathtub. All treatment rooms open onto a courtyard, also with garden and fountains.

At the far end of the courtyard are three pools—a small infinity-edge soaking mineral pool (warm), a plunge pool (cool), and a hot tub.

The spa now has an herb garden, so it can infuse and make up its own special potions. The treatments are categorized into four groups—the Valley (based on mud and minerals), the Grove (olive oil), the Garden (herbs and flowers), and, my choice, the Vineyard (grapes). Each group features massages, facials, exfoliation, wraps, and foot/scalp/hair treatments. The spa service is really the big reason to book here, and there's no question about the magic in those magic fingers—you just have to choose your treatment. I opted for the Virtual Head to Toe, which began with a full-body massage with grape-seed oil and rose hips (I could have sworn it was Smucker's jam).

Accommodations here consist of 50 suites, each with terrace and valley view; rates vary from $450 (in low season) to $3,000 per day. No pets or children under 16 are permitted. For reservations, call © 800/348-5406. Local phone © 707/63-1211. www.aubergedusoleil.com.

CALISTOGA RANCH
580 Lommel Rd., Calistoga.

I chose Calistoga Ranch right after it opened—unaware of the press, the word, or the whispers—knowing only that the property was the newest member of Leading Hotels of the World and sounded good enough for me. Perhaps the lack of expectations was responsible for the way the Ranch hit me emotionally. On the other hand, since in all my years of visiting hotels, I've never seen nor felt about a property to this extreme, you may just have to accept that it was a simply staggering experience.

Calistoga Ranch functions as both hotel and private club with residences for sale. (My birthday is April 13, for those of you who wonder what's on my wish list.) Guests stay in one of 46 private redwood lodges, each separate but set up in village style (you get around by golf cart). The lodges themselves are built around the concept of integrated space—not all of the rooms adjoin one another, but are, instead, spaced apart

Auberge or Ranch?

Since the Auberge du Soleil and the Calistoga Ranch are owned by the same hotel group and are only about a 5-minute drive apart, which one is right for you? How do you tell them apart? Sarah Lahey, Born to Shop news director, reports:

I went to Auberge du Soleil hoping I wouldn't be disappointed after my stunning stay at Calistoga Ranch. Nothing could top Calistoga Ranch, I thought nervously. The Auberge will be old hat, old-fashioned, ho-hum, I worried as I parked, sulking.

Not so.

In fact, I found just the opposite. Where Calistoga Ranch is new, sexy, cutting edge, and sophisticated, the Auberge is tranquil, luxurious, yet low-key . . . and the service is supreme. In fact, part of the charm of Calistoga is the get-away-from-it-all aspect—there's plenty of good service, but you ring for it when you need it. At the Auberge, in contrast, I was awash in being cared for.

I didn't feel as if they were putting on a show for me, or that someone had been prepped to pamper me. I didn't feel like I was on a movie set, as can happen elsewhere. This was down-home luxury with a human touch. Calistoga Ranch is therapeutic with a sense of renewal, but Auberge is healing because of the personal comforts. The hospitality seemed simply a natural extension of the inn itself.

If I were booking a weekend away with my husband of 25 years, I'd be very tempted by the drama of Calistoga Ranch, but I'd probably choose Auberge. On the other hand, if I were running off with George Clooney, well, in that case, then perhaps Calistoga Ranch.

by an outdoor area or even an indoor/outdoor fireplace. While there is, of course, a complete bathroom suite in each lodge, there is also a private outdoor shower that's an extension of the bathroom itself.

Because the property was once a tannery, water is an important presence here. A creek runs through the resort, and dinner is served in a dining lodge next to a small lake. Meals are offered indoors or out; expect to pay about $100 per person for a complete dinner, which includes a glass of local wine. The wine cellars, which can be toured, are across from the restaurant and sunken into natural stone.

The spa is called the Bathhouse and offers treatments for singles or couples, along with a small gift shop selling a variety of tonics and treatments. Treatments make use of local and all-natural ingredients, such as the Harvest Fruit enzyme facial or the Vineyard Crush antioxidant rubdown. Naturally, the property has its own natural hot springs as well: The Healing Waters Soaking Pool is a comfortable 102°F (39°C).

Rates vary with the season, but are generally $550 to $850 per cabin. For reservations, call Leading Hotels of the World at © 800/223-6800. Local phone © 707/254-2820. www. calistogaranch.com.

COTTAGE GROVE INN
1711 Lincoln Ave., Calistoga.

Insider's secret advice: Stay across the street from Indian Springs (described below) at Cottage Grove Inn, which is a slightly more upscale property. You can then walk over to Indian Springs for the mud, pool, and spa (and a glimpse into the magic mirror). Besides, rooms at Indian Springs are often booked up, especially on weekends—making Cottage Grove a true find.

Each cottage has a king-size bed with luxe linens, down pillows, and duvet. Several of the cottages will accommodate a third person on a twin sleeper sofa; children over 12 are welcome. Rates vary with the season and range from $215 to $350. Packages with wine tours are available. For reservations, call © 800/799-2284. Local phone © 707/942-8400. www.cottage grove.com.

INDIAN SPRINGS
1712 Lincoln Ave., Calistoga.

For the poor man's posh visit to Napa, try to book at Indian Springs, perhaps the most famous of the mud-inclusive resorts in downtown Calistoga. As you drive through town, you'll be drawn to it by the need to follow the plumes of steam that seem to be lifting heavenward right from its rooftop.

An Olympic-size mineral pool is naturally heated to between 90° and 102°F (32°–39°C), depending on the season. The pool lies adjacent to a mission-style bathhouse, built in the 1920s. The bathhouse has a gift shop selling local spa products, but the best part? Outside the shower room is one of those old carnival wavy mirrors that distorts your image. Gals, take note: This mirror makes you look 6 feet tall with endless legs and huge boobies.

If the image of the new you puts you into shock, there's the newly opened Dragonfly Geyser Pond to enjoy before or after your spa treatment. In a peaceful parklike setting, a Buddha watches over guests and inspires meditation.

Rates for the 18 bungalows range from $185 to $450; hotel prices are $235 to $550 on weekends and in high season, May through October. A classic mud bath goes for $75 and includes use of the Olympic-size mineral pool. ✆ 707/942-4913. www.indianspringscalistoga.com.

Eating in Napa Valley

Not too much goes better with wine than food, so Napa and Sonoma have both become well known for their kitchens. Napa Valley, in particular, is home to some of the most famous chefs in the United States, like Thomas Keller of the **French Laundry**, 6640 Washington St., Yountville (✆ 707/944-2380; www.frenchlaundry.com), where an over-the-top, nine-course tasting menu will set you back a whopping $175 per person. Many of the restaurants in Napa Valley are hard to get into and require booking a table months in advance. Since all of the options are listed in general food and travel guides, below I've shared some of my own shopper's secrets of the area.

ANDIE'S CAFE
Classic Car Wash, 1042 Freeway Dr., Napa.

So, before you get deep into wine country, it's time off for the outlet mall, right? Of course! And for lunch? Nothing will do except Andie's. Yes, the place is attached to a car wash. That's just part of the charm. The rest of the charm lies in the simply fabulous burgers and damn good onion rings. You can order takeout by calling ☎ **707/259-1107.**

BOUCHON
6534 Washington St., Yountville.

Bouchon is French for traffic jam, which is what you'll find here among those foodies trying to get into the French Laundry's baby sister. It's got the same chef, Thomas Keller, but is more casual. A new cookbook has recently been published; there is another branch of this restaurant in Las Vegas. ☎ **707/944-8037.** www.bouchonbistro.com.

OAKVILLE GROCERY
7856 St. Helena Hwy., Oakville.

Oakville Grocery has branches in both Napa and Sonoma. The one in Sonoma (p. 211) is actually larger and better. Nonetheless, whether you are in need of a snack, a meal, a picnic, or a bathroom—this is the place to stop.

The store has become so chic that its blue-and-white stripes are now a logo statement sold on tote bags and paper goods. This is the "in" place to buy groceries, pick up picnic fare, or simply be seen. The shelves are endowed with local and imported gourmet foodstuffs, and you'll also find a bakery counter, a deli, and—you guessed it—plenty of local wines. Good bagels, too. ☎ **707/944-8802.** www.oakvillegrocery.com.

TRA VIGNE
1050 Charter Oak Ave., St. Helena.

This Mediterranean-style restaurant makes its own fresh mozzarella and prosciutto, presses its own olive oil, and grows its own table grapes. Within several dining environments—grand dining room, courtyard, and small cantina—you'll find creations that pay homage to traditional Italian cookery while incorporating a bit of Napa Valley innovation and a local twist or two. The excellent wine list includes an extensive selection by the glass. © 707/963-4444. www.travignerestaurant.com.

The Towns of Napa Valley

NAPA

Napa, Napa, Napa. Hmmm. I don't know if Napa has just changed so much that I didn't recognize it, or perhaps I was just too blown away after my visit to the outlets, but Napa did not knock me out with opportunities to jump out of the car and browse or shop. The "cute" that I had remembered from a visit years ago was mostly gone; I felt an overwhelming desire to sing "Is That All There Is?"

Local merchants claim I'm wrong, that newer and varied stores are arriving all the time; that the north-south divide has brought an entire crop of newcomers; that Napa is where it's happening.

CAFE SOCIETY
1000 Main St., Napa.

If you haven't stopped at Andie's for a burger, perhaps you need a fix in French style– and French-bistro food. You can simultaneously eat, shop, and marvel at how much French influence can be seen throughout the Napa area at one of the cuter (and nicer) of the French-style properties—all the merchandise here comes directly from France, including antiques and flea-market finds, foodstuffs, and tabletop items. This is a great place to make a pit stop and shop for house gifts all at the same time. © 707/256-3232. www.cafesocietystore.com.

COPIA
500 First St., Napa.

Where wine meets science meets art meets community and more—this is the wine center of the area, with tastings, teachings, events, classes, films, concerts, gardens, and special exhibits meant to explain or enhance your understanding of the wine-growing process and wine itself. Yeah—and, of course, there's a gift shop.

Copia specializes in all-day or even weekend programs, so you can often buy one ticket that entitles you to speeches, tastings, presentations, book signings, and more. The space is also home to a well-known restaurant, Julia's Kitchen, and a tasting table hosted by *Wine Spectator* magazine.

Copia is open Wednesday through Monday. Admission ranges from $7.50 to $13, depending on your age; a 1-day pass is usually included in the price of any special event you may book. For reservations at Julia's Kitchen, call © **707/265-5700**; the six-course chef's tasting menu costs about $60 per person. © **707/259-1600**. www.copia.org.

NAPA TOWN CENTER
1290 Napa Town Center, at First St., Napa.

You can park in the garage or take the city's trolley before exploring this small mall that caters to the Napa lifestyle (which boils down to: shop, eat, drink). There's real-people shopping (**Waldenbooks, Gary's Tux Shop, GNC Vitamins**), but also cafes, an ice-cream shop, and **Wineries of Napa Valley** (© **707/253-9450**). © **707/253-9282**.

RED HEN
5091 St. Helena Hwy., Napa.

This is a must-do stop only for those who like junk and are attracted to kitsch and newer antiques (from the '50s and '60s). Prices are low to moderate, as befits the quality. Rummage around and enjoy it, or don't even bother stopping. © **707/257-0882**.

Winery Gift Shops: The Best of the Bunch, Part 1

Almost every winery will sell you something besides wine, but some are worth visiting for the gift shop alone. Most offer a selection of gifts, tableware, and specialty foods—and, of course, items emblazoned with the winery's logo. You won't find a ton of bargains, but you will see merchandise that you can't buy elsewhere.

The wineries below feature some of my favorite gift shops, though not necessarily my favorite wines.

- **Beringer Vineyards,** 2000 Main St., St. Helena (© 707/963-7115; www.beringer.com).
- **Clos Du Val,** 5330 Silverado Trail, Napa (© 707/252-6711; www.closduval.com).
- **Domaine Chandon,** 1 California Dr., Yountville (© 707/944-2280; www.chandon.com).
- **Freemark Abbey Winery,** 3022 St. Helena Hwy. N., St. Helena (© 707/963-9694; www.freemarkabbey.com).
- **The Hess Collection,** 4411 Redwood Rd., Napa (© 707/55-1144; www.hesscollection.com).
- **Mumm Napa,** 8445 Silverado Trail, Rutherford (© 707/942-3434; www.mummnapa.com).
- **Niebaum-Coppola,** 1991 St. Helena Hwy. (Hwy. 29), Rutherford (© 707/968-1100; www.niebaum-coppola.com).
- **Robert Mondavi Winery,** 7801 St. Helena Hwy. (Hwy. 29), Oakville (© 707/226-1335; www.robertmondaviwinery.com).
- **Silver Rose Cellars,** 351 Rosedale Rd., at Silverado Trail, Calistoga (© 707/942-9581; www.silverrosecellars.com).
- **Sterling Vineyards,** 1111 Dunaweal Lane, Calistoga (© 707/942-4219; www.sterlingvineyards.com).
- **V. Sattui Winery,** 1111 White Lane, St. Helena (© 707/963-7774; www.vsattui.com).

YOUNTVILLE & RUTHERFORD

Oh dear, what to say—eat and forget about the shopping? Do I dare be that blunt? Yes, I dare to do so.

For those who haven't already memorized the latest pages in foodie guides, Yountville is home to a handful of the most famous chefs in the region, if not the country. It's also the destination for those making the pilgrimage to the French Laundry, reigned over by Thomas Keller, said by many to be the best chef in the U.S. But most of the organized shopping here is very, very touristy.

Don't get me wrong: Yountville is cute, and I found a few nice antiques shops there, like **Antique Fair,** 6512 Washington St., Yountville (© 707/944-8440; www.antiquefair.com), right next to Bistro Jeanty, one of the most famous places in town to eat.

But overall, Yountville has tried to woo visitors to its stores with a few touristy malls, which are just that—touristy. My advice? Forget the stores and dream about the meals. Once in Yountville, serious shoppers will know they aren't very far from St. Helena, which has many adorable stores—so eat and run. And en route to St. Helena, make a stop in Rutherford at the following winery.

Niebaum-Coppola Estate, Vineyards & Winery
1991 St. Helena Hwy., Rutherford.

If you ever doubted the connection between show business and retail, you have only to stop by Niebaum-Coppola. Movies are shot here, shoppers are happy here, there's plenty to sip and taste, and one corner of the store is even devoted to shopping choices made by Francis's dad. Nonshoppers will have fun here, too. (They can drink.) © 707/963-9099. www.niebaum-coppola.com.

St. Helena

Dean & Deluca
607 S. St. Helena Hwy., St. Helena.

Dean & Deluca is a foodie's paradise of gourmet this and that, with an emphasis on local producers. © 707/967-9980. www.deananddeluca.com.

FIDEAUX
1312 Main St., St. Helena.

It's a pet store, silly. Sound out the name (i.e., Fido). It's a mecca for upscale cats and dogs, offering gear, beds, totes, and, yes, clothes. © 707/967-9935.

FOOTCANDY
1239 Main St., St. Helena.

This Beverly Hills-esque shoe store features catch-me-if-you-can stilettos and designer high heels—perhaps not perfect for dancing on grapes, but ideal for those who want to stagger without aid of alcohol. Designers represented include Manolo Blahnik, Edmundo Castillo, Jimmy Choo, Hollywould, Lambertson Truex, and Christian Louboutin. © 707/963-2040. www.footcandyshoes.com.

JAN DE LUZ
1219 Main St., St. Helena.

Proving that you don't have to be French to be rude, the owners here have a great thing going . . . but are pretty snotty about it. The linens and French country–home style are Basque in origin—homespun, natural, with one or more colored stripes. This look is cleaner and more a la mode these days than the cluttered *tissues Indiennes* of Provence. Jan de Luz also does personalized stitching and monograms. It's a large store with sensational merchandise; too bad about the attitude. © 707/963-1550. www.jandeluz.com.

ST. HELENA PREMIER OUTLETS
3111 N. St. Helena Hwy., St. Helena.

An incredibly tiny outlet mall with just a few stores; see p. 199 for more information. © 707/963-7282. www.sthelena premieroutlets.com.

CALISTOGA

The town of Calistoga is a smaller, less fancy version of Aspen—all Western-style storefronts and no Gucci, no Pucci. There's a small emphasis on the cowboy and Western shtick, but more of a focus on the wine and the mud. Everywhere you go, even from shop to shop, you'll note the rising smoke plumes and the siren call of that glorious goop.

Outlet Malls

NAPA PREMIUM OUTLETS
629 Factory Stores Dr., Napa.

This large outlet mall is a tad difficult to get to if you're not paying attention. After you exit the highway and try to turn into the mall, you may very well find yourself back on the highway. If you're heading straight to the outlets, exit at First Street, Napa; turn left, thus passing over the highway, and then follow the signs.

Once you get past that hurdle and wind onto Factory Stores Drive (welcome to scenic Napa), you will come to a sprawling parking lot and a series of strip malls that house factory outlets for such brands as Ann Taylor, Barneys New York, BCBG Max Azria, Calvin Klein, Coach, Cole Haan, Dockers, Ellen Tracy, Izod, J. Crew, Jones New York, Kenneth Cole, Levi's, Max Studio, Timberland, Tommy Hilfiger, and TSE Cashmere. © 707/226-9876. www.premiumoutlets.com.

ST. HELENA PREMIER OUTLETS
3111 N. St. Helena Hwy., St. Helena.

The secret to enjoying these outlets is to expect nothing. If you go into it thinking this is going to be a big mall or offer a lot of shopping ops, you will be crestfallen. In fact, this tiny center has only a handful of shops, a soft-drink machine, and large, clean bathrooms. It's in a wood-shingle, outdoorsy type of ranch dwelling with just a few quality stores: Brooks Brothers, Coach, DKNY, Escada, Jones New York, Movado, Tumi. Stop here

Mud-Slinging in Calistoga

Because of the importance of spas and spa products in the local culture and shopping baskets, herewith, a report on mud not in your eye.

The Wappo Indians, the original inhabitants of the Napa Valley, were the first to discover the natural hot mineral springs and geysers in what is now Calistoga. Recognizing the healing properties of the water, they built three sweat lodges (Native American day spas?) in the area. Rich in magnesium and calcium, the thermal mineral waters were created when Mt. Konocti erupted millions of years ago. This volcanic eruption created fissures in the earth, where layers of volcanic ash were deposited; now residing about 4 feet beneath the earth's surface. (And you thought *Six Feet Under* was a hit?)

The mineral water rises through ancient sea beds, absorbing rich minerals and salt traces. This water is then mixed with hand-sifted ash to create the warm black ooze used in the local resorts' famed mud baths. After each mud bath, the mud is sterilized with geyser water that is constantly replenished. (Phew.)

We tested the mud at **Indian Springs** (p. 192). First you're given a locker and instructed to strip down and wrap yourself in the provided towel; you're then led to the mud room, where a warm mineral shower is the top item on the agenda. The routine is not for the modest: Although the treatment areas are segregated boy/girl, there are no shower curtains or partitions between mud troughs or soaking tubs. Yeah, that means lotsa naked ladies running around in a fashion that makes Loehmann's dressing room look timid.

The mud tub is about 5 feet long by 3 feet wide and 3 feet deep. You sit on the side, grab the opposite wall, and lower yourself ass backward/legs up into the goop. Despite your expectations, you do not sink, but instead seemingly float on the mud. It's coal black with the gritty consistency of a good-quality facial mask. Or maybe quicksand.

The attendant then scoops up the mud and covers you, from neck to toes. If you want mud on your face, just say so.

(Mud on the face is good for those with an oily skin type.)
The goop is the temperature of a hot bath; the claustropho-
bic may need a few minutes to adjust. Then you just settle in
for about 10 minutes and let go of it all. Goodbye, real world.

To get out of that stuff, you must lift one leg at a time (when
did they add the weights?). As you lift, the attendant scrapes
off the mud. Again, not for the modest! Once outta there,
you head to another warm shower, followed by a soak in an
old-fashioned claw-foot tub with plenty of citrus cucumber
water to drink. Then it's the steam room. The final segment
is naptime in a private room, wrapped in towels with cucumber eye compresses. After the cat nap, you can move to the
pool and float around on a foam raft.

Farewell, toxic waste. Hello, ooze and aahs!

if you need a fix, need the bathroom, or can't resist. Otherwise,
you can forget it—the mall is small and not particularly memorable. ✆ 707/963-7282. www.sthelenapremieroutlets.com.

SONOMA VALLEY

Getting There

To get to the Sonoma Valley, you can stay on Highway 101
from San Francisco until you reach Santa Rosa. The area
weaves around a tad, so there is no one-road-does-the-trick
system. The major east-west route is Highway 12, while the
main north-south route is Highway 116.

The Lay of the Land

The Sonoma Valley is not nearly as straightforward as Napa.
Exploring it is not a straight-up-and-down drive like the little
30-mile wander along Highway 29 through Napa Valley, nor
is the retail as easy to grasp. The roads here are twisty and curvy;
in stores and restaurants, the merchandise and feel are funkier.

Sleeping in Sonoma Valley

FAIRMONT SONOMA MISSION INN & SPA
100 Boyes Blvd., off Hwy. 12, Sonoma.

For the most part, the fancy hotels and spas are on the Napa side, whereas Sonoma has more of the small, family-operated B&Bs. The exception is the most famous hotel in either valley—and the one that started it all when it comes to life's luxuries combined with spa treatments. The Sonoma Mission Inn was recently bought by the Fairmont group, which has made enormous changes and investments to the place.

The property is huge—sort of like a village unto itself—so be prepared to walk and possibly get lost . . . or else pay close attention when you are taken to your room, if you're not in the main building.

As the "mission" part of the name implies, the architecture here is mission style. My room was enormous, with a Jacuzzi tub placed sort of in the middle of the space, not far from my very own private fireplace. Because I visited in winter, I got a rate of $300 for this splashy room. Otherwise, it would have cost $450.

Everywhere you go in the hotel—your room, the lobby, the public loo—there's a dispenser of the spa's famous apricot body lotion. The spa itself is extraordinary, with a famous ritual bathing session (for which I was forced to buy a bathing suit) that seems part mikvah and part celebration of water.

About the location: The inn is actually in Boyes Hot Springs (that's the name of the town); I'd call ahead for location information if I were you, or else use a computer printout with specific directions. This area is a lot bigger than you expect it to be, and, frankly, I would have been lost or in a panic if someone else weren't driving.

Rooms begin at $250. For reservations, call © 800/257-7544. Local phone © 707/938-9000. www.sonomamissioninn.com.

HOTEL HEALDSBURG
25 Matheson St., Healdsburg.

This newish boutique hotel is right where some travelers will want to be—on the edge of the plaza in the town of Healdsburg. Many of its 55 rooms and suites come decked out with soaking tubs, private balconies, CD and DVD players, Frette bathrobes, and down duvets. Guests can indulge themselves in this setting of moderne serenity, take dips in the 60-foot garden pool, splurge on massages and treatments at the nearby Spa Hotel Healdsburg, and dine extravagantly at Dry Creek Kitchen, the hotel restaurant that's run by well-known New York chef Charlie Palmer.

Rack rates are between $290 and $790, but call and check online for information on packages and special promotions. ℂ 707/431-2800. www.hotelhealdsburg.com.

MacArthur Place
29 E. MacArthur St., Sonoma.

If you can't—or don't want to—spend the big bucks to stay at Sonoma Mission Inn, I've got another secret find for you. Located in the middle of the town of Sonoma and only 4 blocks from the plaza, MacArthur Place has the perfect shopping location: You can walk just about everywhere. If you check around for special deals, you will spend less here than at the Sonoma Mission Inn.

This former estate of the Burris family (which founded Sonoma Valley Bank) is now a resort, with accommodations in a two-story Victorian hotel and an additional 15 separate buildings. All of the 64 guest rooms and suites come with DVD and CD players, oversize showers, bathrobes, and duvets; some have Jacuzzis as well. A complimentary wine and cheese reception is held daily in the library, where you can relax in front of the fire, sit and play chess or board games, use the computer to check your e-mail, or borrow a bestseller to read or a DVD to watch in your room.

Despite all that luxury, the best part of my stay here was still the spa treatment—not the spa building itself, mind you, which was a bit ordinary, but the signature "Rose Garden" treatment, the most famous one in the house. It starts with a sugar/rose-petal exfoliation, followed by a rose-infused bath and rose (again) oil massage.

This is a four-star property, though not in the same luxury class as the Sonoma Mission Inn, Auberge du Soleil, or Calistoga Ranch. But then again, the prices are lower and you won't be unhappy here. Rack rates begin at $299, but fellow guests at the wine reception reported paying around $200 (and advised researching the online hotel sites to book). The signature "Rose Garden" treatment costs $199 for 100 minutes. For reservations, call ✆ 800/722-1866. Local phone ✆ 707/938-2929. www.macarthurplace.com.

Eating & Drinking in Sonoma Valley

THE BIG 3
Fairmont Sonoma Mission Inn, 100 Boyes Blvd., off Hwy. 12, Sonoma.

Secret find: This casual bistro-style diner, part of the Sonoma Mission Inn (see above), has been serving hearty country breakfasts and eclectic American fare for over 50 years. It's a secret from tourists, though obviously not locals.

Favorites include lemon pancakes, eggs Benedict, butternut-squash ravioli, and pizza. The restaurant will even give you its recipes upon request. At odd hours, you can walk right in, but otherwise reservations are recommended. ✆ 707/938-9000, ext. 2410. www.sonomamissioninn.com.

BISTRO RALPH
109 Plaza St., Healdsburg.

Stop here for the perfect shopper's lunch break. The menu offers simple bistro food in the French style, great wine, and a chocolate sundae made with Valrhona chocolate. ✆ 707/433-1380.

DELLA SANTINA'S
133 E. Napa St., Sonoma.

Located just off the plaza in downtown Sonoma, Della Santina's is the epitome of a traditional Italian trattoria. This informal, family-run eatery has a cozy dining room with a marble fireplace. On a nice day, opt for outdoor dining.

The rustic patio is covered in vines and wisteria, but the real draw here is the rotisserie, where a mouth-watering selection of meats is slow-roasted over a wood fire. Other options on the Tuscan menu include to-die-for homemade pastas, fresh fish, and great salads. Dessert could be a meal on its own; homemade gelato is a favorite. The extensive wine list features local vintners, with most selections well priced. Dinner for two will cost about $100, including wine and tip. © **707/935-0576.** www.dellasantinas.com.

KENDALL-JACKSON WINE CENTER
5007 Fulton Rd., Santa Rosa.

Kendall-Jackson is one of the most famous of the local wineries, and a big winner in local competitions. Its wine center offers tastings, garden tours, a viticulture exhibit, and grounds open for picnicking. © **707/571-8100.** www.kj.com.

The winery also operates the Kendall-Jackson Healdsburg Tasting Room, described on p. 211.

The Towns of Sonoma Valley

PETALUMA

Petaluma is one of those places like Timbuktu—it doesn't sound like it's an actual city. But it is a real city, and it's coming along. The "cute" is arriving; meanwhile, there are outlet stores to hit.

PETALUMA VILLAGE PREMIUM OUTLETS
2200 Petaluma Blvd. N., Petaluma.

The good news about this mall: It has some stores you may have missed either in Napa or on your wine-tasting adventures farther north. The bad news: It's a rather small mall and not that great, as these things go. But don't panic—you can still spend half a day here and go broke with glee. Shop, among

Winery Gift Shops: The Best of the Bunch, Part 2

Below are some of my favorite Sonoma winery gift shops. See p. ### for my recommendations in Napa Valley.

See p. ### for my recommendations in Napa Valley.

- **Landmark Vineyards,** 101 Adobe Canyon Rd., Kenwood (© 707/833-0053; www.landmarkwine.com).
- **Ledson Winery & Vineyard,** 7335 Sonoma Hwy. (Hwy. 12), Santa Rosa (© 707/833-2330; www.ledson.com).
- **Sebastiani Vineyards & Winery,** 389 Fourth St. E., Sonoma (© 707/938-5532; www.sebastiani.com).
- **St. Francis Winery & Vineyards,** 100 Pythian Rd., Santa Rosa (© 707/833-4666; www.stfranciswine.com).
- **Viansa Winery,** 25200 Arnold Dr., Sonoma (© 707/935-4700; www.viansa.com).

others, stores like Bass, Brooks Brothers, Coach, Gap, Guess, Lancôme, Jones New York, Mikasa, Puma, and Saks Off 5th.

Note: Driving directions vary depending on which way you're headed. If you're on Highway 101 going south, get off at the Petaluma Boulevard North exit. If you're heading north, use the Old Redwood Highway exit. © 707/778-9300. www. premiumoutlets.com.

SANTA ROSA

MONTGOMERY VILLAGE
2323 Magowan Dr., Hwy. 12 at Farmers Lane, Santa Rosa.

This shopping center includes **Sur La Table,** the famous Seattle tabletop and cookware store; many national multiples like **Chico's** (there seems to be a Chico's everywhere these days); and harder-to-find stores such as **J. Jill** and the **Pendleton Shop.** You'll also see an excellent art-supply store, called **Village Art Supply,** and **Reverie Linens,** described below.

Reverie Linens
Montgomery Village, 2321 Magowan Dr., Santa Rosa.

The name of this shop is a bit of a pun in French, since the store sells luxury (and expensive) bed linens, the stuff that dreams (*rêve* in French) are made of. It also carries a good selection of Lampes Berger, a little-known French contraption with a catalytic converter inside so that when it burns, it can absorb and eliminate pet or smoke odors. As the name implies, it's more like a lamp than a candle. This store is a great source for style and bed-making inspirations—and you can always go on to Ross Dress for Less to copy the luxe look with less expensive goods. ✆ **707/544-3252.** www.reverielinens.com.

Ross Dress for Less
800 Farmers Lane, Santa Rosa.

Hey, you never know. ✆ **707/575-1690.** www.rossstores.com.

SONOMA

The town of Sonoma itself is the main squeeze for tourists who head over to Sonoma Valley. Even sophisticates I know from San Francisco think that a day spent shopping here is charming. I find it very touristy and not at all my favorite; in fact, if I were you, I'd keep on driving until you get to Healdsburg. But if you insist on being part of the legendary town, you'll want to get to the central plaza.

Here you'll find many original stores, and even a few chains that are nice enough to be a welcome sight. My problem is that the town caters to a very broad image of the yuppie as consumer. I went into some fancy chocolate joint and found even that a mediocre and made-for-tourists experience.

The addresses in Sonoma follow an unusual system: The main drag is called First Street, but it's divided into First Street East and First Street West, which do not connect at any point. The East portion is east of the plaza and the West portion is, well, yeah. Things revert to tradition on one of the other main streets alongside the plaza—Spain Street has east and west portions that merge at the middle, just about at the Sonoma Cheese Factory.

BAKSHEESH
423 First St. W., Sonoma.

This home-style source is much like Pier 1 Imports and assorted other third-world, ethnic-fashion-and-tchotchke stores. It works with alternative trade organizations and stands by a fair-trade ethic. Choose from jewelry and accessories, some garden items, toys and games, musical instruments, and lots of home accessories. ✆ 707/939-2847. www.vom.com/baksheesh.

There is a second store in Healdsburg, at 106-B Matheson St. (✆ 707/473-0880).

SIGN OF THE BEAR
436 First St. W., Sonoma.

In order for a kitchen store to survive when it's located right on the main square in prime real estate, it's gotta be good. Sign of the Bear is one of the best stores in town—it's always crammed with shoppers and foodies who fondle the utensils and dishes, cookbooks and cookwares. ✆ 707/996-3722.

SONOMA CHEESE FACTORY
2 Spain St., Sonoma.

This large and airy gourmet food store, located right on the plaza, specializes in—how'd you guess?—cheese. There are many kinds displayed in the fridge cases, alongside the factory's own famous California jack. ✆ 800/535-2855 or 707/996-1931. www.sonomajack.com.

SONOMA HOME
497 First St. W., Sonoma.

This is the granddaddy chic shop in Sonoma and probably the one that made the town's rep as a place to feel good about the cute. The large store features antiques and reproductions as well as gift items—the merchandise is often French, but the look is simple country. I call the style "Weathered Birdhouse Chic"—you know the rest. ✆ 707/939-6900.

Sonoma Wine Hardware
536 Broadway, Sonoma.

This small conglomerate of three stores has made a business out of supplying small vintners, as well as stocking electric wine cellars, wine books, wine racks, wine equipment, gift items, and so on. ✆ 707/939-1694.

Summervine
100 W. Spain St., Sonoma.

Pick up gifts here for the hostess or yourself; there's an emphasis on tabletop items and wine-country needs with vine motifs. ✆ 707/933-8810.

HEALDSBURG

Among the more northerly destinations in Sonoma Valley, Healdsburg is popular for the very reason that it's not too popular. Locals tend to come here because the area is not overrun with day-trippers and has fewer overnight visitors than the towns farther south.

Like most of the villages in the valley, Healdsburg is laid out around a good-sized plaza. Most directions and store addresses are given or written in terms of their relationship to the plaza.

Most of the worthwhile shops and galleries are located around the rather large plaza, but some of the side streets are worth exploring as well. Also note that the stores here are a little more original in scope than those further south. Even the ones that sell French merchandise—and there are several of them—tend to be more thoughtful and avoid offering the same old stuff.

ELAINE GREENE POTTERY
70 W. North St., Healdsburg.

This studio, located 2 blocks from the plaza, features color-ful ceramics that are made and painted by hand. They're a tad Italian in feel, with designs that tend to be related to grapes, olives, or flowers. These chic pieces make a bold statement and can be ordered in custom shades or inscribed with a custom message or important date. Prices begin around $35; a large pasta bowl is $65. © 707/431-8979. www.elainegreene.com.

FIDEAUX
43 North St., at Healdsburg Ave., Healdsburg.

Here's the Sonoma Valley branch of the pet store named Fido-with-a-French-spelling (same pronunciation). See p. 198. © 707/433-9935.

THE GARDENER
516 Dry Creek Rd., Healdsburg.

The store in Berkeley is the flagship, but this branch location is filled with gifts, tabletop items, baskets, and accessories for an outdoor lifestyle—bird feeders, pots, gardening tools, and even trees. In keeping with the nature of the visiting hordes, the store is open only Thursday through Monday. © 707/431-1063. www.thegardener.com.

JIMTOWN STORE
6706 Hwy. 128, Healdsburg.

Sneeze and you'll miss this place. Located on the road into town, this one-stop-hangout joint offers wine tastings and gourmet food from a small-town deli counter, but is still able to sell sou-venirs, mementos, local crafts, and some kitsch. © 707/433-1212. www.jimtown.com.

KENDALL-JACKSON HEALDSBURG TASTING ROOM
337 Healdsburg Ave., Healdsburg.

Kendall-Jackson is one of the most famous labels in the area. If you don't make it to its wine center in Santa Rosa (p. 205), make sure to stop by its Healdsburg tasting room, where a manager hostess will help you select wines or gifts from the wide range of tabletop and wine-related products, all more stylish, expensive, and high-end than is usual for this sort of store. © 707/433-7102. www.kj.com.

OAKVILLE GROCERY
125 Matheson St., Healdsburg.

With a location right on the plaza, an outdoor terrace, and a wood-burning oven, this branch of the now-famous food and pit stop is more like a restaurant than a country grocer. Nonetheless, alongside the deli counter and refrigerated yummies, you'll still find tables and shelves piled high with tempting foodstuffs. © 707/433-3200. www.oakvillegrocery.com.

21 ARRONDISSEMENT
309 Healdsburg Ave., Healdsburg.

First for the inside joke: Paris has only 20 arrondissements, so the name of this store implies that it is an extension of the City of Light. Indeed, everything here is French, but not Philippe Starck French—it's a home-style and gift collection that's more soft and country, yet still chic and fun to collect or live with. © 707/433-2166.

Chapter Eight

....

THE EAST BAY

Welcome to the Berkeley area. You knew these folks years ago as "Berkeley People." Not a band like the Village People, but a group of people who lived on "the other side" of San Francisco, people who made it (gasp) chic to live in the East Bay. In those days, it was only chic—intellectually chic, of course— if you lived in Berkeley. Now, you can even live in downtown Oakland and have people consider it interesting.

With the growth of moneyed suburbs has come lots more shopping, so there's not only the cutie-pie funky retail associated with Fourth Street in Berkeley, but also various villages of charm and malls of off-pricers. Moraga, did someone say Moraga?

THE LAY OF THE LAND

The East Bay is that portion of the Bay Area located across from San Francisco via the Bay Bridge—it's not the same direction as the area's more famous bridge, the Golden Gate.

OAKLAND AIRPORT ALTERNATIVE

What was once considered a hokey little airport across the bay from a very famous city is now the home to smart shoppers and travelers alike. **Oakland International Airport** (© 510/ 563-3300; www.oaklandairport.com) is small, but far from hokey, and has gates for more than 200 daily nonstops to and from various domestic and international destinations. This airport is much easier to use than SFO, and flights here may be significantly cheaper—especially since Oakland is the home of several low-cost carriers, such as **Southwest** (© 800/I-FLY-SWA; www.southwest.com) and **JetBlue** (© 800/538-2548; www.jetblue.com).

GETTING THERE BY BART

I don't want to sound like a total idiot, and I do want to remind you that I live in France, where I ride public transportation daily, but I had a very hard time figuring out the BART trains for my first ride to the East Bay. Trains are not marked well; signs to explain the system are almost nonexistent. You'd sure better know where you're going and what you're doing before you get into that station. Or else ask a kind local for help.

Bay Area Rapid Transit (BART) is the San Francisco subway system, not to be confused with the bus system called Muni. BART is a commuter train system connecting San Francisco with the East Bay and with Oakland International Airport. It also runs south to San Francisco International Airport. It's clean, it's relatively modern, it works great—once you're in the train. Even the connection stops are well announced (though only in English—but there is signage in Chinese as well).

From the Market Street Station, it takes about a half an hour to get to Oakland. Not that you're going to Oakland, but at least you know where Oakland is. For my money, you can get off the train at Emeryville and start shopping almost immediately. Note that the Amtrak trains also use Emeryville as their point of arrival to San Francisco. For more on Emeryville, see below.

For my tours of the East Bay, I was guided by my friends Karen and Wendy, who picked me up at the Orinda train station. They told me to take the BART train marked Pittsburgh. This was a lot easier in the telling than the first-time doing.

ADDRESSING ISSUES

The city limits and county lines in this area all seem to blur, so it may be hard for a visitor to know if he or she is in Oakland or Berkeley or wherever. In most cases, it doesn't even matter. In the listings below, the city is included in the address. However, in some cases, a shopping experience may involve a wander down a street that is in two different cities.

ABOUT OAKLAND

California's former governor Jerry Brown is now mayor of Oakland; he's trying to make a difference—to clean up the city, bring in jobs, get people shopping, and grow the area. Oakland itself does need an image revival. Few people outside the area know abut the changes made and the changes yet to come. On the other hand, there's an undertow of know-how—when people come from San Francisco to shop in Oakland or the surrounding area, it's because they know they've found something more than worthwhile. Now then, about Oakland.

Oakland is working on its comeback and now has a fair amount of razzmatazz, some of it different enough to make you sit up and notice.

Yes, there are 6 blocks of restored Victorian buildings that make up a string of restaurants and eats, shops and souvenirs— all just past the Oakland Convention Center. The redeveloped restaurant row is called Washington Street; the **Old Oakland Farmers' Market** (www.urbanvillageonline.com/old oakland) is held here year-round, every Friday from 8am to 2pm. Washington Street runs perpendicular to 10th Street, which is where both the convention center and the Marriott City Center are located. This section of town is sometimes marketed as Old Oakland; you can arrive via the 12th Street Station on BART.

Oakland has a strong ethnic community, including a well-known Chinatown (well known, that is, to locals who avoid San Francisco's Chinatown as too touristy) and also a Koreatown, which is sometimes nicknamed Kimchi Row. Telegraph Avenue is the main drag; from the cross streets in the low 20s running up to the upper 40s, there are plenty of Korean shops, markets, and chances to eat barbecue.

Part of the magic of the new Oakland is that the city is trying to reflect its ethnic mix and offer something other than the same old lily-white faces that you see in every other restored downtown or shopping district. For instance, there are stores that specialize in African fashion. One of my favorite sources is **Urban Skin Solutions Center**, 401 29th St., Suite 111 (© 510/893-7546), which specializes in the care of "multiethnic" skin.

And for those who think that perhaps the East Bay is all marketing gimmicks or ethnic markets, get a look at the **Claremont Resort & Spa**, 41 Tunnel Rd. (© 800/551-7266; www.claremontresort.com), which offers full spa services and has become more than just the hotel where parents stay when they come to visit the kids at school in Berkeley. You can stay at the Claremont as an overnight guest, or opt instead for just the spa services. Choose a single treatment, or treat yourself to a decadent full day at the spa. See p. 222 for more information.

OAKLAND BARGAINS

If the Alameda Point Antiques & Collectible Faire isn't enough for you, then you need to plan your trip to Oakland around the annual **White Elephant Sale** (www.museumca.org/events/elephant.html). Created as a benefit for the Oakland Museum of California, this sale is a 2-day event held once a year, usually in March. But wait! There's also the **Preview Sale** in January, for those who can't make it to town for the regular sale or who are too impatient to wait any longer. You can buy your ticket to the Preview Sale in advance for around $13, or buy it at the door for $15. Items get marked down as the sale progresses, but they start off so low that your head will spin. Our reporter bought a designer fur jacket (needing a repair) for $30. Her furrier said he could make the repair for $50.

ALAMEDA

You already know about the **Alameda Point Antiques & Collectibles Faire** (read: flea market), held the first Sunday of every month (p. 10); you also know that Alameda is the old Navy yard on the edge of Oakland. What you might not know is that the Alameda area is trying to attract shoppers and tourists for more than just its once-a-month flea market. There's now a development called **Park Street,** which is Alameda's historic downtown area, born again as a tourist attraction. See www.shopparkstreet.com for details.

EMERYVILLE

Nestled between downtown Oakland and the joys of Berkeley is a whole other kind of joyful experience—a shopping trip to Emeryville. Teaming Emeryville with Berkeley is indeed a full day out and worth the cost of car rental.

Just a few years ago, Emeryville was more or less a downmarket dive of warehouses and street people. But you know what's been happening to warehouses these days—they become shops and condos and even hotels, and then they get very chic. While Emeryville is not quite chic yet, it is a fabulous shopping city with all sorts of retail experiences, from a large regional mall to a series of furniture warehouses where smart shoppers come for Japanese antiques.

Besides the mall and the furniture warehouses, there are assorted big-box stores, mainstream chain hotels, and even a **Trader Vic's,** 9 Anchor Dr. (© 510/653-3400; www.tradervics. com), where you can get cocktails in coconut shells with floating flowers and pretty straws and be gone with the wind after you blow the family fortune at all the stores. The sober will not confuse Trader Vic's with Trader Joe's.

While in Emeryville, look for shopping ops at Ikea, Old Navy, Ross Dress for Less, Jo-Ann Fabrics, Circuit City, and Home Depot's Expo Design Center (all in the shopping centers listed below)—and don't miss that ocean view.

For those who have a good eye and a real sense of adventure, head a little past the Emeryville border to what is termed the **San Pablo Flea Market**—it's actually a storage yard that calls itself the San Pablo Flea Market, and not a flea market in the true sense of a weekend event with a lot of dealers and stalls. In fact, this is a salvage yard, located at 6100 San Pablo Ave. Call ✆ **510/420-1468** for exact directions.

Getting Around

The **Emery Go Round** (✆ **510/451-3862**; www.emerygo round.com) is a free shuttle-bus service connecting Emeryville shopping centers with BART every day of the week. During weekday commuter hours, buses run every 10 to 12 minutes.

Emery Go Round serves Bay Street Emeryville, East Bay Bridge Center, Emeryville Public Market, Ikea, and Powell Street Plaza, as well as corporate centers, hotels, and some residential areas.

Shopping Ops

The following listings are included just to give you an overview. The shopping here is neither glam nor luxe. The crowd is very real-people: multiracial, multimoneyed, multi-age range.

BAY STREET EMERYVILLE
Bay St., Emeryville.

Among the tenants in this 3-block-long urban village: Abercrombie & Fitch, Aldo, Apple Computer, Banana Republic, Barnes & Noble, Bath & Body Works, Coach, Chico's, J. Jill, Old Navy, Pottery Barn Kids, See's Candies, Steve Madden, Talbots, and Williams-Sonoma. Dining and entertainment options include California Pizza Kitchen, Cold Stone Creamery, and P. F. Chang's China Bistro, along with a multiscreen movie theater. www.baystreetemeryville.com.

EAST BAY BRIDGE CENTER
40th St. and San Pablo Ave., Emeryville.

At this big-box shopping center, watch for Home Depot's Expo Design Center, Michaels Arts & Crafts, OfficeMax, and Toys "R" Us.

ELIZABETH ARDEN WAREHOUSE
4550 San Pablo Ave., Emeryville.

This outlet's opening hours are a little unusual, but you'll probably be willing to cope when I whisper the number 80%. That's what the Arden folks take off the retail price on discontinued and sell-by-passed-by perfumes and beauty treatments. Open Thursday through Sunday from 11am to 6pm. The store accepts plastic. ✆ 510/601-1251.

There's also an outlet store in San Francisco, at 1222 Sutter St., near Polk Street (✆ 415/346-7144); its hours are Tuesday through Saturday from 11am to 6pm.

EMERYVILLE PUBLIC MARKET
5959 Shellmound St., Emeryville.

Here you'll find over 25 food retailers, restaurants, and stalls, as well as a branch of Borders Books & Music and a multiscreen movie theater. ✆ 510/652-9300. www.emerymarket.com.

IKEA
4400 Shellmound St., Emeryville.

Disneyland for grown-ups—especially college students and first apartment dwellers, young couples and newlyweds—is surely Ikea, the Swedish maker of knock-down furniture. It provides a lifestyle in a box—you build it from there. ✆ 510/420-4532. www.ikea.com.

POWELL STREET PLAZA
5700 Christie Ave., off I-80 at Powell St., Emeryville.

Featured stores here include Ethan Allen, Copeland Sports, Jo-Ann Fabrics, Circuit City, Lane Bryant, Pier 1 Imports, Trader Joe's, Shoe Pavilion, and Ross Dress for Less.

THE PROMENADE
San Pablo Ave., between 45th St. and Park Ave., Emeryville.

The Promenade is home to two of my faves: IHOP (International House of Pancakes) and Longs Drug Store. It's more like a small strip center with real-people places; I guess I just like to eat Swedish pancakes and hang out in drugstores.

BERKELEY

Make love not war, as we used to say. Berkeley is a mere 10 miles from San Francisco, but light-years away in terms of intellectual—and now shopping—snobbery. After all, hoi polloi like San Francisco—anyone can do it; they've done so for years. In contrast, discovering and then knowing Berkeley takes smarts. Even knowing how to dish, or diss, the Claremont takes insider information. Berkeley is all about insider information. It remains the domain of the student body (poor), their parents (well off), and commuting yuppies (rich). Real estate has gone sky high. And if you think there's anything unsophisticated about Berkeley, dump your SDS button right now and return to the Haight.

The Lay of the Land

Telegraph Avenue is the main drag of beautiful downtown Berkeley, leading directly into the campus gates at U.C. Berkeley. Not that we came for a higher education. Our mission is art.

The main action on Telegraph is between Bancroft and Dwight ways, where you have the usual suspects—coffee shops, coffeehouses, coffee cups, and bookstores. The 2400 block of Telegraph has two famous bookstores, **Cody's** (at no. 2454) and **Moe's** (no. 2476). You'll need a rolling suitcase to cart away all the books you're going to buy, since one of the world's best selections of used and new titles is right here in this bit of intellectual heaven.

Telegraph Avenue also has, thank God, plenty of shopping. You might want to skip directly into the real-people stores or cruise the whole area for the usual suspects, such as the **Gap** (no. 2310). **Urban Outfitters** (2590 Bancroft Way) rules the roost, but there are a lot of vintage shops—a good place to start is **Buffalo Exchange**, 2585 Telegraph Ave.—along with many branches of retailers who also trade on Haight Street. Power to the people, man.

Fourth Street

ANTHROPOLOGIE
750 Hearst Ave., at Fourth St., Berkeley.

I love the look perfected by this chain of stores, vaguely ethnic and homemade and vintage and French country all rolled into one. Wander in and start browsing the pretty clothes, the sweetly chic housewares, and the soaps, books, and other gift items. ✆ 510/486-0705. www.anthropologie.com.

CP SHADES
1829 Fourth St., Berkeley.

CP Shades has mastered what I call the "California casual" style of clothing—drapey, natural fabrics in soft, muted tones, with an emphasis on textures and layers and detail. The elastic, drawstring, and wraparound styles are especially flattering for larger women. ✆ 510/204-9022. www.cpshades.com.

CRATE & BARREL OUTLET
1785 Fourth St., Berkeley.

Nothing could be better for a constantly renewing population of students in shared apartments, young couples, and career strategists on the rise than a large Crate & Barrel outlet store

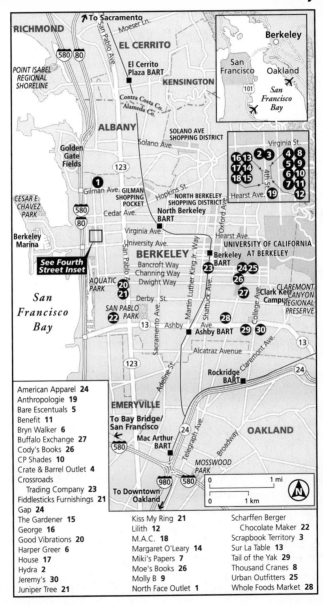

Berkeley

RICHMOND

To Sacramento
Moeser Ln.

Berkeley

San Francisco   Oakland

San Francisco Bay

EL CERRITO

KENSINGTON

El Cerrito Plaza BART

POINT ISABEL REGIONAL SHORELINE

Contra Costa Co.
Alameda Co.

SOLANO AVE SHOPPING DISTRICT

ALBANY

Solano Ave.

Golden Gate Fields

Virginia St.

CESAR E. CHAVEZ PARK

Gilman Ave.   GILMAN SHOPPING POCKET

Hopkins St.

NORTH BERKELEY SHOPPING DISTRICT

North Berkeley BART

Hearst Ave.

Berkeley Marina

Cedar Ave.

Virginia Ave.

University Ave.

See Fourth Street Inset

BERKELEY

Bancroft Way
Channing Way
Dwight Way

Hearst Ave.

UNIVERSITY OF CALIFORNIA AT BERKELEY

Berkeley BART

AQUATIC PARK

Derby St.

CLAREMONT CANYON REGIONAL PRESERVE

Clark Kerr Campus

San Francisco Bay

SAN PABLO PARK

Ashby Ave.

Ashby BART

Alcatraz Avenue

Rockridge BART

EMERYVILLE

To Bay Bridge/
San Francisco

Mac Arthur BART

OAKLAND

MOSSWOOD PARK

To Downtown Oakland

0   1 mi
0   1 km

American Apparel **24**
Anthropologie **19**
Bare Escentuals **5**
Benefit **11**
Bryn Walker **6**
Buffalo Exchange **27**
Cody's Books **26**
CP Shades **10**
Crate & Barrel Outlet **4**
Crossroads
  Trading Company **23**
Fiddlesticks Furnishings **21**
Gap **24**
The Gardener **15**
George **16**
Good Vibrations **20**
Harper Greer **6**
House **17**
Hydra **2**
Jeremy's **30**
Juniper Tree **21**

Kiss My Ring **21**
Lilith **12**
M.A.C. **18**
Margaret O'Leary **14**
Miki's Papers **7**
Moe's Books **26**
Molly B **9**
North Face Outlet **1**

Scharffen Berger
  Chocolate Maker **22**
Scrapbook Territory **3**
Sur La Table **13**
Tail of the Yak **29**
Thousand Cranes **8**
Urban Outfitters **25**
Whole Foods Market **28**

Luxury Pampering

Parents of U.C. Berkeley students have made up an interesting market segment in the Berkeley-Oakland area. In short, they're people with extra money to spend. It didn't take long for a famous hotel to get established and to then reinvent itself and add on spa facilities. Welcome to the **Claremont Resort**, 41 Tunnel Rd. (© 800/551-7261; www.claremontresort.com).

Originally built in the style of an English castle in the days of the gold rush, then reborn as a Mediterranean resort after a fire in 1901, the Claremont has been through more renovations than your average Beverly Hills home. The latest was completed in 2003, with California contemporary decor. Hot tub, anyone?

My spa treatment was the "Philippine Journey—Moisturizing, Tonic, Warming, Antioxidant." This routine involved a bath in ginger tea water followed by a ginger and brown-sugar scrub. I was then hosed down by a carwash apparatus, which swished overhead, and moved to yet another room for a massage with coconut and neroli oil. Each of these services began with a "tray presentation" featuring plastic coconuts bearing oils graced by plastic orchids. No mai tais, though.

The hotel is a controversial conversation point among visiting parents and area locals—is it as good as it used to be, is it worth it, how many awards has it won, is it the best in the area? You'll just have to try it yourself to find out.

Rates vary by type of room; prices begin around $270 and go up to $1,000 per night. During a promotional special, rates can fall to $175. Spa treatments range from $75 to $350. Local phone © 510/843-3000.

—Sarah Lahey

in a great, easy-to-get-to location. Did I mention that the place is mobbed on weekends? But then, that's no surprise: This is lifestyle in a box, and at the right price to boot. There's everything from kitchen utensils and dishes to home-office and entertaining needs. © 510/528-5500. www.crateandbarrel.com.

THE GARDENER
1836 Fourth St., Berkeley.

The Gardener holds the anchor position on a strip of stores that aptly reflects the glory of shopping Fourth Street. It sells mostly home-style and tabletop items, with, as the name implies, an emphasis on outdoor and garden design. We're not talking redwood picnic tables here; think hand-thrown pots, dishes in muted shades, torches that blaze in the night, and more chic than you ever expected. © 510/548-4545. www.thegardener.com.

GEORGE
1844 Fourth St., Berkeley.

It's pet heaven for dogs, cats, and owners who scramble for the custom-made collars with pet's name and phone number embroidered right into the weave. © 510/644-1033. www.georgesf.com.

HOUSE
1848 Fourth St., Berkeley.

There's a very distinct look here: sort of girly, moderne yet retro, pastels and polka dots, but not *cher* or square. I call it the Tocca school of design. The housewares are mostly bedroom oriented; the fabrics create a total look that is soft, pretty, and not found elsewhere—it's young but hip at the same time. © 510/549-4558. www.houseinc.com.

LILITH
1833 Fourth St., Berkeley.

Lilith is the French designer of unparalleled creative, droopy chic, which, with a strong euro, seems very, very expensive right now. These are the ideal clothes for rock stars and mothers of invention. © 510/849-4281.

MARGARET O'LEARY
1832 Fourth St., Berkeley.

The local Irish designer Margaret O'Leary creates a flirty, gamine look, mixing her own designs with alternative brands like Dosa in her local area boutiques. Check out her collection of sweaters, knit from cashmere, silk, wool, and cotton. ✆ 510/540-8241. www.margaretoleary.com.

MIKI'S PAPERS
1801 Fourth St., Berkeley.

Asian inspiration manifests itself in notepapers, wrapping paper, notebooks, cards, and more. The Japanese papers are sublime. ✆ 510/845-0530.

MOLLY B
1811 Fourth St., Berkeley.

The wares at this small boutique were selected with a certain eye for the whimsical and slightly over the top. The stylish, look-at-me fashions enhance the local rich-hippie look. ✆ 510/548-3103.

SUR LA TABLE
1806 Fourth St., Berkeley.

Give credit to this Seattle-based store for introducing the mainstream public to French imports, expensive brands, and the idea of cooking classes. If you're a serious foodie, you'll want to stop by the Maiden Lane location as well. ✆ 510/849-2252. www.surlatable.com.

THOUSAND CRANES
1803 Fourth St., Berkeley.

Thousand Cranes features vintage Japanese chic, from housewares and home style to kimonos. The prices are much higher here than in San Francisco's Japantown, but the look is something that works very well in this part of the country. The college kids buy futons here and get introduced to the Japanese style, which now permeates the Bay Area. ✆ 510/849-0501.

Introducing WJBRossera

Because of the insider nature of many of the East Bay communities, I needed the help of some insiders. I turned to Wendy and Karen, the two dream designers and super shoppers who head the firm **WJBRossera,** based in Orinda (℃ 925/254-0317; wjbrossera@aol.com). Not only did they drive me, teach me, and feed me, but they also shared some of their own secret sources and best bets, which lean toward interiors (of course, since their business is interior design) and exhibit the true spirit of the chase. And oh yeah, they also turned me onto Mycra Pac (p. 230).

Owned by award-winning florist Ron Morgan, **Loot Antiques,** 5358 College Ave., Oakland (℃ 510/652-3996), features French and Dutch antiques, gilded mirrors, hand-painted furniture, steamer trunks, toile linens, and a wonderful assortment of decorative items. Everything is of the highest quality.

Another source for furnishings is **Swallowtail Interiors,** 5332 College Ave., Oakland (℃ 510/595-1240; www.swallowtail home.com), which offers both eclectic and classic antiques as well as collectibles for home and garden.

Poppy Fabric, 5151 Broadway, Oakland (℃ 510/655-5151; www.poppyfabric.com), boasts floor-to-ceiling racks of upholstery fabrics, tassels, trims, and vintage buttons, all at amazingly low prices. There are literally aisles of Scottish laces, designer brocades, and Italian woolens. The sales staff is made up of seamstresses and students from the California College of Arts and Crafts; they'll be happy to estimate yardage, decipher the small type on the pattern envelope, or inform you of the latest shipment of embroidered tulle.

Pimlico Place, 4125 Piedmont Ave., Oakland (℃ 510/655-7333), specializes in "smalls" from England and Italy—antiques and new merchandise such as handmade decorative pillows, cups and saucers, vintage flatware, and crystal chandeliers. Walk down to the Annex, at 4135 Piedmont Ave., for furniture, prints, and beaded bags.

> For a lunch break, try **Garibaldi's,** 5356 College Ave., Oakland (© 510/595-4000; www.garibaldis-eastbay.com). Its California-Mediterranean menu offers reasonably priced specialties such as quesadillas with pork loin and gourmet burgers on sourdough rolls.

San Pablo Avenue

My part of San Pablo Avenue is the 2500 block, where there's a string of stores, all tiled with the same storefronts from the early 1960s. One leads to the next on this strip, home to fun shopping and good vibrations. Uh, make that **Good Vibrations.** See below.

FIDDLESTICKS FURNISHINGS
2524 San Pablo Ave., Berkeley.

This gift shop tries to offer things you've never seen elsewhere, like a kit with all the makings for a custom-made dog collar ($20). © 510/486-1800.

GOOD VIBRATIONS
2504 San Pablo Ave., Berkeley.

Here's the East Bay branch of the San Francisco institution—a women-owned and -operated resource for literature, movies, and sex toys. © 510/841-8987. www.goodvibes.com.

JUNIPER TREE
2520 San Pablo Ave., Berkeley.

Juniper Tree seems like a regular old soap store (yawn) until you find the make-your-own soap stuff—molds, ingredients, recipes, the works. © 510/647-3697.

KISS MY RING
2514 San Pablo Ave., Berkeley.

Kiss My Ring sells gorgeous handmade jewelry, much of it exotic and funky at the same time, with a touch of 1,001 Arabian nights and perhaps the dance of the seven veils. There are other small luxuries as well. Closed Tuesdays. ✆ **510/540-1282.** www.kissmyring.com.

College Avenue/Ashby Avenue

College Avenue runs the length of Oakland right to the U.C. Berkeley campus, so various pockets of enterprise and fun retail pop up along the way. Some are in Berkeley; some are in Oakland—same street, different ends.

JEREMY'S
2967 College Ave., Berkeley.

This is a small, local branch of the larger San Francisco off-pricer specializing in designer threads that are damaged and are therefore marked down to low, low everyday prices. I bought an Italian hand-embroidered handbag for $35. Yeah, some of the threads were coming unraveled. Do I care? ✆ **510/ 849-0701.** www.jeremys.com.

TAIL OF THE YAK
2632 Ashby Ave., Berkeley.

I've named this one of the best stores in the Bay Area (p. 6) and urge you to pop into the tiny domain, where antiques, picture frames, soaps, and gift items are sold in what feels like a fairy-tale atmosphere. ✆ **510/841-9881.**

College Avenue/Oakland

This part of Oakland is best found through Rockridge. In fact, you can even get here on BART. It's basically an upper-middle-class neighborhood filled largely with commuters who like expensive (read: gourmet) foodstuffs.

Attention, Scrapbookers

The largest supply store in the entire Bay Area for those who pride themselves on their scrapbooking skills is called **Scrapbook Territory**, 1717-A Fourth St., in Berkeley (© 510/559-9929; www.scrapbookterritory.com).

It sells everything you'd expect—special papers, scrapbook pages, rubber stamps, stickers, ribbons, and more—and offers lots of classes, die-cut machines, and even a computer workstation with thousands of fonts.

MAISON D'ETRE
5640 College Ave., Oakland.

The name of this store is a French pun; the merchandise is mostly home decor and tabletop items, but there are also good ideas for house gifts, such as the high-tech wine-cooler packs for single or double bottles. © 510/658-2801. www.maisondetre.com.

THE PASTA SHOP
5655 College Ave., Oakland.

This is one of the several food stalls at the Rockridge Market Hall, a European-style marketplace selling gourmet foodstuffs. The Pasta Shop carries fresh pastas (naturally), California and imported cheeses, olive oils and vinegars, and even gift-basket items for your favorite foodie back home. © 510/652-4680, ext. 219. www.rockridgemarkethall.com.

Choc It to Me

BITTERSWEET
5427 College Ave., Oakland.

Somewhat new to the Rockridge district, this shop is the chocolate version of Starbucks. There are over 150 kinds of chocolate, with five different flavors of hot chocolate alone.

Of course, the store is one of a kind right now—but watch out; the idea is, uh, hot. © 510/654-7159. www.bittersweetcafe.com.

HOOPER'S CHOCOLATES
4632 Telegraph Ave., near Shattuck Ave., Oakland.

Located at the far end of Telegraph Avenue from the Berkeley campus, Hooper's was once the insider chocolate place, rising to fame after World War II. Like many family businesses, it then fell onto hard times and closed. The firm was bought by a larger, local chocolate-making firm and now operates as a developmental work project for people with disabilities. There is a factory store right in the factory itself. © 510/653-3703. www.hooperschocolate.com.

SCHARFFEN BERGER CHOCOLATE MAKER
914 Heinz Ave., Berkeley.

Not only does Scharffen Berger make its own chocolates, but it also produces its own cocoa powder in order to provide the quality control the company craves and demands. To reserve a space on a free public tour of the factory, call © 510/981-4066 in advance. The tour includes a factory walk-through, a lecture on how chocolate is made, and a tasting. Participants must be age 10 or older and wear closed-toe shoes. © 510/981-4066. www.scharffenberger.com.

XOX TRUFFLES
Montclair Village, 6126 LaSalle Ave., Oakland.

North Beach residents have long kept secret the address of their branch of XOX Truffles (p. 147), but now that the firm is expanding, the word is getting out. While the house specialty is French-style chocolate truffles, there is a wine truffle that makes the perfect gift to take back for the friend who has everything. © 510/339-9969. www.xoxtruffles.com.

MORAGA

....

MYCRA PAC DESIGNER OUTERWEAR OUTLET
Rheem Valley Shopping Center, 535 Center St., Moraga.

One of the highlights of my exploration of the Bay Area was the discovery of this line of micropore all-weather coats—and then my visit to the outlet store, where they're sold for half price. Generally, figure that a $225 coat will sell for about $125 here; if you hit a sale, the prices are even lower. While there are many styles, I love the large and flowing coats that are particularly great for bigger women like me. The colors, the details, the quality, the embroidery, the buttons, the flocking, the tote bags—all will convince you that you, too, can be singing in the rain. Note the hours: Monday through Friday only, from 10am to 4pm. ✆ 925/631-6878.

Chapter Nine

....

THE PENINSULA, SOUTH BAY & POINTS SOUTH

Area shoppers may be quite delighted that San Jose has a new luxury shopping mall, but those who want the personal shopping experience still head farther south to Carmel-by-the-Sea, one of the most famous cutie-pie towns in the United States. Watch out for tourists—they walk out right in front of your car without looking, and have the right of way in the state of California. Eeeeeekkk honey, watch it!

PALO ALTO

....

—*by Sarah Lahey*

STANFORD SHOPPING CENTER
680 Stanford Shopping Center, at El Camino Real and Sand Hill Rd., Palo Alto.

So you've decided to travel south to shop, or maybe you're delivering your firstborn to Stanford. Whatever the reason, stopping in Palo Alto is a good idea. I've been driving down to the Stanford Shopping Center with my daughters for years, and though both girls moved east for college, they still prefer shopping here when they return home to visit. Silicon Valley residents are affluent, politically aware, and culturally sophisticated; this shopping center reflects and serves that lifestyle.

In addition to the world-class stores, you'll find several good restaurants and a European-style produce market. Even the McDonald's has a piano player, a la Nordstrom's signature feature. Some stores face the open-air interior mall, while others face the parking lot; I recommend driving around to get your bearings before deciding where to park. I usually find a space near Neiman Marcus.

The anchor stores are Bloomingdale's, Macy's, Neiman Marcus, and Nordstrom. In between are 140 more opportunities to spend your money, including Aldo, BCBG Max Azria, Brooks Brothers, Cartier, Coach, Crate & Barrel, Eileen Fisher, Furla, J. Crew, J. Jill, Kate Spade, Kenneth Cole, Kiehl's, Louis Vuitton, Max Mara, Oilily, Sephora, Smith & Hawken, TSE, Wilkes Bashford, and Williams-Sonoma. Grab a bite at Oakville Grocery, Playa Grill, or Max's Opera Cafe (where the servers will serenade you).

To get here from San Francisco, you can take either Highway 101 or Interstate 280 south. I recommend the latter—it's a beautiful drive. From 280, take the Sand Hill Road East exit and follow Sand Hill Road approximately 4 miles. If you insist on fighting the traffic on 101, take it south and exit on Embarcadero West; head toward Stanford University for approximately 3 miles. Turn right (north) onto El Camino Real; the mall will be on your left. © 650/617-8200. www.stanfordshop.com.

SAN JOSE

—*by Sarah Lahey*

Do you know the way to San Jose? It's easy to find: Go south on either Highway 101 or Interstate 280 from San Francisco. In about 45 minutes, traffic will back up and then slow to a stop. Welcome to San Jose. San Jose is actually bigger than San

Francisco, but everyone I know in that area still heads north to shop.

For years, San Jose had a reputation as a tired, boring city. Enter the dot.com era, which brought money and style. As a result, San Jose has cleaned up its act and transformed itself into an attractive business and convention destination. I've never really considered it a shopping destination and still don't, but if you're staying there, you may want to check out the fancy new shopping center. Drop us a line and let us know what you think.

SANTANA ROW
355 Santana Row, San Jose.

Santana Row is the South Bay's new premier living, shopping, and entertainment destination. There are restaurants, spas, Sunday markets, and a movie theater; summer brings jazz concerts and outdoor dining. You can buy a condo, rent an apartment, or stay in an adjoining hotel. There's even a concierge service to help you with dinner reservations, personal shopping, and transportation.

This is a huge complex, and although it's new and gorgeous, I've heard nightmare stories of traffic jams, difficult parking, and getting lost once you're there. Most of the retailers are high-end, but you'll also find the same multiples you left behind at home. This isn't my idea of a fun shopping excursion, but if you're looking to stay, eat, shop, and never get into your car, this may be the ticket.

Stores include Anne Fontaine, Anthropologie, BCBG Max Azria, Best Buy, Borders, Brooks Brothers, Burberry, Camper, Cole Haan, Container Store, Crate & Barrel, Design Within Reach, Diesel, Donald J. Pliner, Escada, Gucci, Nanoo and Oilily for kids, St. John, Sur La Table, Taryn Rose, Ted Baker, Theory, Tod's, Tourneau, Tumi, Urban Outfitters, Wolford, and Z Gallerie.

To get here from San Francisco, take Interstate 280 south and exit at Winchester Boulevard. Turn left on Moorpark Avenue, left again on Winchester, and then right on Olsen Drive. © 408/551-4611. www.santanarow.com.

GILROY

If Gilroy means garlic to you, you're right—but it should also mean outlets. And if you're heading south from San Jose toward Monterey and Carmel, you owe it to yourself to stop in the garlic capital of the world . . . for some shopping, of course.

GILROY PREMIUM OUTLETS
681 Leavesley Rd., Gilroy.

Among the Northern California outlet malls, this is one of the biggest. It also has one of the more comprehensive mixes of name designers and useful brands, along with places to eat, like the Garlic Cafe (natch) and a Starbucks. I always encourage my travel agent to book me through airports where I can get my fix of Auntie Anne's soft pretzels, but here's the outlet store! If you aren't as into food as I am, consider these possibilities: Adidas, Anne Klein, Banana Republic, Bath & Body Works, Birkenstock, Bombay Company, Calvin Klein, Coach, Crabtree & Evelyn, Ecko, Eddie Bauer, Hugo Boss, J. Crew, J. Jill, Le Creuset, Levi's, Nike, Polo Ralph Lauren, Puma, Skechers, and Sony. And there's more, too! © 408/842-3729. www.premiumoutlets.com.

MONTEREY

In its early days, Monterey was the capital of the Spanish territory of California and the first capital of the state of California. Many of its historic buildings and Spanish adobes have been restored; a walking tour of these buildings around Old Monterey, called the Path of History, might be a good way to entertain your husband while you shop. Or perhaps he'd like to play golf at Pebble Beach.

Today, Monterey is a real-people town with a military base and two very touristy areas—Cannery Row and Fisherman's Wharf. Don't stop by on our account.

In the last 30 years, these areas have seemed more tacky, touristy, and frustrating each time we've returned. It's impossible to park; tour buses are everywhere, blocking streets and bringing hordes of people to town; tourist traps (TTs) sit side by side by side. It's just flat awful.

But if you insist, yes, you can shop in Monterey. Below are some sources from Born to Shop news director Sarah Lahey, who in real life is also an antiques dealer.

AMERICAN TIN CANNERY FACTORY OUTLETS
125 Ocean View Blvd. (about 2 blocks up from the aquarium), Pacific Grove.

This isn't the greatest outlet mall and certainly doesn't compare with the shops in Gilroy, but it's convenient, it has a parking lot (but don't even think about parking here to visit the aquarium), and you may find some good deals. There are around 30 shops, including Izod, Reebok/Rockport, Nine West, and Bass. When I visited, everything in the Izod shop was marked down 50% to 65% and the selection was good, especially in golf wear. © 831/372-1442. www.canneryrow.com.

CANNERY ROW ANTIQUE MALL
471 Wave St. (about 3 blocks from the aquarium), Monterey.

Housed in the former Carmel Canning Company Warehouse #2, this antiques mall is located in one of the few remaining authentic and unchanged Cannery Row structures from the John Steinbeck era. An antiques collective since 1994, it has over 150 dealers on two floors. These aren't high-end goods, but lots of "smalls," with some furniture thrown into the mix. You'll find kitchen items and an extensive selection of vintage *Life* magazines (great for milestone birthday gifts). Complimentary coffee and tea are available on the second floor. © 831/655-0264. www.canneryrowantiquemall.com.

DEL MONTE CENTER
1410 Del Monte Center, Hwy. 1 at Munras Ave., Monterey.

This is a real-people shopping alert for those who love malls and the suburban-American lifestyle. The Del Monte Center has 85 locally owned shops, family restaurants, and retail chains, including Macy's, Macy's Furniture Gallery, Mervyn's, Bath & Body Works, Chico's, Express, and See's Candies. For something less mass-market, stop by Thinker Toys (described in greater detail on p. 243). Real people will hit the Whole Foods Market and Rite Aid pharmacy as well. Dining and entertainment options include California Pizza Kitchen, Chipotle, Cold Stone Creamery, and a multiscreen movie theater © 831/373-2705. www.delmontecenter.com.

CARMEL

—by Sarah Lahey

Carmel-by-the-Sea is a quaint village of fairy-tale cottages and hidden courtyards where well-heeled residents tend to be preppy, artsy, and/or retired. Did I mention rich?

There's an idyllic charm to this small town full of specialty shops, boutiques, and more than 70 art and photography galleries. Don't look for billboards or neon signs; you won't find any. High heels may be worn by permit only (rarely enforced!), and dogs are welcome in the many hotels and restaurants with outdoor seating.

Yes, the streets are often crowded with tourists, but the pace is slow, the shoppers have class, and there is so much to see and buy, who cares? Shopping hours vary by store; all are open on weekends. You can't always rely on the hours posted below—I've returned to shops that were supposed to be open, only to find them closed, so call ahead to be certain. The art galleries are among the few shops open in the evening. Also note that the stores—and homes, for that matter—do not have street numbers in Carmel. Just go with it.

Practicalities

It's not too difficult to find a parking space in Carmel, but be aware that most have a 90-minute limit. Keep an eye on the clock: Your tires will be marked and you will be ticketed as soon as your time runs out.

There are public restrooms in the park in the middle of the town, but do yourself a favor and walk across the street to the third floor of **Carmel Plaza,** on Ocean Avenue between Junipero Avenue and Mission Street, where the facilities are clean and convenient.

Sleeping in Carmel

CYPRESS INN
Lincoln Lane and Seventh Ave., Carmel.

Known for its classic interior and stately Moorish Mediterranean facade, the Cypress Inn has been recently restored with beauty, comfort, and grace. Owned by actress Doris Day, the inn is situated in the heart of Carmel. I saw a handful of rooms, each beautifully decorated with classic California design and featuring standard luxury amenities such as bathrobes and decanters of sherry. You can choose from a variety of accommodations, some of which include sitting areas, wet bars, verandas, and ocean views. When you reserve, your dog's preferences are noted and the correct size fleece bed and turn-down dog treat will be waiting. If you aren't traveling with your four-footed friend, you can opt to stay in a new wing of the hotel that offers pet-free lodging.

Along with the obvious charm, the rates here are impressive. A small single goes for $125; classic queen and king accommodations are under $250 per night. Huge king suites with full balconies and ocean views run $550. This is a popular place, so reserve as far in advance as possible. © 800/443-7443. Local phone © 831/624-3871. www.cypress-inn.com.

QUAIL LODGE
8205 Valley Greens Dr., Carmel.

Decades before Quail Lodge was deemed one of the finest resorts in the world, it was home to several cows. It was, in fact, the Carmel Valley Dairy, owned by Dwight Morrow, Jr., brother-in-law of aviator Charles Lindbergh. Forty years and many renovations later, Quail Lodge's California-country ambience still pays homage to the region's rustic, romantic essence. A $25-million makeover in 2003 transformed nearly every facet of the resort, while retaining its legendary character and charm.

We were greeted upon arrival with a glass of Bernardus wine, produced at the nearby Bernardus Winery and Vineyard. Registration was completed in our room, where we were given a quick lesson in how to use the many remote controls (fan, fireplace, DVD, and *42-inch,* flat-screen plasma TV!). We were impressed with the complimentary in-room refreshment center, stocked with chips, salsa, trail mix, soft drinks, beer, Bernardus wine, and more bottled water than we could ever drink.

I'd rather shop than play golf, but couldn't help but be wowed by the Robert Muir Graves–designed golf course and clubhouse (the snack bar is strategically located so that golfers may phone their orders in from the 9th tee). The Spa at Quail Lodge offers a comprehensive menu of treatments, including facials, massages, a hydrotherapy tub, and Vichy showers. Manicures, pedicures, waxing, and hair treatments are all available in the salon.

Rack rates range from $225 to $435 for rooms, $325 to $825 for suites and villas. Golf and spa packages are available. © 888/828-8787. Local phone © 831/624-2888. www.quail lodge.com.

Eating in Carmel

There are so many wonderful restaurants in Carmel, you won't have trouble finding a great meal. Most require reservations at night, especially on weekends—but grabbing a quick bite as you shop is easy to do.

ANTON & MICHEL
Court of the Fountains, Mission St., between Ocean and Seventh aves., Carmel.

My husband, Tom, and I have enjoyed excellent romantic dinners here for over 25 years—and it just seems to get better and better. Try the chateaubriand or fresh Monterey Bay seafood, but leave room for the flambé desserts, prepared tableside. Reservations are imperative. ✆ 831/624-2406. www.carmelsbest.com.

THE COVEY RESTAURANT
Quail Lodge, 8205 Valley Greens Dr., Carmel.

After having a fabulous dinner here to celebrate our anniversary, we planned to make it a regular tradition. The Covey serves California contemporary cuisine, inventively prepared with fresh local ingredients. The menu is complemented by an extensive list of well-priced regional wines. Views of the lake, gardens, and Carmel's rolling hills provide a beautiful setting. I recommend the signature rack of lamb; Tom loved the duck. Reservations required, of course. ✆ 831/829-8787. www.quail lodge.com.

FLAHERTY'S
Sixth Ave., between San Carlos and Dolores sts., Carmel.

My favorite lunch spot serves far more than just lunch—it's open daily from 11am to 10pm. The menu offers fresh regional and specialty seafood, including local sand dabs, Monterey Bay spot prawns, live oysters, and award-winning Manhattan and New England clam chowders. ✆ 831/622-8850. www.carmels best.com.

The Shopping Scene

Ocean Avenue, from Junipero to Monte Verde, is the main street in town. The adjoining blocks and cross streets stem out to

Close Encounters of the Clint Kind

The **Hog's Breath Inn**, on San Carlos Street between Fifth and Sixth avenues (© 831/625-1044; www.hogsbreathinn.net), is one of Carmel's most famous restaurants. It used to be owned by ex-mayor and number-one resident Clint Eastwood, and everyone still thinks of it as Clint's place. It serves great drinks and bar food on a cozy outdoor patio with six fireplaces. Fido is welcome here. Lunch is served from 11:30am to 3pm, dinner from 4 to 10pm, and cocktails and hors d'oeuvres at the bar during other times.

Now, if you want to run into Clint himself, you'll have to go to his **Mission Ranch**, 26270 Dolores St. (© 831/625-9040; www.missionranchcarmel.com), where he often hangs out in the bar on weekdays. The place is always crowded with people waiting for tables, especially at Sunday brunch, but if you can make eye contact with Clint's baby blues, it could make your day. We've had drinks at the bar, which has a lively reputation and draws locals as well as visitors.

provide great shopping opportunities; don't miss the tiny alleyways and courtyards, either, where you'll find more boutiques. Art galleries are scattered throughout the area, but most seem to be on the north side of Ocean Avenue. Since art is a personal choice, I can't make any specific recommendations—but the variety and price range here are endless. The wonderful thing about shopping in Carmel is that most boutiques are small, privately owned, and stock unique items.

Carmel Plaza, on Ocean Avenue between Junipero and Mission (© 831/624-0137; www.carmelplaza.com), mentioned above for its bathroom facilities, is also home to both local boutiques and national chains. Tenants include Banana Republic, Coldwater Creek, Cole Haan, J. Jill, Louis Vuitton, Sur La Table, Talbots, Tiffany, and Yves Delorme.

Local Heroes

A BEAD ABOVE
San Carlos St., between Seventh and Eighth aves., Carmel.

This is a full-service bead store, with everything from glass, stone, and freshwater-pearl to semiprecious and metal beads. The stock comes from around the world—India, Germany, Japan, China. You can also buy all the supplies you'll need to create jewelry and more. © 831/622-9932. www.letitbead.com.

CARMEL HAT COMPANY
Doud Arcade, Ocean Ave., between San Carlos and Dolores sts., Carmel.

Need a boater, sun hat, beret, or any other type of chapeau? This is the place. It's a tiny space with hats stacked up to the ceiling, but it carries a huge selection—and will even steam your purchase to fit your head. Hang 'em high, as someone around here once said. © 831/625-9510.

DIGGIDY DOG
Southwest corner of Mission and Ocean aves., Carmel.

Diggidy Dog has dog clothes like I've never seen before. Does your puppy need a Chanel-style fringed tweed jacket? Or maybe a T-shirt that says "I'm a bitch"? Outfit your pooch in motorcycle gear or even a down parka. There's also a full range of collars, dog beds, treats, and more. © 831/625-1585. www.diggidydogcarmel.com.

JAN DE LUZ
Dolores St., between Ocean and Seventh aves., Carmel.

Jan de Luz features French linens and Basque home style, from antiques and small furnishings to bath products and imported foodstuffs. There's another branch in St. Helena, in Napa Valley; see p. 198 for more information. © 831/622-7621. www.jandeluz.com.

LOES HINSE
Lincoln Lane, between Ocean and Seventh aves., Carmel.

Loes studied in Europe and then opened this boutique in Carmel, featuring elegant Armani-inspired designs in fabulous fabrics. Her speciality is the "California casual" look, somewhat similar to what Eileen Fisher does in New York. However, here you can buy off the rack or order custom pieces, ready in about 2 weeks. The colors are contemporary; the styles are seasonal, classic, and comfortable (with elastic waists); and the prices are reasonable. Most jackets cost under $250; knit tops are also well priced. © 831/620-1060. www.loeshinse design.com.

MADRIGAL
Carmel Plaza, Ocean Ave., between Junipero and Mission sts., Carmel.

Madrigal sells classic clothing for men and women, including golf wear and everything you need for that next country-club outing. © 831/624-3477.

MARK FENWICK
Carmel Plaza, Ocean Ave., between Junipero and Mission sts., Carmel.

Contemporary knits and outerwear are the main draws here. I loved the polar-fleece coats and jackets, which come in a dozen colors and many styles. These are not boring zip-up jackets, but rather swing styles, three-quarter coats, and much more. If what you want isn't in stock, you can select the style and color, and the store will send it to you in 7 to 10 days. If you can't get to the Mycra Pac outlet in Moraga (p. 230), Mark Fenwick also carries Mycra Pac raincoats and a nice selection of sweaters. © 831/624-1174.

RED HAUTE
Ocean Ave., between Dolores and San Carlos sts., Carmel.

It's a pun in French, get it? Red Hot? Red Haute is a cute boutique that will offer you a glass of champagne or bottled water while you shop. Look for hip embroidered blazers and coats, soft leather jackets in yummy colors, and many other items that will appeal to both mom and her teen daughter. © 831/625-6333.

THINKER TOYS
Seventh Ave. and San Carlos St., Carmel.

This isn't just a great toy store—it also has a seating area where you can read to your kids and let them play with the toys. The company is dedicated to the theory that fun, learning, and personal growth go together perfectly. Thus you'll find quality toys here that inspire creativity and stand the test of time. The temptations include everything from arts and crafts to games and puzzles, dress-up clothes to erector sets, collectibles, furniture, and on and on. This shop is a treat for kids of all ages. © 831/624-0441. www.thinkertoys.com.

INDEX

See also Accommodations and Restaurant indexes, below.